HUNTER LIGGETT

No. 15
C. A. Brannen Series

U.S.
U.S.

HUNTER LIGGETT

A SOLDIER'S GENERAL

Michael E. Shay

Texas A&M University Press
College Station

First edition

This paper meets the requirements of ANSI/NISO Z39.48-1992 (Permanence of Paper).
Binding materials have been chosen for durability.
Manufactured in the United States of America

Library of Congress Cataloging-in-Publication Data

Names: Shay, Michael E., 1945– author.
Title: Hunter Liggett: a soldier's general / Michael E. Shay.
Description: First edition. | College Station: Texas A&M University Press, [2019] | Series: C. A. Brannen series; no. 15 | Includes bibliographical references and index. |
Identifiers: LCCN 2018037115 (print) | LCCN 2018039410 (ebook) | ISBN 9781623497460 (ebook) | ISBN 9781623497453 | ISBN 9781623497453 (cloth : alk. paper)
Subjects: LCSH: Liggett, Hunter, 1857–1935. | Liggett, Hunter, 1857–1935—Military leadership. | Generals—United States—Biography. | World War, 1914–1918—Biography.
Classification: LCC E745.L3775 (ebook) | LCC E745.L3775 S53 2019 (print) | DDC 940.40092 [B]—dc23
LC record available at https://lccn.loc.gov/2018037115

To the Honorable Stanley Novack
friend, colleague, and mentor

Unquestionably, there is such a thing not only as
being too old to fight, but too fat. That disqualification
is the more serious if the fat is above the collar.

—LT. GEN. HUNTER LIGGETT

The real object of an Army is to prepare for war.

—ELIHU ROOT

CONTENTS

ILLUSTRATIONS

Photographs

Maps

PREFACE

Lt. Gen. Hunter Liggett is somewhat of an enigma. Large of frame and overweight, as commander of the 41st ("Sunset") Division, he was certainly not on Gen. John Joseph Pershing's short list for active command—that is, at first. Yet the latter relented, and Liggett went on to direct and win in the Meuse-Argonne sector, in what was at that time the largest single battle in American history. If Pershing assembled the pieces of the American Expeditionary Force (AEF), Liggett made it work. In fact, when he took command of the First Army from Pershing himself in October 1918, it was Liggett who went on to succeed, whereas Pershing had been bogged down.

That is not to say that Liggett lacked ambition—far from it. He courted friends and acquaintances and was not shy about asking them to use their influence on his behalf. When an opening for promotion occurred, he was quick to submit his application. Liggett also developed a reputation as a scholar and a hard worker, and he received uniformly excellent reviews from his superiors. Although he gained very little combat experience along the way, he did serve once in Cuba and twice in the Philippines as a line officer. After 1900, with the creation of the US Army general staff and the implementation of other reforms recommended by Secretary of War Elihu Root, including making promotions a matter of more than just seniority, Liggett's reputation and experience served him well, and his upward movement was accelerated.

Liggett's story is an important one. Like many officers of his generation, he grew up listening to stories of family members who had fought in the Civil War. His mother's brother John Hunter had survived, but two other uncles had not. When he began his service, the frontier was beginning to close, so his tours in Texas and the northern plains involved rounding up scattered members of smaller tribal bands—general constabulary duty. Although he would later serve in Cuba and the Philippines, much to his dismay, he did not experience combat after Montana. Nevertheless, during his early career with the 5th Infantry Regiment, he had the good fortune to learn the art of soldiering from three superb leaders, Nelson A. Miles, Frank D. Baldwin, and Samuel Ovenshine. All three were Civil War veterans, but none was a West Point graduate. Later in his career, in addition to his self-study, he would turn to a young George C. Marshall, a graduate of the Virginia Military Institute, for more formal lessons in leadership.

It has always been surprising to me that in the eighty-plus years since his death, his complete story has never been told, just the broad strokes. My decision to tell his story was made all the more difficult because I had been initially misinformed that his Compiled Military Service Record had been destroyed in the devastating fire at the National Personnel Records Center in St. Louis, Missouri, on July 12, 1973. Not to be deterred, I was aided by a helpful archivist at the National Archives in Washington, DC, who indicated that in fact there was a file, and it had a number. Armed with that information, I had the good fortune to hire Ann Gillespie, an independent researcher, who with her dogged determination was able to literally pry the file loose, opening up a treasure trove. In addition, by sheer happenstance, the Berks History Center in Reading, Pennsylvania, had a copy of Liggett's official Statement of Military Service, which proved to be an enormous help in creating the timeline.[1]

Hunter and Harriet Liggett had no children, so perhaps there was no incentive to save important family records. In 1925 and again in 1927, Liggett published books about his experiences in World War I, each of which offers a glimpse into his personal background and philosophy of leading and soldiering. In order to find more, in addition to his personnel record, it has been necessary to search many other sources, two of which stand out from the rest.

First and foremost is the remarkably detailed diary of Lt. Col. Pierpont Langley Stackpole, who served as Liggett's aide-de-camp in France. Robert Ferrell has done a superb job in editing the diary, and his annotations are invaluable in placing the story in context. Stackpole was a Boston lawyer from an old New England family who at various times comes across as opinionated, judgmental, stuffy, or sanctimonious. All that aside, Stackpole's personality quirks do not detract from the importance of the work itself, and Liggett found him to be "thoroughly efficient" and an "admirable companion" with an "intuitive social sense." His older brother, Markham Winslow Stackpole, served throughout the war as a chaplain in the 102nd Field Artillery Regiment. The unit was part of the 26th ("Yankee") Division under the command of Maj. Gen. Clarence Ransom Edwards, for whom the diarist displayed nothing but disdain. Stackpole family gatherings certainly must have been interesting![2]

Another source is an unpublished master's thesis by Charles Francis King at the University of Oklahoma, written in 1964. Although based in large part on published materials, King gives a good overview of Liggett's life and career. Some conclusions by the author, especially with regard to the actions of the 26th Division and its commander, Maj. Gen. Clarence Edwards, are too narrowly drawn, based only upon Stackpole's account. Nevertheless, it is another good place to start.[3]

More than forty years ago, no less an authority than noted historian Allan R. Millett lamented the dearth of scholarship for the man: "Hunter Liggett . . . rates at least a memoir and several biographies." I could not agree more wholeheartedly, and this volume will hopefully be a good start to finally give this great soldier the recognition he rightly deserves.[4]

I am, as always, very grateful for the many people who have helped me with this project:

Richard L. Baker, senior technical information specialist, Military History Institute, Carlisle, PA

Sabina Beauchard, reproductions coordinator, Massachusetts Historical Society, Boston, MA

Michael Bellacosa, information services manager, and Catherine Steele, interlibrary loan manager, Wilton Library, Wilton, CT

Nan Card, curator of manuscripts, Rutherford B. Hayes Presidential Center, Fremont, OH

Suzanne Christoff, associate director of unique resources, and Alicia Mauldin-Ware, archives curator, special collections, West Point, NY

Ann Gillespie, independent researcher, Fredericksburg, VA

James Ginther, archivist, US Marine Corps History Division, Quantico, VA

John Heiser, historian, Gettysburg National Military Park, Gettysburg, PA

Jeffrey S. Kozak, director of library and archives, George C. Marshall Foundation, Lexington, VA

Ruth Shaffer, volunteer, Berks History Center, Reading, PA

Alison Simpson, historian, Florida National Guard and Department of Military Affairs, St. Augustine, FL

Kellyn Younggren, archivist, Mansfield Library, University of Montana, MT

Once again, Chris Robinson has created some superb original maps, which certainly enhance the text.

I would be remiss if I failed to mention the late James J. Cooke, PhD, professor emeritus of history at the University of Mississippi. Jim was always supportive of my efforts. He freely shared his vast knowledge of the subject with me and offered countless valuable suggestions and insights that without a doubt made my books all the better. He will be missed by me and all who knew him.

Thank you to Jay Dew, editor in chief at Texas A&M University Press, and a great staff for a job well done in "making this book."

As always, I am appreciative of my wife Marilyn's support as a patient sounding board and diligent researcher, as well as an overall boon companion. Thanks also to our fellow road warrior "Spike," who doesn't get a vote but does relish a comfortable motel bed at the end of the day.

HUNTER LIGGETT

ONE
The Early Years

THE TAILOR'S SON

Situated just sixty miles northwest of Philadelphia, longer if one follows the twisting course of the Schuylkill River, Reading, Pennsylvania, had long been a jumping-off point on the journey west through the Conestoga Valley. Reading is the seat of Berks County and lies at the lower end of a geological feature called an anticline. Stretching from there northeast to Scranton and Wilkes-Barre, it holds an enormous seam of hard, anthracite coal, sought after for its longer- and cleaner-burning properties. During the mid- to late nineteenth century, this coal was essential to heating thousands of homes in the Northeast and feeding the steam engines plying the nation's burgeoning railroad system and many small local ironworks. Coal made some men rich, and it made those who dug it deep underground hard. Berks County was also full of farms and small villages, populated with a mix of Quakers of English stock and Germans, the children and grandchildren of early residents pushing westward from nearby Lehigh and Chester counties and seizing their own opportunities. Methodism was also making deep inroads.

Tradesmen and small manufacturers served the local farmers and workingmen of Berks County. One of these was twenty-six-year-old James Liggett, a tailor by trade, who had left his home in Chester County in 1847 and settled in what would later become the Borough of Birdsboro in Robeson Township. James was the son of James and Ann Liggett. He married twenty-five-year-old Margaret Hunter in about 1850. She was also born in Chester County and was the daughter of the Rev. George Hunter and his wife, Ann. Although George Hunter was a shoemaker by trade, he was also called to preach the Gospel, which he did part-time. James and Margaret first lived in a frame house in town, just above the locks on the Schuylkill River

1. Hunter Liggett's birthplace, Reading, PA (ca. 2016). Courtesy of Marilyn Shay.

canal, and there James set up his tailor shop. Later on, he and Margaret moved to another home by the river bridge.[1]

By 1856, the couple had moved to nearby Reading, where James set up shop at 145 South Sixth Street (between Franklin and Chestnut Streets) in a modest two-story building, with his business on the first floor and the family residence above. For seven years, the couple remained childless, so there must have been considerable joy when, on March 21, 1857, Margaret gave birth to a healthy son. They named the boy Hunter in honor of his mother's family. Joy soon turned to sorrow when Margaret, age thirty-two, died just three weeks after the baby was born, more than likely as a result of complications related to the birth. Margaret was buried in the Hunter family plot at the Elverson Methodist Cemetery in Chester County.[2]

With the sudden death of his wife, James Liggett was clearly distraught and overwhelmed. He turned his newborn son over to the care of his sister Ann, a dressmaker, who lived nearby in town, and he moved to West Nantmeal in Chester County. There, he boarded at a small hotel run by Samuel Hockassino while he plied his trade as a tailor. It was also there that he met and married Catherine Amole, the daughter of William Amole, a very prosperous local farmer.[3]

By 1860, Ann Liggett and young Hunter had moved to Birdsboro. Soon after, James and his new bride moved back there, too. James immersed himself in his business. For starters, he switched trades and opened a shoe shop on Furnace Street. In addition, he operated a brickyard and built several brick homes in the town. James's hard work paid off, and by 1870, he had achieved a measure of prosperity. In the federal census for 1870, he listed his occupation as "shopkeeper" and valued his real and personal estate at $9,200.00. In addition to his various businesses, James was active in local Democratic politics, serving at one time or another as a burgess, councilman, and assessor. He would later serve two terms in the Pennsylvania state legislature.[4]

Shortly after James resettled in Birdsboro, young Hunter returned to his father's household, where, by all accounts, the boy led a normal life. However, in a case of bureaucracy run amuck, although there was a school just across the street from his home, it was in another district, and the young man was forced to walk to another school a mile away. When he was older, Hunter was sent to a private school in Manayunk.[5]

Meanwhile, Liggett enjoyed a normal boyhood, playing "Indian" with his friends in Hill Hollow and daydreaming in class, as numerous doodles in his textbooks can attest. Like all young boys, he had a little mischief in him. One day, while passing Thomas White's bakery, Liggett had a craving for something sweet, but when it came time to pay, he was ten cents short. Looking down at the boy who obviously had his heart set on the treats and not wanting to disappoint him, the shopkeeper told him to come back later with the money. The boy left happy and no doubt enjoyed the cakes; however, the kindly baker was still waiting for his money five decades later.[6]

DUTY, HONOR, COUNTRY

For many young men, an appointment to West Point was their best, if not their only, chance to obtain a college education and at the same time secure an honorable profession. Pennsylvania had been the site of one of the most significant battles of the Civil War (at Gettysburg, now more than a decade in the past), and the state had supplied thousands of young men to the Union cause, many of whom did not return. Two of Liggett's uncles had died during the war, and he was certainly old enough to hear and appreciate the stories of the others who survived, including his uncle John Hunter.[7]

Whether he chose the soldier's path or it was chosen for him, in late 1874 or early 1875, Liggett set his sights on an appointment to West Point.

Other young men from the Reading area also had the same ambition—six all told, including Hunter. Representative Hiester Clymer, who held the seat for the Eighth Congressional District, announced that he would hold a competitive examination for one vacancy each at West Point and at the Naval Academy. Hearing that, Liggett and his father engaged the services of Henry C. Hunter, more than likely a distant relative, as a tutor. At that time, Professor Hunter served as the supervising principal of the Birdsboro schools.[8]

All the applicants were first given a physical examination, and all passed. The competitive examination itself took place on May 20, 1875, at the boys' high school. Professor John A. Stewart, assisted by several other educators, as well as the congressman himself, conducted the exam. The subjects ranged from algebra to geography and poetry. When it was over, the examining board indicated that they were "much gratified with the aptitude and general intelligence" of the applicants. In the end, the tutoring certainly paid off, as Liggett stood first among all the competitors. Representative Clymer forwarded Liggett's name to the War Department. As a result, he received an appointment to the United States Military Academy, and he quickly accepted it.[9]

Then as now, situated on the west bank of the Hudson River, high above a sharp bend, the United States Military Academy occupies one of the most spectacularly beautiful locations on the East Coast. Ever since its creation in March 1802, in addition to soldiering, West Point–trained officers have gone forth all across the continent and beyond, utilizing their engineering education to design and build the necessary infrastructure, from bridges to railroads, that made expansion possible. The Panama Canal is one example of a major feat made possible with the help of West Point graduates.[10]

At the time that Liggett attended the United States Military Academy, it continued to adhere to a "rigid and highly technical curriculum with its emphasis on mathematics, science, and engineering." Moreover, its system of competitive ranking forced cadets to "fight for rank," which carried forward into their later careers, where ambition often trumped collegiality and led to much jealousy and ill will as certain officers advanced more quickly than others. Also, with limited postgraduation opportunities for further formal study, it was hoped that West Point would also instill a real sense of professionalism that would inspire graduates to engage in self-study. Some, like Liggett, would accept that challenge, while many others would not.[11]

Liggett reported to West Point on July 1, 1875, to begin his time as a "plebe," or member of the fourth class. Prior to the start of classroom work, all plebes

2. Cadet Hunter Liggett. Courtesy of Special Collections and Archives, United States Military Academy.

underwent what one graduate referred to as the "ordeal of Beast Barracks," a three-week mix of examinations, physical activity, and hazing by upperclassmen. After that, the plebes joined the rest of the Corps of Cadets for summer camp and still more hazing. Finally, on September 1, the academic year began.[12]

The class of 1879 started with ninety-one young men ranging in age from seventeen to nearly twenty-two. It would finish four years later with sixty-seven members. It was not that the course work alone was so challenging. Rather, it was the combination of the academics with the harsh, unrelenting discipline and a rigid code of honor that was simply too much for some young men, especially during the plebe year, when many felt a sense of isolation.[13]

"No horse, no wife, no moustache" was the saying, and the expectation was simple—absolute loyalty to the Corps of Cadets. Each cadet was held to the same standard, and each was responsible for his own conduct and that of his fellows. It was an important lesson for a soldier. Students were charged with disciplinary infractions, referred to as "delinquencies," for things most people would consider petty or ridiculous, like "gazing about in ranks" or wearing one's cap "at a jaunty angle." A log (*Register of Delinquencies*) of each cadet's violations was maintained by the school, and a tally of two hundred at year's end meant expulsion, although cadets were permitted extra duty to work the demerits off and thus save their standing.[14]

At the end of his first year, Liggett stood fifty-first in his class. He seemed to have trouble mastering drill and the manual of arms, which was not uncommon for a plebe. In addition, he was frequently cited for keeping a messy room or clothes closet and for infractions regarding his uniform. Once, he failed to return a library book on time. Yet by the end of May 1876, he had only accumulated fifty-eight delinquencies. At the commencement ceremonies the following month, no doubt to the delight of the cadets, Lt. Gen. William T. Sherman was on hand to deliver the address and hand out diplomas.[15]

During his second year, the academics became somewhat more challenging with the addition of Spanish and drawing, the latter with the emphasis on topography, an essential element in map making and reading. It was here that Liggett developed a lifelong passion for maps. "I am as much at home with a land map as an astronomer with his stars," he would write, adding, "and I have studied maps perpetually out of an innate interest, as well as professional need."[16]

Liggett continued to have trouble with drill, in addition to spilling milk at breakfast, laughing in formation, taking fruit from the mess hall, and galloping his horse in the riding hall "after being repeatedly told not to do so." But at year's end, he'd accumulated a total of only thirty-six delinquencies. Moreover, he had improved his class standing to forty-second.[17]

THE PATHS OF GLORY

Promptly at 8:30 a.m. on October 10, 1877, the mayor of Poughkeepsie, New York, along with a delegation of other city officials and distinguished citizens who were assembled at City Hall stepped out into a dense fog and climbed aboard waiting carriages. They then set off to meet an honor guard accompanying a hearse. It bore the remains of Bvt. Maj. Gen. George Armstrong Custer, transporting him from where his casket had lain in a vault at the Poughkeepsie Cemetery since early August. Half an hour later, with thousands of townspeople lining the streets to get a glimpse of the procession, as if on cue, the sun broke through and burned off the fog, and a cool north breeze blew down the Hudson River. The casket was taken to the landing, where it was placed aboard the waiting steamer, *Mary Powell*, at about 10:30 a.m. for the final journey upriver to West Point.[18]

At the south dock at West Point, thousands more lined the bank and the avenues leading up to the school. Distinguished military men and other officials followed the procession to the Cadet Chapel. At 12:30 p.m., Maj. Gen. John Schofield, superintendent of the academy, led Libby Custer into the chapel, followed by Custer's father and sister, where an Episcopal service was conducted. The brigade of cadets was poised in formation outside the chapel and, when the service ended, came to present arms as the casket came into view. The cadets then fell into line and followed an honor guard of cavalry in the procession to the cemetery. At the end of the burial service there, they fired three volleys over the grave. For Liggett and the other cadets, the pomp and ceremony aside, this event must have been a sobering reminder of the risks inherent in their chosen profession.[19]

HITTING THE BOOKS

Liggett showed slow but steady improvement in the 1877–78 academic year. Although the subject matter was more challenging, he remained right in the middle of his class with a rank of thirty-seven. Drawing continued to be his

3. Funeral of Bvt. Maj. Gen. George A. Custer (October 10, 1877). Courtesy of the Library of Congress.

best subject, and he only accumulated a total of twenty-nine delinquencies, including the usual lapses during drill, along with a dirty washbowl and failure to shave properly on two occasions.[20]

Years later, Liggett wrote that his real love was reading history, particularly military history, and at every available opportunity, he frequented the Cadet Library instead of concentrating on his course work. Had that not been the case, he suggested, he would no doubt have stood higher in his class. Throughout his long career, Liggett strove for self-improvement as an officer, while many of his former classmates, who considered their education to be complete upon graduation, "drifted into poker playing, garrison small talk, and a despairing clinch with boredom."[21]

On November 3, 1877, during the fall of his third year, Liggett's stepmother, Catherine, died, leaving James a widower once more. She was buried with her family in Knauertown in Chester County. There is no indication that Liggett asked for leave to attend the funeral.[22]

When the "makes" were published on June 13, 1878, Liggett was pleased with his selection as a sergeant in the battalion of cadets for the following term. Shortly thereafter, his orders were changed with his appointment as a lieutenant. This honor fell to those cadets who were the "most studious, soldier-like in performance of their duties, and most exemplary in their general deportment."[23]

Liggett's final year, called the first class, was perhaps the most demanding of all, yet by then he had adjusted to the routine. Perhaps he had become a little too comfortable, as very uncharacteristically, Liggett accumulated seventy-one demerits during the year, including his continued troubles with drill, a dirty mirror, an unbuttoned coat, and a protruding shirt. His final class ranking slipped slightly to forty-one.[24]

THE LONG GRAY LINE

On June 12, 1879, gray skies and a steady rain marred graduation day, and as a result, the ceremony was moved indoors to the Cadet Chapel. There, Liggett and his classmates, along with a capacity crowd of distinguished guests, both military and civilian, filled the room. Chief Justice Morrison R. Waite was in attendance to see his son graduate. Other guests included Secretary of War George W. McCrary; Lt. Gen. William T. Sherman, the commanding general of the US Army; Dr. Noah Porter of Yale, president of the Board of Visitors; and Maj. Gen. John Pope, the principal speaker.[25]

Maj. Gen. John Schofield introduced the chief justice, who made some very brief remarks, followed by General Sherman, who was greeted with a "spontaneous burst of applause." Sherman told the graduates that "there is no profession in the world in which those who follow it are held to a higher responsibility before God and man than the profession of the soldier," adding, "You will be held responsible for the safety of the Country and the honor of the Flag." Sherman teased the five highest-ranking members of the class, who he was sure would become "highly scientific and accomplished officers." However, it was to the lower ranks, those who would encounter the "rough life" in Montana and Arizona while serving in the infantry and cavalry, that he offered encouragement. Those experiences would, he said, "develop the true soldier—the men who could fight hard and take the lead . . . [and] even the lowest might become the highest in the only school better than West Point—the school of life." The general then told them to enjoy their three-month vacation prior to reporting for duty. The graduates gave Sherman a "long continued applause."[26]

General Pope followed Sherman, and for the graduates his remarks were anything but anticlimactic. "Do your duty thoroughly and conscientiously, regardless of time or circumstance," he told them, even though "it may be, and no doubt often will be, that the sense of duty so performed will be your only reward." For Liggett, what Pope said next would resonate with him throughout his entire career: "Be mindful, too, that in leaving this institution you have not completed your education, but have only begun it." Pope continued, "You have learned here how to learn, and if you fail to avail yourself of that lesson, a large part, indeed the whole of your education here will be useless to you. Self-reliance and self-restraint you will be compelled to learn in the Army, whether you desire it or not, but no man can stand justified of himself who does not use every means and avail of every opportunity to study his profession, and as far as theory and a limited practice can accomplish it, prepare himself for higher position and greater responsibility." Pope did not leave it there but offered one more lesson; it was one thing to learn to obey orders, he told them, but "the far harder task is before you of learning to command." In order to do this, they would need to get to know the men they would lead. Pope reminded them that "the soldiers of a Republic are its citizens . . . [and] in a free country and among a free people, the real heroes of every war are found in the ranks." At the conclusion of General Pope's remarks, General Schofield called the graduates' names in order of their class standing and presented them each with a diploma.[27]

On the day following his graduation, Liggett received his commission as a second lieutenant. His first assignment was with the 5th US Infantry, a crack regiment, at that time stationed in Montana Territory. He joined the regiment after spending the traditional three-month leave following graduation with his family in Birdsboro. Like his son, James would soon embark on a new career: in the fall of 1879, James ran for a seat in the Pennsylvania General Assembly and was elected. He would go on to serve two terms. James continued to live in Birdsboro, though he became a boarder in the Hafer family home on Furnace Street.[28]

TWO

Out West

CANTONMENT AT TONGUE RIVER

Fresh out of West Point, 2nd Lt. Hunter Liggett was assigned to the 5th US Infantry Regiment, then headquartered at Fort Keogh, Montana Territory, and he arrived there for duty on October 9, 1879. Originally designated as the "Cantonment at Tongue River" when it was established on August 25, 1876, the temporary post was intended to serve as a base of operations against hostile bands of Sioux and Northern Cheyenne. The post was located on the southern bank of the Yellowstone River at its junction with the Tongue River. The new cantonment was approximately 220 miles upriver from Fort Buford, Dakota Territory, or about 165 miles overland by rough wagon road. Most likely, the initial site was prone to flooding, and within two years, the post was moved about a mile west, where a permanent facility was built and renamed Fort Keogh in honor of Capt. Miles Keogh, who had recently died with Lt. Col. George A. Custer at the Battle of Little Bighorn.[1]

The first buildings at the cantonment were "vermin infested" one- and two-room huts constructed with roughhewn, perpendicular cottonwood logs chinked with mud. As the green wood shrank, the mud chinking would fall out, necessitating a "replaster" of the gaps to keep out the driving rains and cold, wintry winds. By the time Liggett had arrived, these hovels had given way to more-comfortable wood-framed barracks, as well as two-family officers' quarters. The latter were a story and a half high, with a covered porch running along the front side. Cottonwood or pine logs were burned in the large fireplaces in the parlor and the box stoves in the hallway, and once the open foundations were banked with a mixture of soil and manure to keep out the arctic blasts, these accommodations became very comfortable in winter.[2]

Fort Keogh was by then home to the headquarters and several companies of the 5th US Infantry, commanded by Col. Nelson A. Miles. From time to time, various companies of the regiment would also occupy Forts Custer and Maginnis in the Montana Territory as well as Forts Abraham Lincoln, Buford, and Totten in the Dakota Territory. Miles described much of the countryside within his command area, declaring that "no section of country abounding in such pasturable richness can be found in the United States" and "the horses, mules, and cattle keep in better condition than in any territory that I have ever passed over."[3]

GETTING THERE

Liggett's journey from Birdsboro to Fort Keogh was a lengthy one, taking a little more than three weeks by way of several different means of travel. More than likely, he made his way by train to St. Paul, Minnesota, where he boarded a Northern Pacific train. Those tracks passed through Fargo in the Dakota Territory, past mile after mile of fields of ripening grain, on the way to Bismarck, a bustling town then at the end of the tracks, some twenty-four hours later. There, before boarding one of a half-dozen steamboats tied up at the landing on the Missouri River, he would rub elbows with townspeople, boatmen, rail workers, and soldiers from nearby Fort Abraham Lincoln, as well as local merchants and a few American Indians.[4]

The watersheds of the Yellowstone and Missouri Rivers are covered with vast, golden, rolling grasslands and some rich bottomlands, sporadically interspersed with areas of broken ground and occasional rugged badlands—all new to the young man raised in eastern Pennsylvania. On deck, Liggett, who had a lifelong passion for maps and topography, likely took mental notes of the changing scenery as the steamboat churned slowly northward against the river's steady current, which carried along with it mud and dozens upon dozens of deadly snags, each one capable of hanging a boat up or, worse, ripping through its fragile wooden hull. Snags were such a serious problem that steamboats would tie up to the bank each night.[5]

Four days and three hundred miles later, the boat landed at Fort Buford, situated directly across from the confluence of the Yellowstone River with the Missouri. Following a layover, the steamboat would then turn to ply its way southwest up the Yellowstone, 220 miles and four days later arriving at Miles City, Montana Territory, a mile or so away from Fort Keogh.[6]

At the time that Lieutenant Liggett stepped off the boat, it would be more correct to call Miles City a "settlement." It was populated by a "motley array of every sort and occupation," and seven hundred souls called it home, with more arriving daily. It was a mix of approximately 150 structures, a few of which were substantial brick and frame buildings housing banks, stores, and residences but juxtaposed with "shacks with doors open day and night"—saloons, gambling parlors, dance halls, and less-reputable establishments that beckoned siren-like to each passerby to enter and partake of the pleasures within. Colonel Miles himself called the town "the headquarters for the frontier rough element." He was referring to the loud, rowdy, or drunken cowboys from local stock and cattle ranches "amusing themselves in the peculiar style . . . which usually consists of firing their pistols in all directions, allowing chance to decide whether they kill anybody or not," all too often with that tragic result.[7]

On the other hand, there were some elements of a more civil society, including a small, one-room courthouse constructed of logs. The court had finished its very first session some four months earlier. Though church services were often "sparsely attended," the city boasted several denominations, including Catholicism and Methodism. Miles City was, nonetheless, visible evidence of the advance of civilization and as such was at once a place of diversion for the soldiers at Fort Keogh and a reminder of their duty to protect the citizens of the town and the travelers who passed through it.[8]

THE BRAVE PEACOCK

Theodore Roosevelt called Nelson Miles a "brave peacock." The description is an apt one. There was no doubt that Miles was brave, as he had proven time and again on many a battlefield. Yet bravery is only one of his many attributes. He was first and foremost a superb field commander, one doggedly determined to succeed. He was also vain and thin-skinned, and he saw slights where perhaps they were not always there. He was ambitious and shamelessly pursued promotion. Miles had married well; his wife, Mary, was the niece of both Gen. William T. Sherman and his brother Sen. John Sherman, connections he was not shy about using. Maj. Gen. Henry Ware Lawton, who had served under Miles during the Geronimo Campaign in 1886, observed that Miles "wants his name kept before the people. He wants *everybody* to know that there is a Gen'l Miles in the US Army, and the role of martyr or villain suits him equally."[9]

Nelson Appleton Miles was born in Westminster, Massachusetts, in 1839. The youngest of four children and a tall, thin boy, he left home while still in his teens to seek his fortune in Boston. Miles started out selling fruit but soon

4. Bvt. Maj. Gen. Nelson A. Miles. Courtesy of the Library of Congress.

went to work for an uncle in the clothing business. He was hardworking and thrifty, and he soon achieved a measure of prosperity. Then came the Civil War, and his life took an entirely different course. Under Colonel Miles's leadership, the 5th Infantry was a very reliable regiment, having seen hard service in Oklahoma and the Texas Panhandle in numerous fights with the Comanche and their Kiowa allies. At the time Liggett arrived at Fort Keogh, Miles was still in command of the 5th Infantry, and most recently, he had led the regiment in the final pursuit of Chief Joseph and the Nez Percé.[10]

Lieutenant Liggett was initially assigned to Company G under the command of Capt. Samuel Ovenshine. The captain and his wife, Sallie, along with four of their children, lived on post. Throughout his long career, Ovenshine would serve in a number of important assignments, including in the Plains Wars on the northern plains and the Red River Indian War in the Southwest. He would particularly distinguish himself by leading the attack at the Zapote River bridge during the Philippine War in 1899 and retire as a brigadier general shortly thereafter. His oldest daughter, Emma, would

5. Maj. Gen. Frank D. Baldwin. Courtesy of the Library of Congress.

later marry James Guthrie Harbord, John J. Pershing's first chief of staff in France. In that capacity, Harbord would be in a good position to influence the commander in chief regarding his choice of American Expeditionary Forces (AEF) division commanders.[11]

The post was also home to Capt. Frank D. Baldwin, along with his wife, Alice, and their daughter. Baldwin, another seasoned soldier, would go on to enjoy an active and distinguished military career, retiring as a major general, and Alice Baldwin would write a memoir of her soldier-husband's long career and their experiences along the way. Much later, in his own memoir, Liggett singled out Baldwin as an exceptional officer who was awarded two Medals of Honor. He wrote in the foreword to the book, "He was my real military mentor and taught me all the fundamentals of service, in the field and in garrison. . . . His energy, resourcefulness and courage made him a model for the younger officers." In 1919, then retired, General Baldwin returned the high compliment to his former subaltern: "[Liggett] has no equal in professional ability or noble character among our American generals."[12]

FOOT CAVALRY

Infantry played a vital role in the overall strategy of western settlement. In fact, many posts were manned by just one or two companies of infantry. While the use of cavalry troops was often more advantageous depending on the nature of a particular mission, there were some serious drawbacks. First and foremost, the large cavalry mounts required prodigious amounts of forage daily (both grain and hay) in order to maintain their strength, along with regular care and grooming, including an occasional reshoeing. All this required a large supply apparatus following along with the troop in order to take care of both man and beast. Second, even if well fed and groomed, a cavalry horse did not have the stamina and could not keep up a long, sustained pursuit against the lighter, swifter ponies used by the plains tribes. The fact is that without sufficient quartermaster wagons accompanying the expedition, the individual trooper could not carry anywhere near the necessary forage to supply his mount its full daily ration, thus wearing it down over time. On the other hand, horses were the Plains Indians' stock-in-trade, and the large pony herds accompanying the bands, if kept intact, virtually guaranteed a reliable source of fresh mounts in time of danger or a long hunt.[13]

Lastly, cavalry often fought dismounted, which meant that the horse-holders, one-quarter of the troop, were effectively out of the fight. For its part, a fit, experienced infantry company could march virtually anytime, anywhere, winter or summer. This proved especially effective during winter, when most native tribes had settled into seasonal quarters, awaiting the spring.

When Liggett arrived at Fort Keogh during the fall of 1879, the infantry companies were mounted. That would all change on October 31, 1881, when the regiment was "dismounted" by order of the secretary of war. One hundred ponies were kept within the department to be used for scouting while the remaining animals were sold at an auction held at Fort Keogh on November 14.[14]

HIGH-WATER MARK

With the marriage of the horse and the rifle, the Plains Indians became consummate warriors and hunters. They lived a nomadic existence, roaming far and wide, following the game by season. Shortly after the end of the Civil War, the plains tribes like the Lakota, Cheyenne, Crow, and Arapaho came under increasing external pressure from those who at best wished to shrink their domain and to assimilate them into the dominant culture and, at

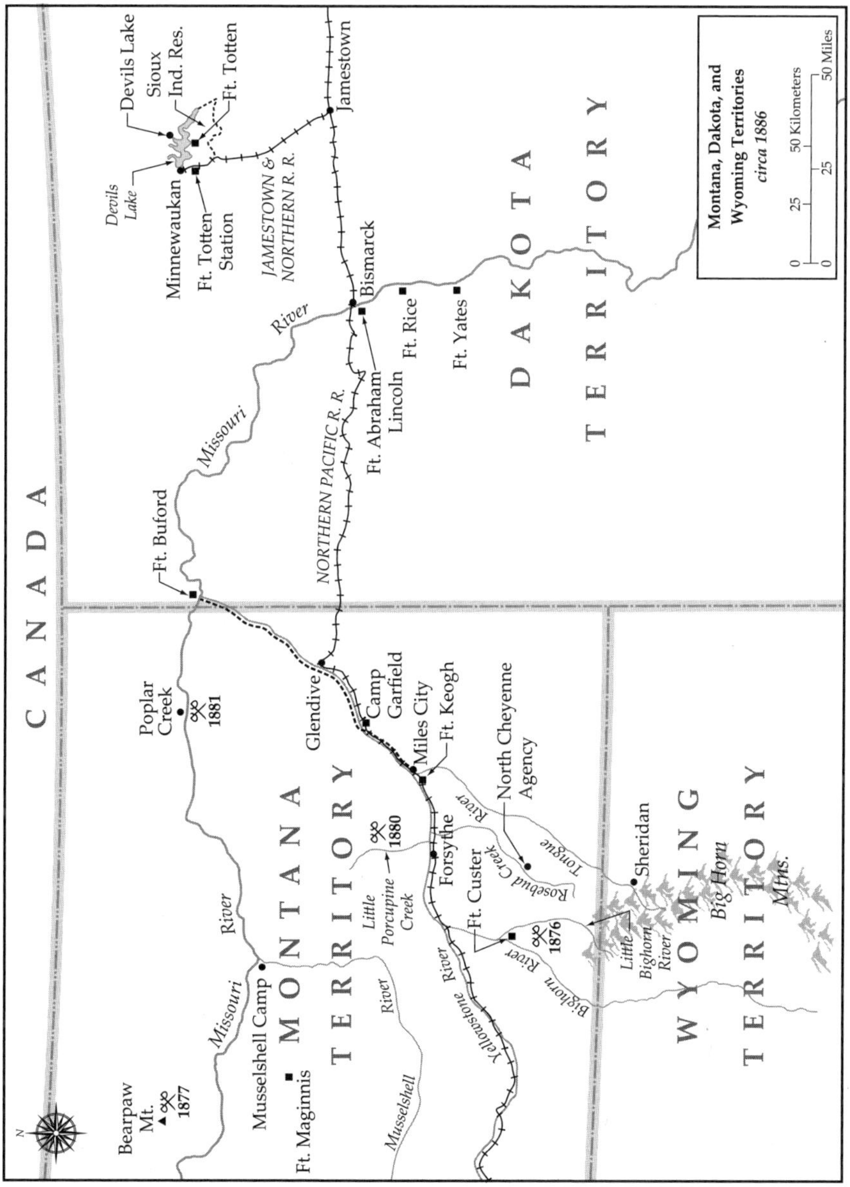

Map 1. Montana, Dakota, and Wyoming Territories (circa 1886)

worst, to exterminate them. Quite naturally, the native peoples resisted the pressure—some successfully, like Red Cloud, who effectively shut down the Bozeman Trail in Wyoming, at least for a time. For the most part, however, such efforts merely resulted in yet more pressure. June 25, 1876, would prove to be their high-water mark, when George A. Custer attacked what was then the largest aggregation of Plains Indians ever assembled in one place.[15]

From that point on, the end was clear, a fact that became slowly and painfully apparent to the various bands. Some reluctantly agreed to live on reservations, while others like Sitting Bull and Gall fled to Canada. Some of those who remained behind allied themselves in small bands and continued to raid the various ranches and settlements, primarily looking for horses. These nonreservation bands were termed "hostiles" by the US Army, and in October 1876, General Sheridan made it his mission to "disarm and dismount them." That was the situation in southeast Montana Territory when Liggett reported for duty at Fort Keogh on October 9, 1879.[16]

THE IRON HORSE

The inexorable pace of the westward migration accelerated during the years following the Civil War. A principal agent of change was the railroad. For presidents Lincoln and Grant, the linking of the West and East Coasts had become a matter of national necessity—an urgent priority. With the coming of the transcontinental railroad, the vast central plains were both physically and symbolically cut in two. Already, the large Cheyenne population was divided into northern and southern branches, as were the formerly vast but now dwindling herds of buffalo upon which the Plains Indians derived their sustenance. Not only did the railroad profoundly affect the native peoples; it also changed the dynamic of the US Army. General Sherman himself recognized this phenomenon when he compared the railroad to an army: "The railroad which used to follow in the rear now goes forward with the picket-line in the great battle of civilization with barbarism." Not surprisingly, a vital component of the US Army's mission was to guard stage drivers as well as the railroad and survey crews who had become the targets of the hostile bands.[17]

FIRST HOSTILE ENCOUNTERS

Except for a brief assignment on detached service at Fort Abraham Lincoln near Bismarck, North Dakota, between December 2, 1879, and February 28, 1880,[18] Liggett would make Fort Keogh his home for the first seven years of his career. There, during his spare time, Liggett continued his course of self-study, something that he would pursue throughout his entire career. Liggett considered himself fortunate as a young officer to have served under General Miles, who, he said, "made a practice of sending his subalterns out on their own on patrols and on scouting to put them on their mettle." Within five months after he had arrived in Montana Territory, Lieutenant Liggett engaged in his first real test.[19]

In early March 1880, reports were received that a band of hostile Indians had been raiding the ranches and settlements near Forsyth, a small town opposite the junction of Little Porcupine Creek and the Yellowstone River, and that the raiders had stolen a large number of horses and mules. While it was believed that the Indians had escaped south of the Yellowstone, several detachments, infantry and cavalry, were dispatched from Fort Keogh both to the north and to the south in order to locate them. On March 5, a small detachment from Company E, 5th Infantry under 2nd Lt. Samuel Miller, encountered the hostiles at their camp some thirty miles west of Rosebud Creek and south of the Yellowstone River. In the ensuing fight, three Indians were killed, but some ponies, a few weapons, and a large amount of ammunition were seized. Two Army scouts also lost their lives in the fight. Although their camp was destroyed, the remaining raiders escaped, crossed the Yellowstone, and proceeded north with the captured animals along the course of Little Porcupine Creek.[20]

Meanwhile, on March 3, Capt. Frank D. Baldwin led Companies I and K of the 5th Infantry on a reconnaissance north of the Yellowstone along Little Porcupine Creek and other tributaries. Liggett accompanied this command. The trail was soon found, and what followed was a determined pursuit up Little Porcupine Creek by means of long marches, night and day, during which temperatures were well below freezing. The soldiers covered a remarkable 100 to 120 miles in thirty hours "over snow and ice." It was all the more remarkable as their rations were exhausted and "the last 30 miles [were taken] at a trot and a run." Both officers and men suffered "severely from the intense cold and from snow-blindness," yet they carried on. It was a valuable lesson in determination not lost on Liggett.[21]

On March 9, the Indian camp was again found near the head of Little Porcupine Creek and quickly surrounded. Another sharp fight ensued, and although the Indians were able to break through the lines on their own ponies, they left behind all their goods and the captured animals. Liggett was among those mentioned by name in Brig. Gen. Alfred H. Terry's report to the secretary of war. Two companies of the 2nd Cavalry that had been ordered to cooperate with Captain Baldwin continued the pursuit. Liggett returned with the command to Fort Keogh on March 13. There was no rest for Liggett, as he led a scout for hostiles along the Tongue and Powder Rivers and Rosebud Creek that commenced on March 20. Liggett finally returned to Fort Keogh on April 3.[22]

The year 1880 continued to be a busy one for Liggett. On June 1, Company G was part of a mixed command of infantry and cavalry sent to pursue some hostile bands of Indians that were raiding stagecoaches and other travelers along the Fort Keogh to Bismarck mail route. The detail covered 240 miles and returned on June 10, at which time Liggett received new orders.[23]

From June 18 to September 16, Liggett led an extended scout during which he was ordered to explore the Bighorn Mountains. At one point during that expedition, he visited the Little Bighorn battlefield, where he walked the entire site with Philo Clark, a first lieutenant in the 2nd Cavalry, as well as several of the Indians who had fought there. Clark served as his scout during the expedition. The visit to the battlefield was likely the first of many like it during his long career. Not only did it provide context to his reading, particularly about such a significant event so close in time and place, but it also presaged Liggett's use of staff rides as a teaching tool. Years later, he would offer his opinion that the outcome of the fight could well have been different had Major Reno "shown some 'bull dog' tendencies and hung on in his second position."[24]

THE WILD WEST

During the decade of the 1880s, the vast area encompassed by the territories of Dakota, Idaho, and Montana was a dangerous place. Towns and military installations were few and far between. Aside from the Indian threat, there were horse and cattle thieves, stage robbers, and drunken cowboys going on sprees. In more remote areas, where the US Army or local law enforcement lacked a meaningful presence, vigilante groups took the law into their own hands, serving up summary justice to those disturbers of peace and order unfortunate enough to fall into their hands.[25]

An important duty for soldiers was the payroll escort, given the presence of this lawless element. Shortly after Liggett returned to Fort Keogh from his scout, Company G, led by Capt. Simon Snyder, was ordered to Fort Buford in the Dakota Territory to meet an Army payroll officer and escort him and the funds back to Fort Keogh. Liggett and the company returned on October 20 after a journey of 330 miles.[26]

Three weeks later, on November 12, Liggett, then in temporary command of Company G, was ordered to proceed to the camp at the mouth of the Musselshell River for unspecified detached service, more than likely relieving other troops on duty there. Liggett and Company G returned to Fort Keogh on December 13, and he reported for sick call the following day. Liggett would remain on sick call until January 17, 1881. From time to time during his career, he would suffer flare-ups of rheumatism, and given the length of his recuperation, this would have been a much more likely diagnosis than the more typical bout of malaria or dysentery that he and other soldiers frequently suffered.[27]

In the meantime, on December 15, Company G—along with Companies A, B, C, and F—set out north for the camp at the mouth of Poplar Creek, Montana Territory, under the command of Maj. Guido Ilges. Although some accounts say that Liggett was at the skirmish at Poplar Creek on January 2, 1881, in actuality, he remained on sick call, and he missed out on the pursuit and ultimate surrender there of a band of three hundred Sioux under Chief Gall, who had returned from Canada.[28]

THE CALL OF DUTY

On March 1, 1881, two companies of the 5th Infantry (D and K) under Capt. Robert M. McDonald left the post for detached duty at Fort Buford, Dakota Territory, and traveled along the south side of the Yellowstone River. However, high water in both the Powder and Yellowstone Rivers due to melting snow and the breaking up of the ice forced their return to Fort Keogh on March 15. Liggett was given temporary command of Company K on March 22 and, later that same day, joined Captain McDonald's detail, which set out once again for Fort Buford. This time, however, the soldiers immediately crossed over to the north side of the Yellowstone River and by April 16 had crossed the Missouri River opposite Fort Buford. Companies A and B, which had completed their detached duty, left immediately for Fort Keogh. Liggett returned with those units, and all arrived back at Fort Keogh on April 22.[29]

Two days later, Liggett applied for a three-month leave of absence to, in his words, "take effect when my services can be spared by my Post Commander." Although he gave as his reason the fact that he had had no leave for nearly two years, the underlying reason was that he had met Harriet Lane, his future bride, and he wanted to carve out some time to marry her and to take a honeymoon trip. How the couple came to meet is not known; however, given the small size of the US Army, it is likely that Harriet was introduced to Hunter by a mutual friend during a visit to Fort Keogh some months earlier.[30]

On Monday, June 13, 1881, Liggett bore witness to a pathetic pageant: approximately three hundred captive Sioux—men, women, and children, young and old—slowly shuffled up the gangplank and onto the deck of the steamer *Josephine*, then moored on the south bank of the Yellowstone River at Fort Keogh. Company G, under Captain Ovenshine, was part of a larger escort detail that had been ordered to transport the captives, 1,641 in all, aboard five steamers, down the Yellowstone and Missouri Rivers to their new home at the Standing Rock Agency at Fort Yates, Dakota Territory (now North Dakota). The flotilla arrived there without incident on June 18. In fact, the two-week trip passed uneventfully, and Liggett and his company returned to Fort Keogh on June 27.[31]

Three days later, Liggett was finally able to take the time to marry nineteen-year-old Harriet Lane at Fort Keogh on June 30, 1881. From the very start of their relationship, Harriet saw that there was something special about the tall, lanky lieutenant, and she never hesitated to sing his praises. She would be his biggest booster throughout their long marriage, frequently importuning his superiors for his promotion or word of his whereabouts while he was deployed overseas.[32]

Harriet was the youngest daughter of Edwin D. Lane and Elizabeth ("Eliza") Richardson. Her parents, both Virginia natives, moved to Texas sometime before 1860, and they settled in the Hill Country near Fredericksburg in Gillespie County, where Edwin became a prosperous sheep rancher. Harriet's older sisters Mary and Fannie were born there. Shortly after 1860, Edwin moved the family to San Antonio, where Harriet (whose family nickname was "Hallie") was born on June 30, 1862. Sometime around 1870, Edwin moved yet again, this time to Fort Sanders, Wyoming Territory, where he served as the post trader and earned a very comfortable living. The fort, which was built in 1866, was located about three miles south and east of present-day Laramie. It was intended to protect settlers along the Overland Trail and, later, railroad workers along the path of the Union Pacific Railroad. Eliza remained behind in San Antonio for a while with her daughters, but by 1880, she and Fannie and Harriet had joined Edwin at Fort Sanders.[33]

The young couple's much anticipated honeymoon, however, was put on hold, as the following day, Liggett was ordered to escort a convict, Pvt. Thomas

Clayton of the 2nd Cavalry, to Fort Snelling, Minnesota. No doubt the unfortunate trooper would ultimately be taken from there to Fort Leavenworth, Kansas, to serve his time. Liggett returned from this special duty on July 5, and he and Harriet set out on their delayed wedding trip. This too was cut short when duty called once again. For Liggett, his duty always came first.[34]

The couple returned to Fort Keogh on August 28, 1881, when Liggett was ordered to rejoin his company, and Harriet began to set up house. Alice Baldwin and the other officers' wives made the young bride feel welcome. The officers and their wives carried on an active social life at Fort Keogh. Cards were a popular diversion, along with dances and suppers; the wives of local ranchers were often invited as well. From time to time there were concerts. Alice Baldwin called the 5th Infantry band "exceptionally fine," and many of the members were foreign born. Standard military fare was supplemented from time to time with imported foods from the east and local game like rabbit or quail. Fort Keogh would be their home for the following five years.[35]

Meanwhile, Liggett and Company G, along with Company C of the 5th Infantry and Company E of the 2nd Cavalry, set out the next day for Camp Garfield, some thirty-five miles northeast, in order to relieve Companies A and F, 5th Infantry, and provide security for the working parties building the Northern Pacific Railroad, which was at the time close by and anticipated to reach Fort Keogh on November 30. Liggett took command of the detail on September 24 and returned with it to Fort Keogh on September 30. For the next several months, other than a three-week leave of absence in February 1882, for Liggett, it would be the usual company routine.[36]

As things turned out, given the relatively mild weather, the Northern Pacific crews were laying track at a rate of five miles a day, and the railroad reached Miles City on November 28, slightly ahead of schedule. The Tongue River was temporarily spanned, and the railroad reached Fort Keogh the following day, where it was greeted by the "firing of cannons, music by the band, and great rejoicing." A more permanent bridge was already in the works, and it was hoped that the tracks would reach Rosebud by January 1.[37]

FORT KEOGH: THE PACE SLOWS

By 1882, the incidents of hostile activity were definitely declining but had not ceased altogether. The new year began slowly enough; Liggett remained on duty with his company except for a three-week leave in February and a brief assignment at Fort Buford, where he served on a general court-martial board from April 23 to May 1. He also served as judge advocate for a general court-martial in July and August and as temporary instructor of musketry during the latter month.[38]

On September 26, 1882, Captain Ovenshine led Company G on a detail to repair the military telegraph line from Fort Keogh to Glendive, Montana Territory, more than likely damaged by hostiles. The repair party first camped at Crackerbox Creek (near present-day Marsh, Montana) prior to moving on to Glendive on October 1. They worked their way back from Glendive to Fort Keogh from October 2 to October 7, covering, all told, 135 miles.[39]

RECEIVING OFFICER

In addition to his normal company duties, sometime in late 1882, Liggett was appointed as the post receiving officer. As such, he was in charge of freight shipments to Fort Keogh, as well as to Forts Custer and Maginnis. His duties frequently took him to Glendive, Montana Territory, in order to sort out the freight arriving there by way of the Northern Pacific Railroad. Accordingly, he made the seventy-five-mile trip to Glendive about once a month from late December through early May. On February 7, 1883, Liggett was detailed to Glendive to escort the loaded freight wagons destined for Forts Custer, Keogh, and Maginnis. Late November found him back in Glendive on detached service for three days.[40]

Throughout most of 1883, when not on detached service at Glendive, Liggett carried out his customary duties with Company G. All was not work, as he was able to take several short leaves of absence to go hunting. During his spare time that year, Liggett continued to improve his skills, taking courses in military and civil engineering and practical surveying and road-making. From January 9, 1884, to the end of the month, he and his company were assigned to the ice detail, the arduous duty of cutting and storing it for use during the upcoming year.[41]

FIRST LIEUTENANT LIGGETT

At this time, promotions through the rank of captain were made strictly by seniority and slow in coming, as they occurred if, as, and when a vacancy arose within an officer's own regiment. Accordingly, in June of 1884, when Capt. James Casey of Company A was promoted to major in the 17th Infantry, his vacancy was filled by 1st Lt. Edward L. Russell of Company F. This left a vacancy for Liggett, who received his promotion to first lieutenant effective June 27, 1884. At the same time, he was reassigned to Company F.[42]

NEW ORLEANS

In November 1884, Liggett requested and was granted a one-month leave of absence, which he postponed so as to attend to his various duties at the post. Finally, on January 3, 1885, he and Harriet journeyed by rail and steamboat to New Orleans to enjoy the delights of that city, including the World's Industrial and Cotton Centennial Exposition that had just opened with considerable fanfare on December 16 in Audubon Park. The main building, reputed to be the largest in the country, covered thirty-three acres and was designed to resemble the Louvre. It contained a music hall capable of seating eleven thousand people, where the couple was treated to music played on a gigantic Pilcher Brothers organ. In addition, there was a horticultural hall (in reality, a large greenhouse). For the price of a fifty-cent admission ticket, visitors were dazzled by exhibitions of the latest industrial and agricultural equipment, as well as steam locomotives from all over the world. Elevators took them between floors, and electric lights, powered by a large Corliss engine, turned night into day. With their memories of the beautiful city and the exhibition, the couple returned to Fort Keogh on January 22, 1885.[43]

MORE OF THE SAME

For the next several months, Company F performed the customary garrison duties. On May 24, Liggett was reported as sick in quarters with an unspecified ailment, more than likely another flare-up of his rheumatism, and he remained on sick report until July 18. In the interim, he was appointed post topographical officer and later acting ordnance officer and instructor of musketry. He was relieved of command of his company on September 18 so that he could devote his energies to his new special duties. As topographical officer, he wrote, he had a chance to "practice map making . . . where the country was only superficially charted." For example, on November 16, he rode out to the Rosebud Agency in order to examine the Northern Cheyenne Reservation boundary lines, and he returned to Fort Keogh on November 20.[44]

At about that time, trouble erupted at the Northern Cheyenne Agency between the Tongue and Rosebud Rivers when it was reported that there were insufficient government rations to feed the population and that there were strong signs of discontent. As a result, the agent there asked for assistance. It turned out that the shortage, if it existed at all, was due to the tendency of many hostile tribesmen (in this case, from Pine Ridge) to return to the reservation during the winter months and take shelter among the permanent residents, thus swelling the rolls. Nevertheless, before the situation was fully sorted out, rumors of an Indian outbreak spread quickly, and a mixed column—5th Infantry and 7th Cavalry, led by Maj. Simon Snyder, 5th Infantry—left Fort Keogh, bound for the Indian camp on the Rosebud River. Lieutenant Liggett led the detachment of 5th Infantry and served as quartermaster in the field. Before the soldiers had reached their destination, the agent sent word by courier that all was under control. Major Snyder ordered the return of the command to Fort Keogh, but he and a small detail went on to the reservation to assess the situation, where he found that things had calmed down. The troops returned to Fort Keogh on December 2, having covered a total of 289 miles.[45]

On a lighter note, in December 1885, Liggett allowed his name to be used in connection with the sale of a patent medicine called "Peterson's Lightning," which was touted as the "Great Swedish Remedy." The product was guaranteed to cure "neuralgia, headache, and all acute pain." Lieutenant Liggett was listed in an advertisement as one of the "leading men of the County" who recommended it.[46]

In January 1886, Liggett put his newly acquired surveying skills to good use again, and at the same time earned some money on the side, when he laid out lots in a subdivision in Miles City. For the next six months, he continued to perform a number of special duties in addition to those of post topographical officer, acting ordnance officer, and instructor of musketry, having also been appointed as acting signal officer. He even served as judge advocate for part of the time.[47]

The weather in the Montana Territory was often marked by extremes. The summer of 1886 was no exception, as no rain had fallen from mid-June to mid-July. During that heat wave, a temperature of 120 degrees in the shade was recorded at Fort Keogh on July 15. Between July 12 and 15, Liggett returned to the Rosebud Reservation for the last time to inspect cattle.[48]

FORT TOTTEN, DAKOTA TERRITORY

Looking back on the previous year, Brig. Gen. Thomas H. Ruger, as commander of the Department of Dakota, reported that the year 1886 was marked by a definite decrease from previous years in "Indian depredations" and raids. He attributed that situation in part to the salutary effects of a treaty reached between several tribes at Fort Belknap that past June. For the most part, he credited the "continued activity" of the troops under his command to suppress outbreaks, as well as the growing number of Indians seeking life on the reservation due to "the extinction of the buffalo, and the loss, owing to settlement of the country and extension of railroads, of all the places of refuge to which, formerly, they went when hostile, for at least temporary security."[49]

In August 1886, Companies F and K of the 5th Infantry were transferred to Fort Totten in the Dakota Territory and would remain on duty there until May 30, 1888. Capt. Edmund Rice and Company F left Fort Keogh on Monday, August 16, at 2:00 p.m. and arrived at Fort Totten the following day, traveling most of the way on the Northern Pacific Railroad.[50] Liggett received permission to remain behind a day or so to be with Harriet, who was ill and would follow after she had recovered sufficiently to travel. The post records covered the situation by indicating that the lieutenant was "detached temporarily" at Fort Keogh "by verbal orders of commanding officer" of the post. Captain Baldwin and Company K left Fort Custer on August 29 and arrived at Fort Totten on September 2. In addition to the two infantry companies, the Fort Totten garrison would be augmented by a troop of cavalry and at full strength would consist of approximately 160 officers and enlisted men.[51]

Hunter rejoined his company several days after its arrival. No doubt to Liggett's relief, Harriet and a companion, Gertrude Sevier, arrived during the first week of September. Shortly after her arrival, Harriet left the post for a visit with Miss Sevier at her home in nearby Minnewaukan.[52]

The original Fort Totten was built in July 1867, as "one of a series of posts built for the protection of emigrants passing via an overland route extending from southern Minnesota into western Montana" and later the Northern Pacific Railroad, which soon followed in their wake. As was the case with Fort Keogh, the original log structures were replaced in the early 1870s with more permanent ones, this time built with bricks made from local clay. The clay, however, proved prone to crumbling due to its high lime content, so the exterior brick was painted in order to help stabilize it.[53]

Situated on the south side of Devils Lake and adjoining the Sioux reservation, Alice Baldwin described the setting as "picturesque." Aside from the beautiful lake, the surrounding vista encompassed pine-covered hills, waving prairie grass, and wild flowers in spring and summer. All this beauty, however, came with a price. In summer, the place swarmed with mosquitoes, and the brutal winters eclipsed those experienced in Montana. "Game was plentiful," according to Baldwin, including deer, wild turkeys, quail, grouse, and prairie chickens. So were hungry wolves that were bold enough to stalk the parade ground.[54]

6. Officers' quarters, Fort Totten, ND. Courtesy of the Library of Congress.

Liggett's stay at Fort Totten was relatively uneventful, his company performing the usual garrison duties. As would be the case throughout his early career, he was soon assigned extra duties, first as range officer and eventually as post adjutant, recruiting officer, and post topographic officer. Liggett was appointed assistant commissary in July 1887 and again in January 1888.[55]

By the late 1870s and early 1880s, target practice and marksmanship had become a regular part of the training regimen for officers and enlisted men alike, which could also include lengthy marches and skirmish drills. Liggett was responsible for supervising the testing of all post personnel in marksmanship. By order of Gen. Philip Sheridan, in addition to the designation of "marksman," the US Army created a new category called "sharpshooter," in order to reward excellent target shooting and perhaps stir up some competitive interest in the sport as well. While at Fort Keogh, Liggett had qualified for the new award, which was in the form of a bronze cross.[56]

Sometime during the evening of October 8, 1886, shortly after the arrival of Companies F and K, the government steam yacht *Tillie Lee* burned to the waterline. The vessel, which carried post personnel and their dependents back and forth across the lake to the town of Devils Lake, had been moored at the Fort Totten wharf when a person or persons unknown doused her with kerosene, set her ablaze, and cut the boat loose from her moorings. The fire was labeled "incendiary," and the post authorities offered a fifty-dollar reward for the apprehension and conviction of the arsonist. Apparently, the firebug was never caught. This criminal act appears to have left the principal competition—another steam vessel, the *Minnie H*—with a monopoly. She was piloted by a genuine character, Capt. E. E. Herman, who called himself an "old salt" and paced the deck of the small vessel with a megaphone shouting a colorful variety of "nautical terms and phrases."[57]

Winter came early in Dakota Territory, and with it came frequent blizzards, with snow drifts sometimes reaching as high as the second story. Ropes were run from building to building so as to assure safe passage during such storms. Double-glazed windows and coal stoves kept the quarters warm and cozy. Families entertained in the traditional manner, with regular card games and dances. In addition, there was frequent interaction with the citizens of Devils Lake, through many dinners and dances. The extreme cold did not dampen Liggett's spirit of adventure, as he and a Will Egan were reported to be the first to drive a sleigh over the ice to visit the town of Devils Lake on November 29. Meanwhile, throughout the months of December 1886 and January 1887, the enlisted men were periodically assigned to the ice detail.[58]

Summer in 1887 brought a change of pace. During the evening of June 14, 1887, the *Minnie H* was the venue for an "aquatic picnic" attended by the officers and their wives, including Hunter and Harriet. Later on, Liggett led Company F on two practice marches. The first, on August 13, involved a ten-mile round trip to the Devils Lake ferry and back. The second march took place on August 27 and 28 and involved an eighteen-mile overnight tramp to a spring northeast of Devils Heart Butte and back.[59]

In September 1887, Liggett was granted a seven-day leave to go hunting, and he left the post on September 13 but returned on September 16, before his leave was up. It is possible that the hunting was poor, but more than likely he had received word that his father had been gravely ill for some time. Liggett requested and was granted a twenty-three-day extension of his leave, and he left the post again on September 19, traveling to Birdsboro, Pennsylvania, to see his father for the last time. James Liggett died there on September 27 at the age of sixty-six. He was buried with other family members at St. Paul's Methodist Episcopal Cemetery in Geigertown, Pennsylvania. Liggett overstayed his leave by several days and rejoined his company at Fort Totten on October 17.[60]

ANOTHER MOVE

In May 1888, the command at Fort Totten was notified of an impending transfer of the entire 5th Infantry Regiment to Texas. Many rejoiced over what they believed would be a more "salubrious" climate, if only warmer. At this time, Liggett was relieved of his extra duties. All ten companies and the band were ordered to assemble in Bismarck in preparation for their journey down the Missouri River. To that end, Companies F and K left Fort Totten at 1:00 p.m. on May 30 and marched to nearby Fort Totten station just south of Minnewaukan. There, they boarded a waiting Jamestown and Northern Railroad train for the seventy-five-mile trip to Jamestown, in order to make a connection with the Northern Pacific Railroad that would carry them all the way to Bismarck.[61]

The mood at the landing in Bismarck was festive on Friday, June 1, despite the early hour. Local dignitaries and other well-wishers mingled amid the usual hustle and bustle attending the loading of men and baggage aboard the waiting steamers, *Helena* and *General Terry*. Both sternwheelers were owned by the Power Line. Hunter and Harriet, like the other officers and their wives, were assigned first-class quarters on the *Helena*. His Company F, along with Companies A, D, and G, were billeted on the *General Terry*.[62]

The passage downstream went smoothly at first, although early on, the *General Terry* became briefly hung up on a sandbar, and later, just below Sioux City, Iowa, she hit a snag. At 6:00 p.m. Sunday, June 10, both boats approached the landing at Douglas Street at Omaha, Nebraska, with the "usual screeching of whistles" for a brief stop to reprovision. Seeing a flag on shore at half-staff, a rumor circulated that General Sheridan had died, although that was quickly dispelled. After more than a week on board, the soldiers were eager to set foot on dry land but were not permitted to disembark, and they became disgruntled. Sensing trouble, an observant officer ordered the band to strike up some lively tunes in order to lighten the mood.

At sunset, both boats slipped their moorings and headed downriver to Kansas City. The *Helena* was first to pass under the new Union Pacific Railroad bridge, followed by the *General Terry*. At that moment, the "strong current swung her sidewise against one of the old piers standing in the river," a navigational hazard lurking just below the surface. The impact tore a hole in her side some eight feet long and six feet high, and water began to pour in. Reacting quickly, the pilot ordered the engineer to proceed at full speed and turned the vessel toward the shore, where she grounded in about eight feet of water. Panic and pandemonium ensued as the startled men, women, and children immediately realized what had happened. The boat was tied up, and order was restored. While the women and children were escorted to local hotels, the men were organized into teams and began to salvage what they could.[63]

Meanwhile, the *Helena*, hearing her sister ship's distress whistle, turned around and steamed back upstream to assist. Local brigands, known as "sandbank pirates," also responded quickly to the situation, looking to profit from the accident. Seizing any small boat they could find along the shore, they retrieved dozens of boxes of military stores and trunks full of clothing and personal effects that had been swept off the decks by the rushing water and had begun to float downriver in the lowering darkness. Sad to say, these items were never recovered by their rightful owners.

At daybreak, the salvage efforts were redoubled as squads of soldiers, led by their officers, combed through the wreckage. Although many of the officers' families lost valuable objects—including furniture, artwork, and sentimental keepsakes—the heaviest burden fell upon the enlisted men who had been situated on the lower deck when the accident occurred, whose meager possessions were simply swept away. Luckily, no lives were lost. An estimate of the total loss amounted to one hundred thousand dollars.[64]

On June 12, Harriet and the other wives reboarded the *Helena*, which resumed her journey to Kansas City, Missouri, arriving two days later. From there, that portion of the regiment traveled the balance of the way to Texas by the Missouri Pacific Railroad. In the meantime, Liggett's Company F, which was involved with the salvage effort, was delayed twelve days in Omaha, and it did not arrive at Fort McIntosh until June 27, when Hunter and Harriet were reunited.[65]

In a sad postscript, no doubt recognizing the futility of the salvage efforts, the "entire cargo," including "furniture, carpets, rugs, curtains, bedding, furs, robes, lamps, [and] Indian relics," was sold at auction on June 28.[66]

THREE
Southern Exposure

FORT MCINTOSH

During the years 1888 to 1890, Liggett was on duty with the 5th Infantry at Fort McIntosh near Laredo, Texas. Although the post had gone through several major renovations during its long history, which dated back to 1849, its mission remained largely unchanged: to protect the ranches of the region from the depredations of Comanche and Lipan Apache raiders, as well as to guard a major ford over the Rio Grande known locally, fittingly enough, as "Indian Crossing." Blistering summer heat, little rain, and a host of insects, snakes, and vermin often proved a challenge for the fort's occupants, particularly the officers' wives.[1]

Fort McIntosh was home to Companies C and F of the 5th Infantry and one troop of the 3rd Cavalry. In overall command of the post was Maj. (Bvt. Col.) Samuel B. M. Young of the 3rd Cavalry. Also stationed there with the 3rd Cavalry was Lt. Joseph Dickman. Liggett would cross paths with both throughout his career. Young would later distinguish himself during the Philippine War and also serve as the first president of the Army War College and the first chief of staff of the US Army. He would retire as a lieutenant general. Dickman would go on to serve in a variety of assignments, including as a corps commander under Liggett during the First World War, where he would play a role in the "Race to Sedan."

Liggett arrived in Texas with Company F on June 27. In July, he was assigned extra duties, as post adjutant, acting assistant quartermaster, assistant commissary officer, and recruiting officer. At the same time, Company F carried on normal garrison and escort duties. In August, he briefly took command of Company C while its other officers were unavailable for duty. He was a busy man. Rather than complain, he no doubt accepted these assignments for what they were—an indication of the confidence his superiors had in his abilities.[2]

Between October 30 and November 3, Liggett remained sick in quarters. He was well enough to leave the post on November 4 for an unspecified purpose, and he returned on November 25. Things must have been slow, since he was able to take a brief hunting trip between December 7 and 10. In January 1889, he was appointed post treasurer and as such was placed in charge of the post schools, a duty usually performed by the regimental chaplain, who had just been transferred out.[3]

When Companies C and F left for the annual target practice at San Antonio for two months from March through May, Liggett stayed behind to carry out his duties on post. Liggett was granted a one-month leave, and he and Harriet left on July 15. He took a leave again between September 10 and September 26, followed by a short hunting trip November 8 through 10. For the next several months, Liggett was ill much of the time. Aside from another short hunting trip in February 1890, he was sick in quarters for two days in mid-November with an unspecified ailment, followed by a bout of acute nephritis that lasted for more than two weeks in late December and early January. Then he caught the flu following his February hunting trip, which laid him up for another ten days, followed by a relapse in early March.[4]

During the years 1890 and 1891, Congress, in concert with the secretary of war, instituted more reform measures in order to further professionalize the US Army. It was at this time that proficiency examinations were mandated for officers seeking promotion, and all commanding officers were required to fill out standardized annual efficiency reports rating their subordinates in certain categories like attention to detail and discipline. As a component of the report, by order of the secretary of war, each officer was required to fill out a one-page form listing his particular skills and the activities in which he participated, including his current reading. This form was then combined with the efficiency report.[5]

Beginning with a report dated May 1, 1890, Liggett enjoyed consistently good efficiency reports, his commanders rating him "excellent" in all areas, from attention to duty and the care of his men. Most, like Col. A. Brackett, the post commander at Fort McIntosh, made specific reference to Liggett's studious habits. Liggett himself would write that he "commenced study of [the] military profession in 1879 and have pursued it since." In his studies of military history, he used "the best maps attainable" in addition to the standard texts like Jomini and the writings of generals Grant, Sherman, and Sheridan. Lest one think he was all work and no play, in 1885 Liggett took up the "pastime" of photography.[6]

Things returned to normal in the spring of 1890, and this time, Liggett was back in command of his company when it traveled to San Antonio in May for the annual target practice exercises. The company left Fort McIntosh by rail on May 29 and, upon completion of that duty, marched 154 miles back to Fort McIntosh between July 15 and 22. Like a rolling stone, the 5th Infantry was frequently on the move. The following month, Liggett and Company F were transferred to Fort Davis in West Texas. The company left by rail at 8:40 a.m. on August 16.[7]

FORT DAVIS

Liggett would remain at Fort Davis, Texas, from July 1890 to July 1891, when the fort was decommissioned by order of the War Department. Built in 1854 by Bvt. Maj. Gen. Persifor F. Smith, it was located on the eastern slope of the Davis Mountains, nestled in a small canyon near Limpia Creek and Wild Rose Pass. Fort Davis was one of several posts in the Trans-Pecos region of West Texas, which were intended to protect the trail from San Antonio to El Paso. Most notably, Fort Davis served as a base during the Apache Wars, particularly during the pursuit of Chief Victorio during the years 1880–81. The original wooden structures gave way to more substantial ones built of stone during the late 1860s and early 1870s. A row of officers' quarters lined one side of a long, dusty parade ground, while enlisted barracks and quartermaster storehouses lined the other.[8]

After a period of about six weeks settling into the post routine, on October 2, 1890, Liggett said good-bye to Harriet and left Fort Davis to take command of a contingent of Seminole-Negro Indian Scouts. This reliable unit of volunteers was based at Fort Clark, which was located just outside of Brackettville, Texas. The unit was used primarily to scout the border in the Big Bend area along the Rio Grande, looking for cattle and horse thieves and hostile Indians, often one and the same. Liggett made his way to Neville Spring, where a small post or camp had been established as a base for the scouts, usually a contingent of approximately twenty men, to use while in the field. In addition to the spring itself, there was a barracks as well as a small officers' quarters.[9]

While on duty at Neville Spring, Liggett received word that Col. Nathan W. Osborne, his regimental commander, had recommended him for training at the Torpedo School at the Fort at Willets Point, New York. This was clearly in recognition of his diligent study and excellent qualities as an officer and was a choice assignment. He took his time to think about it but in the end asked that the recommendation be withdrawn. "While I appreciate the advantages of this detail and the compliment of the selection," he replied, "I feel compelled to ask the Regimental Commander to withdraw my nomination because of my pecuniary situation is at present such that I cannot afford to accept the detail." The nomination was withdrawn.[10]

His assignment at Neville Spring completed, Liggett returned to Fort Davis on December 12, where he resumed command of Company F. At some point during his tour at that post, he met 2nd Lt. Clarence R. Edwards, who, at that time, was assigned to the 23rd Infantry Regiment and as post adjutant. Edwards had been a plebe at West Point at the same time that Liggett was in his final year. He came from a well-to-do and well-connected family in Cleveland, Ohio. His father, a successful wholesale grocery and liquor distributor, rubbed elbows with the likes of Sen. Marcus A. Hanna and Adj. Gen. Henry C. Corbin, and he and his wife, Lucia, were not shy about advancing their son's career. Edwards's and Liggett's paths would also cross from time to time, culminating with the First World War, where Edwards would lead the 26th ("Yankee") Division.[11]

The next several months were marked by the usual post routine, broken only by Liggett's detached duty at Fort Bliss, Texas, from February 9 through March 9. There he served on court-martial duty. He must have contracted something during that trip, as he was reported sick in quarters for an unspecified illness from March 11 to 16. In May, he served on a Summary Court for five days.[12]

No longer deemed useful, Fort Davis was ordered by the War Department to close by June 1891. Accordingly, Liggett's stay there was relatively short. Company F was sent to Fort Sam Houston on June 30, simultaneous with the abandonment of Fort Davis.[13]

FORT SAM

Liggett and Company F arrived at Fort Sam Houston in San Antonio, Texas, on July 4, 1891. The post had a long history, stretching back to a camp built by the US Army in October 1845, two months before Texas was admitted into the Union. Over the succeeding decades, the facilities expanded to include an infantry post, a hospital, and a quartermaster depot. In fact, by the time Liggett arrived, the fort was well on its way to becoming the second-largest US Army post. The sprawling complex had been named Fort Sam Houston in 1890, but many would refer to it simply as "Fort Sam."[14]

Aside from occasional detached service, for Liggett, the following several months found him and his company, for the most part, performing garrison duties. In early August, the post commander, Col. John J. Coppinger, 23rd Infantry, detailed Liggett to attend the state militia encampment in nearby San Antonio. Beginning in the 1880s, these "camps of instruction" also played an important training role for both regulars and militia, as they provided an opportunity for larger-scale maneuvers, as well as instruction in basic skills such as reconnaissance and map reading. This training was especially valuable for the regular regiments, as the scattered companies had a chance to work together. Liggett spent five days in San Antonio from August 19 through 24.[15]

In October, he was able to go hunting from the twenty-second through the twenty-ninth. Later on, in December, he traveled to Fort Bliss, where he served as a member of a general court-martial. The court-martial board ended on December 27, yet Liggett did not return to Fort Sam until January 7, 1892. It is possible that Harriet had joined him and that they took some extra time to travel over the holidays.[16]

In January 1892, while Liggett was still on detached service at Fort Bliss, Colonel Coppinger prepared an efficiency report calling him a "hard student on military works" and "an excellent officer, thoroughly reliable for any duty entrusted to him."[17]

Once back at Fort Sam, Liggett continued his course of independent study that included an eclectic mix of subjects from military history and tactics to engineering, photography, and "electrics." He also believed that it was necessary to complement theory with practice. "Theoretical study would be more satisfactory," Liggett wrote, "if conditions were such that practice could be combined with such study." He added that "in order to keep abreast of the times constant and systematic study [is] a necessity." At some point during the year, he delivered a lecture at the officers' lyceum titled "The Modern Development of Infantry Tactics."[18]

Company duty for the next three months was marked once again by dull routine. Finally, at 6:00 a.m. on April 5, Companies A and F marched out of the post, eighteen and a half miles, to Leon Springs for their month-long annual target practice. Liggett would remain behind once more, but this time he was happy to do so. It seems that his hard work, no matter the task, and his demonstrable talents and sense of responsibility were finally recognized, as he was appointed regimental adjutant. After a brief service as judge advocate on May 9, he left the post on May 11 for his new duty station at St. Francis Barracks in St. Augustine, Florida.[19]

7. St. Francis Barracks, St. Augustine, FL. Courtesy of the Library of Congress.

ST. FRANCIS BARRACKS

Liggett assumed his duties as regimental adjutant at St. Francis Barracks on May 14, 1892. There he joined the regimental headquarters staff, along with Companies D, E, I, and K, and the band. At any one time, the post was customarily occupied by two of the companies on a rotating basis while the other two were off training elsewhere, such as nearby Anastasia Island or Fort Thomas, Kentucky.[20]

St. Francis Barracks was a former Franciscan monastery dating from the Spanish era, located on the Matanzas River in St. Augustine, Florida. As can well be imagined, the post had undergone numerous changes in the years since, as the area passed from Spanish control to British and back over. The enlisted barracks and officers' quarters were nearby, adjacent to the small post cemetery. From the porch of their duplex, Harriet and Hunter could look out over the river and enjoy the cool sea breezes.[21]

As with his previous assignments, Liggett would wear many hats during his tour at St. Augustine. On the day following his arrival, he was appointed post adjutant as well as regimental recruiting officer. The following July, his duties were increased when he was, once again, placed in charge of the post schools. In addition, he would take turns with the other officers to serve as a summary court officer, dealing with less serious breaches of military discipline. In spite of their number, his regimental duties were not onerous, and when Liggett was not carrying them out, he had the opportunity to pursue his real passion—the independent study of military history. For both Hunter and Harriet, the assignment was a real change from the past decade.[22]

In October 1892, Hunter and Harriet enjoyed a fifteen-day leave from the thirteenth through the twenty-seventh. On December 26, under orders, he traveled by rail to Fort McPherson, Georgia, where he appeared the following day before an examination board in order to qualify for promotion to the rank of captain in the Regular Army. In addition to a physical examination, there was a lengthy written test consisting of US Army regulations, firing and infantry drills, the guard manual, and military law. By December 31, he was back in Florida in time to celebrate New Year's Eve with his wife. Liggett was notified by the adjutant general on January 18, 1893, that he had passed his proficiency examination.[23]

The year 1893 passed relatively uneventfully, with Liggett performing his usual duties as adjutant. He continued to participate in the officers' lyceum, and at some point during the year, he delivered a lecture titled "Forcing the Passage of a River in the Face of the Enemy."[24]

From September 1 to 3, Liggett served as summary court officer. He was temporarily relieved of his various duties when he and Harriet left the post at the close of business on September 3 for an extended leave. They returned on October 18. Once back, he picked up where he had left off.[25]

The first part of 1894 was more of the same, although Liggett did take several days off in late January to go hunting. In February, when the inspector general for the Department of the East visited the post, both companies, along with the staff, were marched four miles to north St. Augustine in order to conduct practice exercises, alternating attack and defense. Liggett took another short leave in March, most likely hunting, and the month of April was marked by weekly practice marches by the garrison of anywhere from six to twelve miles.[26]

In the interim, Col. Nathan Osborne prepared Liggett's annual efficiency report. Osborne commended him for his professional zeal and called his conduct and habits "exemplary." He went on to describe Liggett as "cheerful and uncomplaining" in carrying out his duties. In addition, Osborne pointed to his "aptitude for mathematics" and "peculiar fitness for topographical observation." For his part, Liggett reported that he continued his self-study on military law, topography, and infantry drill regulations, among other subjects. He also indicated that he had a "reading knowledge" of both Spanish and French.[27]

During the summer of 1894, Liggett contracted a disease (more than likely dysentery) "in the line of duty," and he was placed on the sick list from August 24 through September 2. He was confined to quarters for the first two days and, for the balance, was cleared for office duty, including briefly serving as summary court officer. On September 5, when Liggett had recovered sufficiently, he left the post on detached service, attending an encampment of the 5th Battalion of the Florida State Guard at Tampa. He returned to St. Augustine on September 15.[28]

At 2:30 p.m. on October 18, 1894, the headquarters staff and the band, along with Companies C and D, left St. Francis Barracks by rail, bound for their next assignment at Fort McPherson in East Point, Georgia. They were replaced by elements of the 3rd Artillery Regiment that had arrived at St. Augustine late that morning.[29]

FORT MCPHERSON

Although a military facility of some kind had existed there for at least fifty years, Fort McPherson officially opened in September 1885. It was named in honor of Maj. Gen. James Birdseye McPherson, who had been killed at the Battle of Atlanta on July 22, 1864.[30]

Liggett arrived at Fort McPherson at 7:30 a.m. on October 19, 1894, after a journey of 389 miles. Eventually, eight companies of the 5th Infantry would be consolidated there. With so many other regimental officers on post, the usual duties were spread around. Liggett was appointed post adjutant as well as regimental recruiting officer. His duties being relatively light, he and Harriet were able to take two short leaves in November and December.[31]

Capt. Leonard Wood joined the regiment as medical officer. His transfer to Atlanta from Fort Spokane, Washington, in about 1893 was not to his liking, and he spent much of his time in Georgia importuning Gen. Nelson A. Miles, with whom he had become acquainted during the Geronimo Campaign, as well as his other friends for a transfer to Washington, DC. Wood referred to Fort McPherson as a "dull, stupid post, absolutely without interest." Bored, he enrolled in a class at Georgia Technological School (now Georgia Tech) so that he could coach and play on the football team. He even studied languages and learned how to ride a bicycle. Otherwise, he endured Fort McPherson as a minor pause in his steady path to advancement. Eventually, in September 1895, his efforts were rewarded: he was appointed as an assistant attending surgeon, treating officers and their families in Washington, DC. He and Liggett's paths would cross again after Wood became chief of staff.[32]

In May 1895, as a member of Col. William Kellogg's staff, Liggett, along with Companies E and H, traveled to Camp Schofield in Memphis, Tennessee, to "participate in an encampment of the National Guard" with units from several states. The detail left Atlanta, Georgia, by rail at 3:20 p.m. on May 10 and arrived in Memphis the following morning. After the encampment was over, the detail returned to Fort McPherson during the early afternoon of May 23.[33]

In early July 1895, Liggett received his annual efficiency report, which covered much of the previous year, including his final months at St. Francis Barracks. It was prepared by the regimental commander, Col. William L. Kellogg, who was pleased with Liggett's performance and found him to be "well fitted to any staff duty." From his own standpoint, Liggett reported that he continued to pursue his course of self-study, reading "standard works on munitions, entrenchments, and topography." In addition, he participated in a lyceum course at the post, where he prepared and read an essay titled "The Tactical Training of Infantry."[34]

At the same time, Liggett traveled to Key West Barracks, where he served as a member of a court-martial board. He was back on post by July 15, and he took another short leave at month's end.[35]

In September 1895, a battalion of the regiment (Companies A and D) received orders to attend the Cotton States and International Exposition in Atlanta. The nation had been in the throes of a severe depression for several years. Especially hard hit were the former Confederate states. The exposition was intended to showcase the industrial and agricultural advancements of the nation—in particular, of the South. It also heralded the advances made by women and African Americans. The battalion encamped on the fairgrounds just outside of Atlanta on September 18, and it took part in the opening ceremonies. After speeches by prominent men, including Booker T. Washington, at precisely 6:54 that evening, President Cleveland, who was vacationing 1,100 miles away at Buzzards Bay, Massachusetts, pushed a button that instantly activated the machinery in Atlanta, to the absolute delight of the sixty thousand visitors. Over the course of the next three months, various companies of the regiment were detailed to Atlanta during the period of the exposition.[36]

In December 1895, Maj. J. P. Sanger from the inspector general's office conducted an inspection at Fort McPherson, including the 5th Infantry. In his report, he specifically commended Liggett, who was then serving as post adjutant, as "an efficient adjutant with many, if not all the qualities that grace that position." The following May, inspector general of the US Army,

Brig. Gen. Joseph C. Breckinridge, passed this comment on to the secretary of war on Liggett's behalf regarding his application for the next captain's vacancy in the regiment.[37]

With the spring of 1896 came a series of daylong practice marches to condition the men. The regiment stepped out on March 3 and 10 in "heavy marching order" for fourteen- and fifteen-mile marches, respectively. The final practice march took place on March 26, in "light marching order" for a distance of sixteen miles. The following month, after four years as regimental adjutant, Liggett was relieved of that duty as well as that of regimental recruiting officer. He was attached to Company D and was finally back where he wanted to be—leading troops.[38]

In late June 1896, Liggett received his annual efficiency report. In the absence of Colonel Kellogg, that year it was prepared by Lt. Col. George D. Russell, who found him to be "an excellent officer in every way," including his capacity for command, his professional zeal, and the condition of the men under his command. Liggett reported himself that he continued to participate in the lyceum on post, where he delivered a lecture titled "The 30 Caliber Magazine Rifle."[39]

Marksmanship and physical conditioning continued to be part of the training regimen. On July 14, Liggett led Company D on a nearly sixty-mile march to the target range in Waco, Georgia. The company left the post at 7:00 a.m. and arrived at the range four long days later at 9:00 a.m. Their target practice completed, the detail left the range on August 31 and marched all the way back to Fort McPherson, arriving there at 7:00 a.m. on September 4.[40]

By order of the secretary of war, the regiment was sent to attend the inauguration ceremony for the governor of Georgia on October 31. The troops were taken by rail to Atlanta and back that day. After a busy few months, Liggett took a couple of days off in early November to go hunting. Other than detached service from January 5 to 7, when he participated as a member on a general court-martial panel at Fort Barrancas, Florida, the next several months passed without incident.[41]

During April 1897, Liggett's 2nd Battalion conducted two short practice marches of four miles each on the eighth and fifteenth of the month. Then calamity struck when Col. William L. Kellogg, the regimental commander, died of heart failure at Fort McPherson on April 17. The entire regiment participated in the funeral and acted as his escort as the caisson traveled nearly five miles from the post to Westview Cemetery. From April 19 to 26, Liggett remained sick in quarters with acute pharyngitis.[42]

Liggett was ordered on detached service with the Florida militia from May 15 through the 26. He was back in command of Company D when it and five others, along with the band and a medical detachment, were detailed to attend the Tennessee Centennial in Nashville at Westside Park. The soldiers left the post at 6:30 p.m. on May 30 and boarded a train for the nearly three-hundred-mile journey.

As was the case with the Cotton States and International Exposition in Atlanta two years earlier, this exhibition celebrated the industrial, scientific, and agricultural accomplishments of Tennessee and the country at large. Of the more than a dozen new buildings, including the reconstruction of a roughhewn eighteenth-century log cabin, the highlight of the fair was a full-scale reproduction of the Parthenon, complete with the Elgin Marbles and a statue of Pallas Athena. Aside from the various exhibits, visitors could enjoy a wide variety of foods, bands, a Chinese parade complete with a dragon, and a "coochee-coochee" show. Liggett's men certainly must have enjoyed this assignment, and no doubt many of them flocked to the last of those exhibits when off duty![43]

All troops returned to Fort McPherson at 1:00 a.m. on June 4. Liggett hardly had a chance to settle back in when his company was ordered to attend an encampment of the Georgia Volunteers in nearby Griffin, from June 7 to 22. In between these assignments, his battalion conducted a series of practice marches of anywhere from four to ten miles in length.[44]

The highlight of that summer, however, came on June 24 when the forty-year-old Liggett received his promotion to the grade of captain effective June 1, 1897. Prior to 1890, all promotions through the grade of captain were lineal and based on seniority within the regiment, which made the process glacially slow. An act of Congress in October of that year extended the process to all grades through colonel and expanded the field to include the entire branch, which helped ease the situation. Still, an officer had to wait until a more senior captain retired, which is exactly what happened on June 1, when Capt. Henry Romeyn of Company G retired at the mandatory age of sixty-four. As an indication of just how slowly the promotion process went, Romeyn was a forty-six-year-old first lieutenant in the 5th Infantry when Liggett joined the regiment fresh out of West Point. Liggett was promoted into the slot vacated by Romeyn (i.e., Company G) and simultaneously "reassigned" to Company D. He had worked hard for the promotion and was justifiably proud. Without a second thought, Liggett immediately began the process to seek promotion to the next grade.[45]

That summer, Captain Liggett received a copy of his annual efficiency report, this one prepared by Col. Henry C. Cook, who had replaced Colonel Kellogg. Cook rated Liggett "excellent" in all categories; however, since he had not known him for the full year, he hedged, "as far as observed and known to me." For his part, Liggett reported that he had read a paper at the Fort McPherson post lyceum, the same one that he had delivered four years prior, "Crossing Rivers in the Presence of the Enemy." He continued his course of self-study—including military history, as usual—but he also specifically addressed the question of how to maximize the efficiency of the National Guard.[46]

On September 3, Company D, now part of the 1st Battalion, marched out of the post bound for the target range at Waco, Georgia, some fifty-five miles away. Liggett and his company arrived there two days later. The exercise complete, the battalion marched back to Fort McPherson between September 28 and October 1.[47]

While at Fort McPherson, Liggett made the acquaintance of several prominent Atlanta businessmen, in particular Robert J. Lowry, president of the Lowry Banking Company as well as the American Banking Association. In July 1897, when word of the imminent retirement of a Colonel Hughes as inspector general reached Lowry, he wrote to his friend Sen. Marcus A. Hanna on behalf of Liggett. "Captain Liggett came here a stranger, but soon found himself among friends," he wrote, "[and] by his genial manners, military bearing and gentlemanly conduct . . . I feel fully satisfied he would fill the office he desires with credit to himself and the government." In January 1896, Lowry followed up with a letter directly to President McKinley. Lowry would go on to write two more letters on Liggett's behalf.[48]

Liggett picked up the endorsement of the governor of Georgia, who had become acquainted with him during his tour at Fort McPherson and was impressed with the young officer's work at the camps of instruction for Georgia troops. The governor praised Liggett's qualities as a staff officer, and he added that his appointment as a major "would greatly please our people, who know him well." In addition, he was endorsed by US District Court Judge William T. Newman from Georgia, the adjutant general of Florida, and W. L. Strong, a former mayor of New York City. The campaign was somewhat successful, as President McKinley asked the secretary of war to give some consideration to a promotion for Liggett in the office of either the inspector general or the adjutant general. In reply, he was advised by the adjutant general that none would occur based on retirement for age until April 18, 1901.[49]

The entire 5th Infantry Regiment conducted a march from Fort McPherson to Chickamauga National Park, site of that bloody Civil War battle. The troops left the post at 8:15 a.m. on October 6 and, through a series of daily marches, covered the 124 miles to the park by 10:00 a.m. October 15. They spent a week there.[50]

Each night along the route, Company D would pause to make camp. The march served a dual purpose: it conditioned the men, but it also gave Captain Liggett an opportunity to give his troops a valuable history lesson about war and the tides of battle. As a student of military history, he believed that even from a thirty-five-year-old battle, lessons could be learned and applied to more modern warfare.

It was on one night during this march that Liggett met and became friends with a correspondent by the name of George T. Fry. The man had driven out to Liggett's campsite at the edge of a wooded area when, in Fry's words, a "balky army mule had brought havoc to our buggy." It was then that the "tall, lanky" Liggett came along, his uniform covered in a coat of dust from the march, to take charge of the situation and welcome the visitor to his camp. Fry was impressed with the poise and determination of the officer. Their paths would cross again two years later in the middle of the Pacific Ocean, when the adversities would be more challenging than a balky US Army mule.[51]

The return journey to Fort McPherson was a bit more complicated. Early on the morning of October 22, the regiment began a march to Kingston, Georgia, sixty-six miles distant. It arrived there during the early afternoon of October 25. That evening, it boarded a train to Nashville, Tennessee, to take part in that city's still ongoing centennial exposition and arrived there the following morning. The regiment camped on the exposition grounds, and when the festivities were complete, on October 31, it entrained for Atlanta. The regiment was back home at Fort McPherson on November 1.[52]

After October, the pace slowed, at least for a while. In December, Liggett took two days to go hunting. In the new year, he returned to Fort Barrancas, Florida, as a member of a general court-martial board, from February 14 through 16. It was at this time that the *Maine* blew up in Havana Harbor, and from that point on, things took a different turn.[53]

With April 15, 1898, came orders reassigning the regimental headquarters and staff, along with the band and Liggett's battalion, to Tampa, Florida, as the US Army geared up for war with Spain. The troops left Fort McPherson for the last time at 3:30 p.m. on April 19 for the journey by rail to Florida.[54]

FOUR
Cuba and the Philippines

A SPLENDID LITTLE WAR

The sinking of the battleship *Maine* in Havana Harbor in February 1898 triggered a series of events that, fanned by the press, quickly led to war with Spain. No longer the far-flung and powerful empire that she once was, Spain had struggled of late to contain insurgencies in both the Philippines and in its crown jewel, Cuba. Things were somewhat quiet in the Philippines, where, thanks in large measure to a sizeable payoff, Philippine nationalists were enjoying a fairly comfortable exile in Hong Kong, just biding their time for a return to the islands. Not so in Cuba, where insurgents were actively engaged with Spanish forces. The fight there had attracted hundreds of filibusters from the United States—young men like Frederick Funston from Kansas—who were drawn to the cause of Cuban independence.[1]

With a total strength of approximately twenty-eight thousand officers and enlisted men, the US Army was in no position to take on a major war, even against Spain. So the call went out for volunteers, and the response was overwhelming. For many career officers in an army notorious for slow promotions, this was an opportunity to advance, and so they sought commissions in the volunteer force or other departments. Liggett was no exception. He asked for a transfer to the quartermaster department, which was not granted as there were too many other applicants with more political pull.[2]

At this time, there was considerable movement of units, and confusion reigned. Decisions had to be made regarding temporary encampments, embarkation points, and overall logistics and supply. Despite all the confusion, Tampa became the center of gravity—a poor choice but, as it turned out, the best one from among a host of worse choices.[3]

Still a captain in the 5th Infantry, Liggett left Fort McPherson on April 19, 1898, bound for Tampa, Florida, where he served briefly. On the move once again, Liggett, along with a junior officer and Company D, 5th Infantry, arrived at Fort St. Philip, Louisiana, on May 10 at 3:30 p.m. He assumed command of the post, which at that time also included Company D, 23rd Infantry, and Battery D of the 1st Artillery. While there, he accepted a commission as a major and assistant adjutant general of US Volunteers, effective June 3, and he was assigned as adjutant general of the 3rd Division, Fourth Army Corps. Liggett was granted leave "while awaiting further orders," and he left St. Philip and Company D on June 26. Eventually, Company D, without Liggett, returned to Tampa, Florida, from which it sailed by steamship on August 20, arriving in Santiago de Cuba eight days later, where it would perform garrison duties.[4]

VOLUNTEER SERVICE

On July 1, Liggett reported to his new assignment. The Fourth Army Corps was under the command of Maj. Gen. John J. Coppinger, an Irish immigrant who had served valiantly during the Civil War. General Coppinger had been the post commander at Fort Sam Houston when Liggett reported there seven years before. Another staff officer in the Fourth Army Corps was Clarence R. Edwards, who had, like Liggett, also accepted a commission as a major and assistant adjutant general in the volunteer service.[5]

It soon became clear that an alternate location was necessary to assemble and equip the thousands of volunteers swelling the ranks of the Fourth Army Corps, and Fernandina, Florida, just north of Jacksonville, fit the bill. Liggett reported there on July 29. However, even at that location, supply would be a problem. Worse than that, many camps proved unhealthy, as adequate sanitation and shelter were lacking.

Liggett would spend the month of August in Florida. Then in September, he moved from Fernandina to Huntsville, Alabama, and six weeks later, he was assigned as adjutant general of the 3rd Division, Second Army Corps, then stationed at Athens, Georgia. In January 1899, he was reassigned, this time to the 2nd Division, Second Army Corps, as adjutant general. The division was then stationed at Greenville, South Carolina, where he would serve in that capacity from January 12 until April 12, 1899, at which time he was discharged from the volunteer service once again.[6]

It would be fair to say that Harriet was Hunter's biggest advocate, and she was not shy about sending a letter to the adjutant general on his behalf from time to time, presumably without her husband's knowledge. On February 14, 1899, while Liggett was still in Greenville, she did just that. On March 22, when he found out that she had done so, he immediately requested that the adjutant general's office return the missive to him, which it did. We will never know the contents of the letter, because Liggett presumably destroyed it. As with many career soldiers, Liggett wanted to be where the action was, and he no doubt felt that he had been left out of the Cuban Campaign. We can only speculate that he was concerned that the timing of the letter or its contents would have been harmful to his career.[7]

BACK BRIEFLY WITH THE FIFTH

Until May 2, Liggett enjoyed a brief respite at Fort McPherson while he awaited further orders, and he no doubt took that time to see Harriet and to make his farewells. He then left the post to report to the Santiago Barracks, located on Morro Castle Road in Santiago de Cuba, on May 18. Once there he awaited transport to rejoin his Company D, 5th Infantry, which he did on June 8. He took command the following day. On June 10, Company D, now mounted, established an outpost in the small village of El Caney, about six miles northeast of Santiago, with Liggett in command. El Caney—and, in particular, a stone building there called El Viso—had been the scene of a bloody, daylong battle on July 1, 1898, where Maj. Gen. Henry Ware Lawton had overcome determined Spanish resistance while another, more well-known battle raged nearby at San Juan and Kettle Hills. Liggett, as a student of history, certainly was aware of the significance of his assignment. While there, the regimental commander, Col. Richard Comba, filed Liggett's efficiency report, finding his performance in all respects "excellent." But Liggett's tenure at the post would be short, as he received telegraphic orders on July 14 to proceed at once to New York. He was, once again, appointed as a major in the US Volunteer Service, effective as of July 5. He left Cuba the following day and arrived in New York on or about July 22, ready to join the 31st US Volunteer Infantry Regiment.[8]

On August 2, Liggett reported to Fort Thomas, Kentucky, which was located on the south bank of the Ohio River, opposite Cincinnati. The 31st Volunteer Infantry had established its camp at the rifle range. There, Liggett was assigned to command of the 3rd Battalion as it prepared to go overseas. The regiment was under the command of Col. James S. Pettit, and its executive officer was Lt. Col. Webb C. Hayes, son of the former president. While at Fort Thomas,

Liggett replaced Hayes as summary court officer. As with many volunteer regiments, which were either freshly recruited or converted state militias, discipline could be an issue. Most of the volunteers were young men in high spirits, anticipating the "excitement" of war before the numbing drudgery of daily life in the US Army set in. So it came as no surprise when it was brought to Colonel Pettit's attention that some of the men had been stealing apples, honey, and other produce from nearby farms, while others were bathing naked in the Ohio River "in the presence of women living near the shore." Pettit took immediate steps to nip that behavior in the bud. He told the men that any further thievery would be "punished with the utmost vigor," and as to the swimming, he ordered that the "indecent practice [be] stopped at once."[9]

The regiment entrained for San Francisco, California, on August 25 and arrived there on September 1. Liggett and his battalion remained in camp at the Presidio until September 19, when the regiment was taken to the quarantine camp at Angel Island, California, prior to embarking for the Philippines.[10]

The 3rd Battalion boarded the aging US Army Transport *Immanuense* on Wednesday, October 25, and departed San Francisco the following morning. She sailed in convoy with the transports *Tartar* and *Newport*, which carried the 28th Infantry Regiment. The first port of call would be Honolulu, Hawaii. The remainder of the 31st Infantry boarded the larger transport, *City of Peking*, which sailed two days later. The *Immanuense* was older and smaller than her sister, and although the convoy encountered no weather problems during the first leg, it soon became apparent that there were serious questions regarding the ship's seaworthiness and the state of her mechanicals. Lieutenant Colonel Hayes, who kept a diary of the voyage, referred to her as a "tub" and frequently commented upon her lack of speed. Hawaii was sighted at daylight on November 3, and the ship docked at Honolulu early that morning.[11]

The battalion filed off the *Immanuense* and quickly formed up on the dock. Following the lead of their own drum and trumpet corps, with Hayes and Liggett at their head, the men, dressed in new khaki uniforms, marched smartly through the streets of Honolulu at a "rattling pace." Their destination was a park near a race course and the artillery post at Camp McKinley. Liggett would drill them there then, as well as the following day. At night, the men returned to the ship to sleep and for chow. After dinner, they were given leave to explore Honolulu until midnight.[12]

While in Hawaii, Colonel Hayes sought the assistance of the local quartermaster and commissary, Maj. George Ruhlen, in order to secure necessary

8. Lt. Col. Webb C. Hayes. Courtesy of the Rutherford B. Hayes Presidential Library.

repairs to the ship. For one thing, the generator that provided electricity to the lower decks was inadequate at best—that is, when it worked; more often than not, it was broken. That meant that the fans below decks could not move the hot, fetid air, particularly during bad weather, when the men were confined to quarters and could not be up on deck. In addition, the ice maker was broken, as was the condenser. The former was necessary to keep the meat and other perishables from spoiling. The latter, though, was particularly troublesome. It was supposed to not only provide an adequate supply of drinking water for the more than four hundred men aboard but also supply freshwater for the boilers. Lastly, a freshwater line was needed to connect the freshwater tanks to the front main deck.

Major Ruhlen put men to work on the various problems, and the ship's departure was held up for an additional day in order to complete the repairs. The results were decidedly mixed. The ice maker was a lost cause, so spoiled meat would still be a problem, but Ruhlen was able to connect the water line to the forward main deck. In addition, the quartermaster did deliver a quantity of ice to the ship and filled the forward water tanks with good, clean fresh water. It was thought that the condenser was fixed but not the electrical system, despite every effort. To top things off, unbeknownst to Hayes at the time, the chief engineer turned out to be incompetent and the cause of many subsequent problems.[13]

On Sunday, November 5, just as the ship was getting ready to depart, the chief engineer told the captain that virtually all his firemen had deserted, prompting the formation of a joint search party composed of soldiers and local policemen. In the meantime, a call went out for volunteers from among the 3rd Battalion, and soon the quota was filled by men eager to earn an extra supplement to their own meager soldier's pay. Three of the deserters were eventually brought back four hours later, and the ship sailed out of the harbor at 5:00 p.m. to the cheers of the men lining the deck of the *City of Peking*, which had arrived the day before.[14]

THE VOYAGE FROM HELL

The following day, the first of many calamities befell the ship, when the overloaded electrical generator that supplied the lower decks totally gave out. There were no spare parts to repair it, despite the diligent efforts of 2nd Lt. Wilford Twyman of Company K; the troops below deck would simply have to endure the heat, especially on stormy days. Fortunately, the weather held good for the next ten days or so, and the ship sailed on without further incident.[15]

This all changed on November 17, when, suddenly and without warning, the *Immanuense* developed engine trouble, stopped dead in the water, and began to drift rudderless in the heavy seas. The *City of Peking*, responding to a distress signal, sent a lifeboat over to investigate, with instructions to return with Colonel Hayes to make his report. The lifeboat had just reached the *City of Peking* when the *Immanuense* signaled by whistle for her to return, as they were able to restart the engines.

However, no sooner had Hayes set foot back on deck than the engines stopped dead again, the crew unable to maintain a head of steam in the boilers. The cause was serious flooding in the engine and fire rooms, as well as the coal bunker. Knee-deep—and at times, waist-deep—in water heated by hot coals, with the decking buckling and shifting, each of the companies took turns frantically bailing and manning a bucket brigade for three straight days. At the same time, other soldiers and crew were desperately trying to keep up steam by feeding coal to the boilers by hand from baskets lugged by other volunteers. Hayes wrote that the "hissing steam and red hot coals and the rushing water was simply infernal." Things became so dire that the ship first received orders to proceed to Guam, but the destination was quickly changed to Asuncion Island in the Northern Marianas, which was closer.[16]

Liggett himself took turns in the fire room, and it was there that he was observed on one occasion, waist-deep in water, totally composed, encouraging the men at the pumps, doggedly determined that the ship would not sink. He simply refused to quit and would not let his men do so either. When the surprised visitors from the *City of Peking* called down to Liggett and asked him if he needed anything, he paused, first looked at his bedraggled crew and then up at his inquisitors, and shouted back, "Got anything to wear on your boat?" This personality trait would later prompt an older colleague to remark that Liggett could "lick anything from an army mule to the Pacific Ocean."[17]

On November 20, the cause of the flooding was finally determined to be a leak in the starboard boiler, which was then shut down. Nevertheless, the problems continued, as the faulty ice plant could not keep the meat properly cooled, even with the addition of some ice sent over from the *City of Peking*, and nearly three hundred pounds of fresh meat had to be condemned. Liggett was appointed to a three-man Board of Survey to inspect and pass on the remaining supply of meat. Worse yet, a stubborn fire had broken out in the port coal bunker, which had burned through the ceiling to the pantry and the iron wall adjoining the boiler. It continued to smolder, filling the area with dense, "suffocating" smoke, and the entire bunker had to be emptied by hand before the fire was finally extinguished. In addition, the supply of fresh water had been improperly managed through the incompetence of the chief engineer. All the while, the ship's speed had been reduced to a crawl, and soon the *City of Peking* was nowhere in sight.[18]

During the night of Tuesday, November 21, the weather was marked by heavy winds and frequent rain squalls, driving the soldiers, who had been sleeping on deck, back down into the steamy regions below. The following day was no better, and at 9:00 p.m. that evening, yet another squall came up—which, as it turned out, was only the prelude to a tremendous storm that began three hours later and continued unabated for more than two days. The small ship lost speed and was tossed about by fierce winds and large waves. Water poured into the hatches and flooded the boiler room, which kept three companies busy "bailing, passing coal, and firing." The men subsisted on coffee and hardtack. The *Immanuense* and the *City of Peking* became separated once again, and there were anxious moments until they eventually found each other. At that time, a hawser was tied to the smaller ship in hopes that both vessels would remain together, but the rope was abruptly snapped by the rising and falling sea. Nevertheless, the larger ship remained close by from that point on.[19]

Eventually, the storm subsided—"after a wild night." The *Immanuense* arrived off Manila at 2:00 a.m. on Tuesday, November 28, and all began to file ashore later that morning. Assured that Aguinaldo's "days [were] numbered" and that the fighting was subsiding in Luzon, the 3rd Battalion was informed that it would be sent to the Department of Mindanao and Jolo.

The island of Mindanao lies in the southernmost part of the Philippine archipelago and is second in size to the island of Luzon, being nearly three-hundred-miles long and the same wide. The department was under the command of Brig. Gen. William August Kobbé, who had succeeded Brig. Gen. John C. Bates. Kobbé maintained his headquarters in Zamboanga, a city situated at the western tip of the island of Mindanao with a population of approximately twenty thousand. His adjutant general was Maj. John J. Pershing, US Volunteers. The headquarters of the 31st Volunteer Infantry was also in Zamboanga. The various companies of the regiment were soon scattered about Mindanao at small, one- and two-company posts.[20]

Accordingly, after a brief stay in Manila, on December 1, the regiment boarded steamships, bound for the city of Zamboanga. Liggett's 3rd Battalion was broken up. Companies L and M would continue on the *City of Peking*, while Companies I and K, along with the horses, would sail on the SS *Brutus*, a converted US Navy collier, which Hayes referred to as "another *Immanuense*."[21]

HEART OF DARKNESS

The SS *Brutus* arrived at Zamboanga on December 7, and Liggett and his men disembarked the next day. After a ten-day stopover, Liggett and Companies I, L, and M reboarded the aging transport on December 18 and were carried to a post established at the port of Davao, which was a subdistrict on the southern coast of Mindanao, 250 miles east of Zamboanga by rough trails and at least a three-day sail by water. The troops disembarked at Davao on December 21. Upon arrival, Companies L and M were separated once again and sent to other locations. Also assigned to Post Davao were a surgeon and a small number of hospital corpsmen. In all, Liggett's initial command there was slightly more than one hundred men. However, in May 1900, Company K,

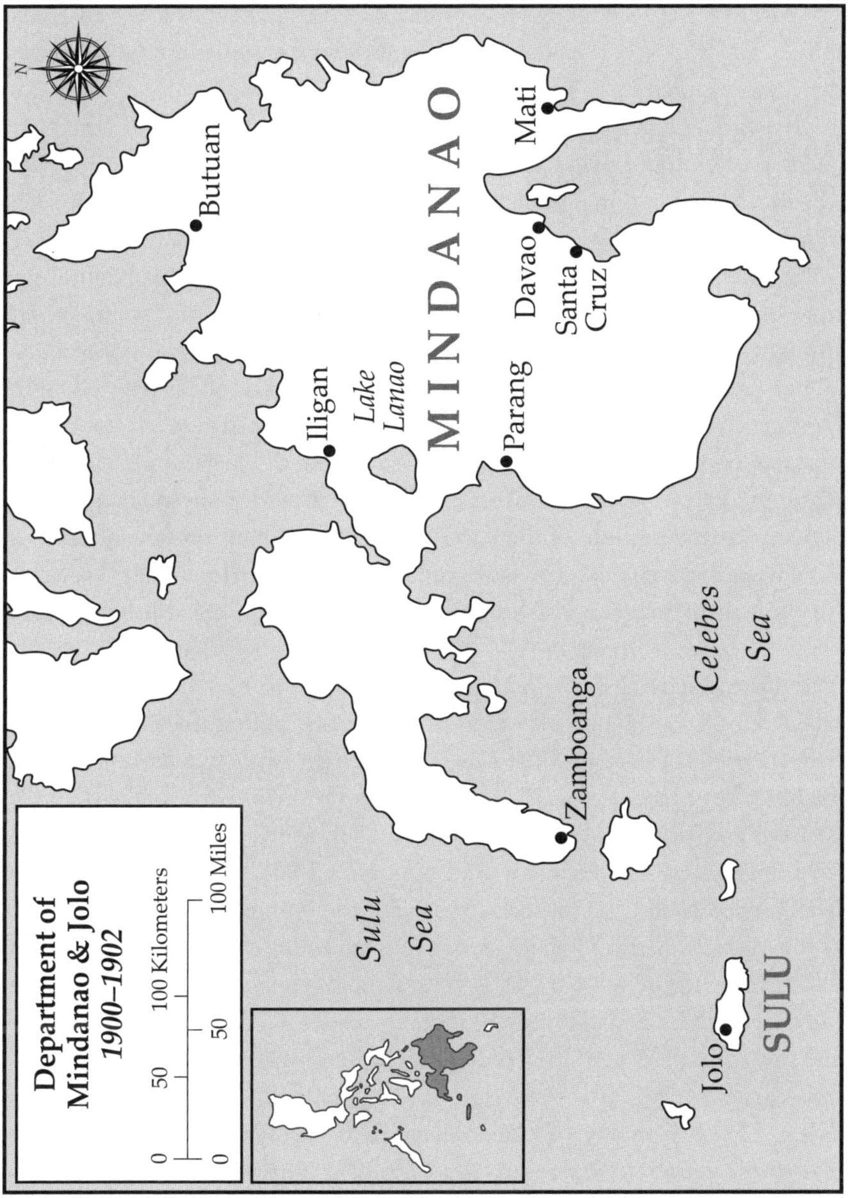

Map 2. Department of Mindanao and Jolo, Philippines (1900–1902)

also part of the 3rd Battalion and initially stationed at Parang, was transferred to the post at Davao, thus doubling Liggett's total command to a little more than two hundred men.[22]

The large island of Mindanao and the smaller island of Jolo are the heart of Moro country. At that time, the Moros, immigrants from Borneo and Malacca several hundred years before who had long ago embraced Islam, had a well-deserved reputation as fierce fighters. Many of them still derived their living from the sea, including piracy and slave trafficking. Local chieftains or headmen, called *datus*, controlled their traditional areas from well-fortified strongholds called *cottas*. Southern Mindanao was relatively quiet, since a brutal fight among the *datu* for territory had recently taken place, and none were eager to upset the status quo. Moreover, there was no strong movement for independence at this time, as was the case among the Tagalogs in the north, who were mainly Christian. As a result, there was virtually no cooperation between the two groups. Things would abruptly change a few years later, in 1903, with the outbreak of what have been called the Moro Wars. However, for the time being, the 31st Volunteer Infantry spent their Philippine tour performing garrison duty.[23]

Prior to General Kobbé's arrival, his predecessor had promised the sultan of Mindanao religious freedom for the Moros in return for a pledge to help stamp out piracy and the slave trade, for which he would be rewarded for his efforts. Kobbé was a firm believer in President McKinley's policy of "benevolent assimilation." In fact, Kobbé submitted the draft of the plan to establish local governments that was refined and ultimately adopted by Maj. Gen. Elwell Otis for use throughout the islands. In short, this policy, as it evolved, called for balancing a firm hand militarily with the delivery of "civilization" in the form of roads, schools, and democratic self-government. However, others in Washington, including Vice Pres. Theodore Roosevelt and Secretary of War Elihu Root, felt that the function of the US Army was to establish control over the Moro just as it did with the American Indian tribes. However, many of the soldiers themselves, who had a front-row seat to the action, took the latter tack. "Civilize 'em with a Krag!" were the words of a contemporary US Army song.[24]

Robert Lee Bullard described duty in the Philippines as "four-fifths peace and one-fifth war making." The one exception to the relative quiet on Mindanao at this time occurred on April 24, 1900. On that day, Maj. Lloyd M. Brett and a contingent of twenty-five men from the 31st Volunteer Infantry, accompanied by one hundred Moro fighters, took sides in a punitive action against a rival *datu* near Malabon. As a result, the short-term peace in that area did not last for long. Afterward, General Kobbé speculated correctly that the action was "singularly unfortunate" in that it had sparked "needless antagonism."[25]

As commander of the subdistrict of Davao, Liggett acted much like a governor. He was ultimately responsible for security, as well as for the collection of taxes and customs fees, the operation of the local schools, and the building of roads, for which civilians were hired to do the manual labor. Separate interpreters were hired in at least two dialects to assist Liggett and his officers. Liggett filed quarterly reports with General Kobbé.[26]

On December 26, by way of his first order, Major Liggett formed a small fifteen-man detachment under the command of 1st Lt. F. S. Lowry, the purpose of which was to become acquainted with the people and surrounding countryside. In addition, the detachment was ordered to explore the feasibility of a wagon road along the coast south of Davao. In all, the expedition was to take two weeks. Lieutenant Lowry was ordered to take "careful field notes" so a proper report could be made. Liggett also established a guard mount in Davao City at night. He warned the men to "be on alert constantly [and] to report at once any unusual activity," reminding them that the "challenging" of any person out and about at night "begins at Taps." The soldiers were assisted by native police, who were responsible for patrolling the outlying districts of the city.[27]

Liggett was a careful commander, and he took no chances with what could well have been a hostile native population. Accordingly, the men were "cautioned against placing any confidence in natives where such confidence may endanger a soldier's safety." His troops needed a pass to leave the post or else be accompanied by an officer. Moreover, they were required to be in the company of at least three or four men, one of whom would carry a rifle and ten rounds of ammunition.[28]

On May 19, 1900, after the death of a soldier, more than likely from either typhus or dengue fever, as well as an increase in the number of dysentery cases, the post surgeon expressed his concerns regarding the drinking water supply, which was drawn from the nearby Davao River, as it had been recently contaminated by heavy rains. Liggett immediately issued an order that all drinking water had to be filtered, if possible, and boiled the night before so that it would be cool the following day when drunk.[29]

Three days later, he followed up with a memorandum reiterating the importance of his order regarding drinking water, to which he added a prohibition against eating mangoes and coconuts and drinking native alcohol such as "tuba" and "arrack." Liggett told his men that, based on "expert opinion," the consumption of these while ill with fever could be fatal. While he reasoned that the men were still acclimating themselves to the country, one has to wonder if he was also concerned with the perils of heavy drinking among the ranks on a small post. "If the above directions are faithfully observed," he suggested in a veiled threat, "there will be but little use for guard house or jail or hospital at Davao."[30]

The following month, after two more deaths and the continued rise in incidents of dysentery, Liggett reiterated his order when it was brought to his attention that many soldiers had ignored the first and had been drinking directly from the river or at local stores and homes whenever they felt the urge. He ordered that any soldier found to have drunk unboiled water from anyplace other than the company mess was to be incarcerated. "If the men of this command have not sense enough . . . to protect themselves in this matter," an obviously frustrated Liggett wrote, "they will have to be treated like spoiled children and forced to guard their own health."[31]

In May 1900, General Kobbé sent Liggett three thousand dollars for road building. Not only was this an important part of the "hearts and minds" effort, as it would give a boost to the local economy, but it would also improve communication between outposts. In addition to the normal garrison duties, Liggett's troops performed escort duty for the native road workers. On July 19, he ordered 1st Lt. Charles O. Thomas Jr. to lead a detachment composed of a sergeant and seventeen men from Company I south through Taloma and on to Santa Cruz, to serve in this capacity. The troops were told to draw thirteen days' rations.[32]

Liggett received his annual efficiency report on July 1, in which Colonel Pettit referred to him as "a valuable [and] capable officer in every respect." Later that month, while drawing upon his early experiences in Montana, Liggett organized a small detachment of mounted infantry in order to quickly meet and suppress any potential activity by insurgents. The mounted detachment was broken down into two eight-man contingents, each composed of a corporal and seven privates, one from each company, all under the command of 2nd Lt. H. D. Mitchell. The training regimen followed the cavalry drill regulations "in training of horse and men, [and] in handling and caring for horses." In addition, as it was expected that the soldiers would fight dismounted, Lieutenant Mitchell was also directed to follow the "Infantry Skirmish Drill."[33]

The dull daily routine at Davao was briefly broken on Saturday, August 25, when General Kobbé and Colonel Pettit visited the post as part of an inspection tour. The general and his party arrived during the early morning, and his vessel was mistaken for another steamer. As a result, no one went out to meet it. The breach of military etiquette was quickly rectified when Kobbé sent his aide ashore to ask Liggett to come aboard. After the usual formalities, everyone went ashore for a tour of the town, accompanied by the *presidente* of the subdistrict. Liggett was invited to lunch aboard the steamer, and the afternoon was taken up by an inspection of quarters. Kobbé and his party departed Davao after dinner at the officers' mess.[34]

Colonel Pettit returned to Davao on November 19, along with the inspector general of the Department of Mindanao and Jolo. Of more significance to the men was the fact that he was accompanied by the paymaster, who brought with him two months' back pay. Later that month, Liggett was unable to attend an officers' conference at Zamboanga, as he had to investigate a series of murders.[35]

On December 20, the steamship *Bolinaro* arrived at Davao with a welcome cargo of commissary supplies. The ship left the following day and returned from Mati with Company L aboard on their way to Zamboanga, as Mati and another post had recently been abandoned.[36]

After a year in Davao, Liggett requested leave to visit Zamboanga, which was granted on January 25, 1901. He had to wait for the departure of the steamship *Rosario*, which had been idling in port since January 18. Finally, on January 27, the ship sailed at 5:00 p.m. Liggett returned to Davao on February 20, taking two days, February 18 and 19, to inspect the road projects in his subdistrict before returning to his desk.[37]

In March, word reached Davao that the 31st Volunteer Infantry would soon be mustered out and heading home. Liggett lauded the fact that after the men had heard the welcome news, most of them continued to go about their normal duties. However, as is always the case, there were exceptions. Three men took the occasion to go on a wild bender—so wild, in fact, that Liggett issued a sternly worded memorandum. "There is no justification for such display of ruffianism . . . [as] last evening," he chided. "In over twenty years service with both black and white troops, the battalion commander has never seen such vile behavior." He went on, "What small claim to common decency they may have imagined themselves to possess was forfeited and the true 'bum' [or] 'hobo' in their makeup became manifested. This to the disgrace of the service and uniform they are unworthy to wear."[38]

On April 26, 1901, orders were received from General Kobbé that Companies I and K would be relieved by Company D, 10th Infantry. The men were ordered to draw three days' rations and would be transported to Zamboanga aboard the steamship *Aeolus*. Accordingly, in anticipation of the forthcoming relief, steps were taken to turn in equipment and ammunition and account for lost and damaged property.[39]

The *Aeolus* arrived at Davao on April 29. Aboard were 128 men from Company D, 10th US Infantry, assigned to relieve the 31st Volunteer Infantry, which was then assembling at Zamboanga in preparation for its return to the United States. Although Companies I and K departed for Zamboanga on May 2, Liggett remained behind for the next two months as commander of the subdistrict, no doubt to ensure a smooth transition.[40]

At 5:00 p.m. on Sunday, May 12, 1901, General Kobbé reviewed the whole 31st Infantry, including the entire staff in line, which he described as "very handsome." This was followed by a reception hosted by Colonel Pettit, during which the regimental band played some familiar songs, accompanied by the "officers joining in the chorus." The following day, eight companies boarded the UST *Hancock* and got settled in for the return trip. On the morning of Tuesday, May 14, the last four companies went aboard, and the ship was ready to sail at 3:00 p.m. There was a slight delay when, as the ship weighed anchor, it dredged up an old anchor from the harbor, which first had to be untangled. Finally, at 4:00 p.m., the *Hancock* cleared the harbor, the regimental band on deck playing a variety of tunes, and the men cheered their anticipated homecoming.[41]

At one point during his service in the Philippines, Maj. Gen. Henry Ware Lawton mused to a friend, "We are six weeks behind the world." Such was the case with Harriet and Hunter Liggett. In June 1901, she received word the UST *Hancock* had arrived on the West Coast with the 31st Volunteer Infantry Regiment aboard, yet she had received no word from her husband. Harriet, who was then living in New York City, had recently changed her address and was worried that a telegram from Hunter might have gone astray. When the adjutant general of the US Army, Maj. Gen. Henry Corbin, ignored her first letter, she sent him a second one a week later, seeking her husband's whereabouts, pleading "if you will kindly let me know, for I am anxious to hear." Corbin responded that he had checked the passenger list of the *Hancock* and Liggett was not on it. Perhaps, he suggested, "he has remained on duty in the Philippines." This in fact turned out to be the case.[42]

Liggett, who had remained behind, was mustered out of the US Volunteers on June 18, 1901, at which time he reverted to his permanent rank of captain in the 5th US Infantry. He left Davao on July 3 on another leave of absence, more than likely for a rest and to see more of the country, only to return on August 18, back in command once again. Liggett left Davao for the final time, bound for Manila aboard the chartered transport *Viscaya,* at 6:30 a.m. on October 3. At that time, Company D, 10th US Infantry, was also aboard, bound for Iligan, their places taken by Troop G, 15th Cavalry.[43]

LUZON

Liggett soon rejoined the 5th Infantry at Pidigan in Abra Province of northern Luzon, where he was placed in command of troops until December 18, 1901. Two days later, he was appointed adjutant general of the 1st Separate Brigade in Dagupan, also in Luzon, and served in that capacity until July 4, 1902.[44]

In the interim, on April 9, 1902, Liggett was ordered to report to Manila to appear before a promotion board, where, on April 14, he submitted to a physical examination and was tested on drill regulations, military law, and minor tactics. Liggett, who scored 93.54 percent on the examination, was found qualified, and the board recommended him for promotion. He received a promotion to the grade of major in the Regular Army, effective on May 5, 1902, although official notice did not reach him until July 9. At the same time, he was assigned to the 21st Infantry, and shortly thereafter, he was finally headed back home.[45]

Perhaps encouraged by her exchange of letters with General Corbin the previous year, on June 5, unknown to Hunter, Harriet seized the opportunity to lobby General Corbin for further promotion for her husband. While acknowledging Liggett's recent promotion to major in the 21st Infantry, she asked that Corbin secure a promotion for him to lieutenant colonel in the Puerto Rican Regiment in light of a pending vacancy. She pointed to her husband's good record as well as the hardships he had endured in the Philippines, or as she called it, "that God-forsaken Country." She went on, "You don't know dear General what this promotion would be to us and will you get it for him. This letter is a personal one to you dear General as I am doing this all myself . . . and if you would do this, it would make me the happiest woman in the world. I will count the hours. Might I hear from you and hope for good news?" No one could say that Harriet was not in her husband's corner. There is no record of Corbin's response, if any.[46]

Although he was serving with troops, Liggett was disappointed that his recent assignments in Cuba and the Philippines were far from the fighting. But if his tour in Davao was otherwise without excitement, it was, nevertheless, another valuable experience. Though he had independent command of only a relatively small contingent of troops and not his full battalion, nevertheless, he learned important lessons about the role that the US Army played in governing captured territory.

More important, he had the experience of actually leading citizen soldiers, not regulars, and of learning the difference. Up to this point, his only experience with state militias had been as an observer or trainer during short-term maneuvers or encampments. Citizen soldiers brought a different element to the table, particularly where it came to discipline and US Army routine. In addition to their youth, they were never too remote in time from the perceived freedom of their civilian lives. As a result, Liggett had to issue clear orders and constantly remind the men of the importance of little things like their personal appearance and the wearing of the uniform or the need for the boiling of their water. Colonel Pettit himself had to issue a stern directive after the regiment first arrived in Zamboanga, when it came to his attention that some of his troops were insulting the local women. This experience would hold Liggett in good stead later on in France, where he would need to fit all the disparate pieces together and mold them into an effective US Army.[47]

FIVE

School Days

ARMY WAR COLLEGE AND GENERAL STAFF SCHOOL

HOME IS THE HUNTER

High atop the bluffs overlooking the confluence of the Minnesota River with the Mississippi, Fort Snelling cannot fail to impress all those who approach its imposing main gate. The location was a natural gathering place for early fur traders and explorers, a fact not lost on the US Army. Lt. Zebulon Pike entered into a treaty there with the Dakota on September 23, 1805, thereby securing one hundred thousand acres for future settlement. However, it was not until 1817 that Maj. Stephen Long, a topographical engineer, approved the actual location for a fort. Two years later, Lt. Col. Henry Leavenworth arrived with the 5th Infantry Regiment and began the actual construction. He was succeeded a year later, in 1820, by Col. Josiah Snelling, who completed the project in 1825. Maj. Gen. Winfield Scott conducted an inspection tour of the nearly finished works in 1824, and he was so pleased with the effort that he suggested the post be named Fort Snelling in the colonel's honor. In late 1902 and early 1903, the fort was home to two battalions of the 21st Infantry Regiment, as well as the 10th Field Artillery Battery. Fort Snelling was also the site of a military detention facility.[1]

Major Liggett returned from the Philippines in September 1902, and he was immediately granted a thirty-day leave of absence, which was extended by an additional two months. He and Harriett had a lot of catching up to do after an absence of nearly three years. Liggett reported for duty with the 21st Infantry at Fort Snelling on December 2, and three days later, he assumed temporary command of the 1st Battalion. Duty in Minnesota was not particularly challenging and involved, among other things, periodic service as a summary court officer on January 8, 1903, as well as periodic detached service, such as at Fort Meade, South Dakota, from February 2 through 10. Upon his return from South Dakota, Liggett briefly assumed command of the post for the balance of the month, except for the five days that he was sick in quarters. In late March, he served on a promotion board that had been convened at the post. Liggett took command of the 2nd Battalion on March 30, 1903.[2]

All, however, was not monotonous, routine garrison duties, as the regiment was called upon from time to time to perform in a ceremonial capacity. Pres. Theodore Roosevelt visited the Twin Cities on April 4, 1903, and for that occasion, both battalions of the 21st Infantry, along with the band and the 10th Field Artillery Battery were called upon to participate in a parade in St. Paul in the president's honor. The infantry were transported the three miles into the city by way of the street railway, while the artillery marched.[3]

Later that same month, Alexander Ramsey died at his home in St. Paul on April 22 at the age of eighty-eight. Ramsey was much beloved by his fellow Minnesotans, having served as the first territorial governor and later as governor during the Civil War years, including the short but tumultuous Sioux War of 1862. Reflecting the attitude of the times, he was quoted as saying, "The Sioux Indians of Minnesota must be exterminated or driven forever beyond the borders of the state." Ramsey went on to serve the state as a US senator and in the Hayes administration as secretary of war. Later on, back in Minnesota, he became quite wealthy as a result of various business endeavors. Alexander Ramsey was, in short, Minnesota's "Grand Old Man."[4]

Liggett and his 2nd Battalion, along with the regimental band, were called upon to escort the governor's remains from his home to the state capitol. There, his body would lie in state in the governor's chambers for three hours while an estimated ten thousand people thronged to pay their respects. Once again, the troops were transported to the city via street railway. After the viewing, the casket was escorted back to the family home that afternoon for a brief private service, which was followed by the burial at Oakland Cemetery.[5]

On May 30, the 21st Infantry, including the band, along with the 10th Field Artillery Battery, took part in Memorial Day ceremonies in Minneapolis, including the parade. The infantry used the St. Paul Street railway and the Twin City Rapid Transit each way, while once again, the artillery marched. Earlier in the month, Liggett had served on unspecified detached service at Fort Meade, South Dakota, between May 7 and 13.[6]

Liggett accompanied his battalion when it participated in the annual target practice exercise at the state rifle range at Camp Lakeview in Lake City,

Minnesota. Marching nearly seventy miles each way, the battalion left Fort Snelling at 7:00 a.m. July 18 and returned to the post on August 11. However, Liggett did not return to Fort Snelling with his battalion. He had a homecoming of sorts, as he was detailed to serve as chief range officer at Fort Keogh, Montana, from August 4 to 17.[7]

DEPARTMENT OF THE LAKES

In early September 1903, Hunter and Harriet pulled up stakes once again when he received orders to report to the headquarters of the Department of the Lakes in Chicago, where he would serve the next four years as adjutant general. Certainly this was not as physically demanding as some of his previous line assignments, and like St. Francis Barracks, it would be a change of pace for both of them. The US Army had a practice of alternating staff and line assignments for promising officers, and the forty-six-year-old Liggett was definitely one.[8]

Liggett's duties involved more than just shuffling papers. Between August 28 and September 15, 1904, the US Army staged a massive maneuver at the Bull Run battleground near Manassas, Virginia, that involved twenty-five thousand to thirty thousand regulars and militia from almost every state east of the Mississippi. Mock battles were staged between a blue and a brown division, and Liggett served as a chief umpire for the latter team.[9]

In early December 1904, Liggett suffered a serious attack of "chronic rheumatism," and he was put under a doctor's care. The situation was unimproved after a month, and the attending surgeon reported that his patient was "entirely incapacitated" and "suffering greatly." As a result, he recommended that Liggett be ordered to the Army and Navy General Hospital in Hot Springs, Arkansas, for further treatment. This would likely explain the several lengthy, unspecified illnesses that had laid him low from time to time throughout his career, in addition to the more common ones like dysentery and influenza.[10]

Named for the many thermal springs and mineral baths, for decades, people had flocked to the city of Hot Springs and its "Bathhouse Row" to relax and to enjoy the therapeutic properties of the waters. The US Army, too, had long recognized these benefits, and in 1882, Congress authorized the construction of a hospital on federal land there. Since this large facility opened in 1887, it had become "a mecca for rheumatic personnel of the Army," treating an average of three hundred patients at any one time.[11]

On January 6, 1905, Liggett was ordered to report to Hot Springs, where he remained until February 23, when it was reported that he was fit for duty. He received his orders to report to Chicago two days later.[12]

From time to time, the Department of the Lakes oversaw camps of instruction for various Regular Army and militia units. One such was held at Fort Benjamin Harrison near Indianapolis, Indiana, in September 1906. Liggett attended as part of the division staff, acting in the capacity of military secretary. Attending the camp that year were elements of the 4th Infantry Regiment and the 2nd Wisconsin Infantry. In addition to the inspector general of the US Army, the camp was visited by a military attaché from the Brazilian embassy in Washington, DC.[13]

Liggett was relieved of his duties as adjutant general of the Department of the Lakes on September 3, 1907, and he was reassigned to special duty there until October 27 while awaiting further orders. The following day, he was assigned to the 13th Infantry Regiment, and he was ordered to report to Fort Leavenworth, Kansas.[14]

FORT LEAVENWORTH

Established in 1827, Fort Leavenworth was built on a bluff on the west bank of a bend of the Missouri River above Kansas City. The post was ideally situated to support the massive westward movement of the 1840s and 1850s, with both supplies and a military presence along the pioneer trails. It was known as a major detention facility for military prisoners.[15]

Fort Leavenworth was also the site of a course for company-grade officers called the General Service and Staff College. The school would later be called the Command and General Staff School. It was an outgrowth of the Infantry and Cavalry School formed in 1881 at the direction of Gen. William T. Sherman, then commanding general of the US Army, and it operated at Fort Leavenworth until 1898, when it was closed during the war with Spain and the Philippine War. Classes resumed in 1902. The model for this school, in turn, had stemmed from an earlier artillery school at Fort Monroe, Virginia, which also provided the impetus for the Naval War College. In addition, the US Army operated separate signal and field engineering schools.[16]

The post–Civil War US Army, under the strong leadership of William T. Sherman and John Schofield, gradually emerged as a more professional institution, emphasizing, among other things, marksmanship, service journals, efficiency reports, promotion exams, and camps of instruction as well as other large-scale exercises. Service schools like the one at Leavenworth played a pivotal role in the process, particularly after the curriculum changes effected by then Brig. Gen. J. Franklin Bell and his assistant instructor Maj. Eben Swift. Under their direction, the Command and General Staff School was divided into two one-year courses of study: the School of Application for Infantry and Cavalry (later "School of the Line") and the Army Staff College. The curriculum emphasized practical lessons in officership and the study of warfare, as well as staff rides and general staff duties.[17]

BACK WITH THE TROOPS

The 21st Infantry Regiment had recently been stationed at Fort William McKinley in the Philippines, but it had returned to Fort Leavenworth on October 21. All in all, the post was home to about two thousand soldiers, including infantry, cavalry, and engineers. Liggett was given command of the 2nd Battalion.[18]

In addition to his battalion duties, Liggett was assigned as a member of the examining board for promotion of officers, and he would serve more or less continuously on it during his stay at Fort Leavenworth. He also served from time to time on the competition examination board. The normal routine was broken during the last three weeks of May 1908, when the 2nd and 3rd Battalions participated in the regular annual target practice at the post range. The following month, from June 10 through June 20, the entire regiment, together with three squadrons of the 13th Cavalry, participated in maneuvers with the student officers from the US Army service schools, including Fort Leavenworth.[19]

Up to this point in his career, with some exceptions, it would be hard to distinguish Liggett's overall experiences from those of most of his fellow officers. That would all soon change with this new assignment. He was known in US Army circles as a hardworking and reliable officer. Moreover, since his West Point days, he had engaged in the self-study of military history and strategy, as did only a small number of his colleagues. His previous assignment as adjutant general for the Department of the Lakes was certainly a way of balancing the routine of garrison and escort duties. Liggett wanted more, and he had come to the realization that a more formal course of study was necessary for him to advance to higher rank and to become a more valuable member of his chosen profession.

As a field-grade officer, Liggett was required to have a yearly physical examination. Accordingly, on October 12, 1908, he reported to the base hospital at Fort Leavenworth for the procedure. Liggett would fight a weight problem later in his career, but that would not be the case yet. The surgeon reported that Liggett was just slightly over six feet in height and weighed 192 pounds, and more important, he pronounced that Liggett's general appearance was "good," and, aside from some slight varicose veins, he was fit for duty. A second component of the examination was a series of three lengthy horse rides ranging from almost six hours to more than seven. He completed all three rides within the time allotted, and he was found to be "sufficiently skilled in horsemanship" as a result.[20]

CHANGING TIMES

The Spanish-American War was a watershed between the old US Army and the new, as envisioned by Secretary of War Elihu Root, who had replaced the much-maligned Russell A. Alger. Root believed, quite simply, that "the real object of an Army is to prepare for war." Shortly after his appointment by President McKinley in 1899, Root prepared a report that contained proposals designed to make the US Army a more professional organization from top to bottom. These changes included, among other things, a substantial increase in troop strength, officers chosen by examination, more uniform training for the National Guard, the further education of select officers, and the elimination of the inefficient bureau system—and in its place, the installation of a general staff along the lines of the German model. Many older officers, including Gen. Nelson A. Miles but particularly the bureau chiefs, vigorously resisted many of the changes. Well entrenched in their individual centers of power within the US Army itself, as well as in the halls of Congress, these officers had much to lose.[21]

A FELICITOUS ENCOUNTER

The paths of Hunter Liggett and George Catlett Marshall would continually cross during the course their careers. While at Fort Leavenworth, Major Liggett was in command of an infantry battalion and, at the same time, as an avid reader, he continued his informal course of self-study of military history. If Liggett had the normal ambitions of a Regular Army officer, he also recognized the fact that any profession, including the military, demanded study to master it. In an increasingly complex world, it was simply not enough to learn by trial and error on the job. At some point, it became apparent to his colleagues that he intended to become, in his words, a "military highbrow." Accordingly, while still in Kansas, he saw a golden opportunity to take a more formal approach to his studies. The decision would be a turning point in his career. Considered a studious and reliable officer, and having "one of the finest minds in the Army," Liggett's next steps separated him from most of his peers and placed him on an upward career track.[22]

9. Lt. George C. Marshall. Courtesy of the George C. Marshall Foundation.

Accordingly, soon after he began his tour at Leavenworth, Liggett voluntarily began to audit the courses at both the School of the Line and the Army Staff School. His instructor, a much younger Lt. George C. Marshall, was a serious and studious officer who would later become Liggett's aide-de-camp. He made the course materials available to Liggett, and after every problem had been given to the enrolled students, Marshall also gave it to him. Liggett would, in turn, offer a solution and work out the details, whereupon the younger man would critique and correct his work. If Liggett was bothered by having to learn from a junior officer, he definitely did not let on. In the ensuing years, the relationship would prove very beneficial to both men. Moreover, Liggett benefitted from a more focused, systematized approach to the study of military science.[23]

THE WORK GOES ON

In addition to his studies, for the next year, Liggett continued to carry out his assigned duties, with an occasional break in the routine. In August 1908, the entire 13th Infantry, along with two companies of the 3rd Battalion Engineers, traveled west to Fort Riley, Kansas, to take part in a camp of instruction and maneuvers. After his return, Liggett was appointed as an instructor of tactics at the garrison school for officers beginning in November 1908 and continuing through the following March. In April, his battalion completed its annual target practice at the post firing range, and on May 26 and 27, he led his battalion and Battery E, 5th Field Artillery, on night maneuvers.[24]

While still at Fort Leavenworth, on November 1, 1908, Liggett applied to the War Department for an "Indian Campaign Badge," citing his service in the Dakota and Montana Territories—in particular, his actions at Little Porcupine Creek in 1880. He received notice that his application was approved on December 4. Liggett also reached another career milestone when he was promoted to the grade of lieutenant colonel in the Regular Army on June 5, 1909. At the same time, he was assigned to the 15th Infantry Regiment.[25]

THE ARMY WAR COLLEGE AND THE GENERAL STAFF SCHOOL

One of the first changes implemented by Secretary Root was the establishment of the Army War College. It had been recognized for some time that a West Point education was simply not enough and that more specialized training in leadership and command was essential. The course at Fort Leavenworth was fine for more junior officers, but it was believed that an advanced course of study was necessary for the more senior ones who showed the most promise for achieving high command. In addition, Secretary Root wanted a pool of talent from which to draw in order to form a general staff and, along with it, a war college that would be a "great adjunct," that would not only educate but also gather intelligence and prepare plans for the War Department.[26]

The mission of the Army War College evolved over time as the product of two competing visions. The first was based on ideas of the more cerebral Brig. Gen. Tasker Bliss, who, like Elihu Root, looked upon the school as an extension of the General Staff School. Its function was not academic, per se, but rather long- and short-range planning and gathering of military intelligence. Since Bliss was designated as the president of the War College starting with the first class in 1903–4, his vision initially prevailed. Within a couple of years, however, the model changed when Maj. Gen. J. Franklin Bell became chief of staff. Bell, known throughout the US Army as a man of action, brought his recent experiences in the Philippines, coupled with his direction of the service school at Fort Leavenworth, to the War College. His principal instructor at Fort Leavenworth was Maj. Eben Swift, who believed that what was lacking in the senior officer corps was a solid, practical curriculum that included tactics and military history as well as the duties of a staff officer, all supplemented by staff and historical rides. Swift was transferred to the General Staff School in 1906 and appointed as an instructor at the War College for the academic year 1906–7 and a director on December 27, 1907. Although his stay at the War College was relatively short, his influence was profound and lasting. He would end his tour there with the class of 1909–10.[27]

THE APPLICATORY METHOD

With Major Swift's appointment came what has been referred to as the "deductive or applicatory method" of instruction—that is, the application of theory to practical problems. The thinking behind this methodology was explained in detail in a report to the chief of staff prepared by the general staff dated August 31, 1910. Echoing Secretary Root's dictum that the "real object of an Army is to prepare for war," the report observed that "instruction in any subject is always in danger of falling into the domain of theory. This has happened to the art of war many times, and armies during the long peace have often become inefficient for war." It was referring to the gulf between "practice and theory" that so often discourages many from attempting to bridge it.

The report alluded to the success of German and other European "peace trained" armies that dispelled the "plausible fallacy" that "war alone teaches war." The nature of warfare had changed radically since the Civil War, not only in the area of weapons and armaments but also in the enormous scope of the battlefield itself. Effective leadership no longer depended upon the courage of a single general officer leading from the front. Rather, "it must be assumed at a distance, gradually increasing in time and space." A modern commander needed to secure the "cooperation of many elements" through "team work." The report went on to state that "the applicatory method" moves gradually from principles to "concrete examples" in three stages, utilizing first "manuals and lectures," then "problems and exercises," and concluding with "conferences" to "discuss the lessons learned."

The "object" of the Army War College curriculum, the report continued, was "to develop a school of safe leadership for officers" and "to formulate a consistent and reasonable habit of looking upon military questions, and [to] build up a system which, like the Common Law in jurisprudence, will guide our officers to those principles of leadership which should govern in our armies." It was into this world that Liggett would soon be thrust.[28]

BACK TO SCHOOL

Shortly after his promotion to lieutenant colonel, Liggett received notice that he had been selected as a student officer at the Army War College in Washington, DC, when the new term started on August 16, 1909. He and Harriet took advantage of a twenty-day leave of absence and rented a home on Connecticut Avenue so that Liggett could pursue his studies during the ensuing year. The class included other future general officers like captains Eli Helmick and Malin Craig, as well Lt. Col. John A. Lejeune, US Marine Corps.[29]

Liggett began his course of study with a preliminary course during the months of September and October under the direction of Major Swift. The course was intended to make sure that all the students, particularly the ones who had not graduated from Fort Leavenworth, had an overview of the regular course and what to expect—including, in particular, an explanation of the applicatory method of instruction—and to make sure that all students were on the same page. It also included short, weekly tactical rides.[30]

In the meantime, on October 23, 1909, Liggett reported to the commanding surgeon's office in Washington, DC, for his annual physical examination. The results were virtually identical to the previous year: he weighed in at 190 pounds, and his general appearance was found to be good.[31]

10. Army War College, Washington, DC. Courtesy of the Military History Institute.

The regular course began in earnest in December, covering military history, map exercises and maneuvers, tactics and strategy, the drafting of orders and plans, and the duties of staff officers for all branches. The students went on progressively more detailed tactical rides and, in addition, attended numerous lectures on a variety of subjects from the "Tactical Use of Field Artillery" to "The Causes of the Russian-Japanese War."[32]

In addition to the regular curriculum, from May 2 through May 26, Major Swift led the students on a tactical ride "over the battlefields of Gettysburg and Chambersburg" as well as the Richmond campaign of 1864. During the following month, the students were led on a staff ride to Gettysburg from Washington, DC, from June 10 through June 29.[33] The students remained at Gettysburg and participated in a camp of instruction during the entire month of July 1910, acting as staff officers, umpires, observers, and instructors for the regular and militia units assembled there for training. It was an opportunity for each to put into actual practice the skills that they had learned in the classroom. Liggett did not participate in the camp. In the ultimate compliment to his proficiency, prior to his graduation, he was detailed to supervise the teaching of the preliminary course for the next War College class during the months of July and August.[34]

FROM STUDENT TO TEACHER

Upon graduation in August 1910, in recognition of his excellent performance in the course, Liggett was promptly assigned to the general staff, where he would also serve as a director of the Army War College effective August 16. In the latter capacity, he was the lead instructor and also in charge of curriculum development. As such, he was in a position to "reshape the curriculum along Leavenworth lines." In fact, Liggett had big shoes to fill, as he succeeded Eben Swift, who had been transferred. One of the assistant directors assigned to the college was fellow graduate Capt. Malin Craig, who would later serve as Liggett's chief of staff in the 41st Division, as well as in the American Expeditionary Forces (AEF) in France.

He took his new responsibilities seriously. Even before his appointment became effective, Liggett requested permission to proceed to Fort Leavenworth, Kansas, as well as to the Sparta Maneuver Tract near Sparta, Wisconsin, later called Camp McCoy, to consult and observe. His request was approved, and the orders read that he was to confer "with the authorities of [the] service schools on matters pertaining to instruction at the Army War College," though a similar request to observe the training at Pine Camp, New York, was disapproved.[35]

Liggett left for this detached service on August 12 and returned to Washington on August 17, prior to the start of the academic year, which began on September 1. He brought with him the recommendation that the Leavenworth curriculum include an annual "three-month preparatory course in military art" for field officers, running from January through March. For more junior officers, he recommended that completion of this course or graduation from the Staff School at Leavenworth be made a prerequisite for admission to the Army War College. He reasoned that it would ensure a common foundation for future students attending the War College. No doubt, he had in mind the two-month preliminary course that he went through, which, if eliminated, would allow the basic coursework to begin in August each year instead of November. His recommendation for the course was implemented, and although it did not become mandatory for admission to the Army War College, it did become a permanent part of the curriculum at Fort Leavenworth.[36]

Liggett performed his staff duties for more than four years. During that time, he was fortunate to work under the overall command of the chief of staff, Maj. Gen. Leonard Wood, and his assistant chief of staff, Maj. Gen. William H. Carter, both of whom were fully supportive of the Army War College. Clearly, after more than thirty years of service, Liggett's hard work and study had caught the eye of the more senior ranks. Now he would be the person who would mold similarly talented officers for higher command.

Liggett reported to the commanding surgeon's office on October 20, 1910, for his annual physical examination. Once again, he passed all elements of the exam. However, over the course of the past year, he had gained eleven pounds and more than two inches in his chest measurement. As a result, the surgeon categorized his figure and general appearance as "stout." Whether or not Liggett considered this as a wake-up call in an army increasingly focused on youth and fitness, he well should have, as it was now a matter of record.[37]

The academic year 1910–11, though similar to the previous one, had an ambitious schedule, including sixty-nine problems, twenty-five map maneuvers, and twenty-six lectures. In addition, Liggett led two twenty-day historical and staff rides, both starting from Fort Myer, where the War College detail was stationed. The first ride, which took place from May 11 through May 27, focused on Civil War battles in Virginia, including the Peninsula Campaign, Wilderness, and Spotsylvania. The second ride was composed of three shorter rides of three to four days each, from June 1 through June 17, and included First and Second Bull Run. For each ride, Liggett designated different students to play a role such as chief of staff, supply officer, and commanders of various brigades. In addition, every day, a student officer was detailed to give a lecture, without notes, on an aspect of the particular battle. A conference followed each ride to discuss their findings. Clearly, Liggett was making his imprint.[38]

Liggett's annual physical examination for 1911 took place on October 9. The results were almost identical to the previous year, with one exception: although his weight was about the same at 199 pounds, his chest measurement had increased by another inch. While this may not seem like much to most people, given his physique, the surgeon once again characterized his figure and general appearance as "stout."[39]

With the class of 1911–12, the pattern was much the same as with the one before. The class included several future general officers, such as Col. Robert L. Bullard, Lt. Col. Richard M. Blatchford, Maj. George B. Duncan, and captains Samuel Rockenbach and Duncan K. Major Jr. On July 7, 1911, prior to the start of the academic year, Liggett was ordered to proceed first to Sparta, Wisconsin, and then to Fort Sill, Oklahoma, to observe field practice firing of both light and heavy artillery between July 15 and August 7.[40]

The academic year commenced as scheduled on September 1, and for the next four months, the class tackled approximately fifty map and maneuver problems. During the months of January and February, they worked on the "war plan of the year," based on a hypothetical attack on the northern border with Canada, along with our continental coastline and island possessions. March was given over to the study of military history and the following month to field engineering problems. Through it all, Liggett encouraged the group to talk the problems over among themselves and to use the research library, but he expected each and every student officer to arrive at his own individual solution to the problems presented.[41]

The academic year ended with staff and historical rides of varying lengths, primarily throughout Virginia, Maryland, and Pennsylvania. Liggett loved this part of the assignment, and although he was no longer the lanky junior officer, as he had gained weight over the years, he was still comfortable on horseback. In fact, while at the War College, part of his annual physical exam included testing following a vigorous ride. Given the overall distances involved on his staff rides and the primitive state of many of the battlefields, his stamina was quite remarkable.

Robert Bullard loved the give-and-take nature of the experience as the day's events were discussed nightly among instructors and fellow students. He described it as "exhilarating." Secretary of War Henry C. Stimson and Gen. Albert L. Mills, then president of the War College, both joined the group while camped at the fairgrounds at Frederick, Maryland, and for the next several days participated in the rides. At Antietam, Liggett assigned two student officers to accompany the secretary and explain the various aspects of the battle to him. All told, the class covered 550 miles on these rides.[42]

That spring, Liggett climbed another rung on the ladder when he was promoted to full colonel effective March 12, 1912. Wasting no time, on April 10, he applied for promotion to the rank of brigadier general. That same day, Lt. Gen. Nelson Miles, now retired, wrote directly to President Taft on Liggett's behalf. Recalling their service together in Montana and the officer's later service in the Philippines, Miles called Liggett "an efficient, accomplished officer" who was "well fitted for promotion to the grade of brigadier general" whenever a vacancy occurred.[43]

No doubt, Liggett lobbied Secretary Stimson at some point during their time together during the staff ride through Virginia. Three months later, he and a number of field officers were ordered to report to Governors Island, New York, to participate in the so-called Connecticut Manoeuvers, which in actuality was a mock attack on the city of New York. Liggett and the others were assigned to serve as either observers or instructors to the twenty thousand regular and National Guard troops participating, and the exercise took place between August 9 and 19. There, Liggett served as chief umpire for the blue force. He made a very favorable impression on John Quillin Tilson, a member of Congress from Connecticut, who wrote a letter to Secretary Stimson the following month urging his promotion. Tilson, who had served in the war with Spain and would later serve on the border with Mexico in 1916, told Stimson that Colonel Liggett was "entitled to very serious consideration" for promotion as "one of the ablest officers in the infantry branch."[44]

The class of 1912–13 commenced in September and followed the now usual format of map exercises, lectures, and the drafting of war plans. It included future general officers Lt. Col. Omar Bundy, a student officer, and Maj. James W. McAndrew, an assistant instructor.[45]

On October 20, 1912, Liggett reported to Fort Myer, Virginia, for his annual physical. As with his previous examinations, he was found to be in good physical condition. There were no changes from the year before. At just over six feet tall and weighing two hundred pounds, the surgeon found his "figure and general appearance" to be "normal and good," respectively.[46]

On November 9, 1912, four days after the election, General Miles called upon President Taft, now a lame duck, and urged him to promote Liggett to one of the vacant brigadier generalships. That same day, Lt. Gen. Samuel B. M. Young, former chief of the general staff and then governor of the US Soldiers Home in Washington, DC, wrote to President Taft on Liggett's behalf. Also recalling their service together, Young told the president that he had known Liggett for twenty-five years and "always found him loyal, conscientious and highly efficient." The general went on to offer high praise: "In my judgment he is among the best equipped officers of his rank in the art of war, military training and strategy for the duties of a general officer."[47]

Once again, the highlights of the academic year were the historical and tactical rides conducted throughout May and June. This year was somewhat different, as the longer and shorter rides were interspersed. A camp was established by the War College detachment at the fairgrounds in Frederick, Maryland. Liggett, along with staff and guests, including two visiting British Army officers, arrived there by train from Washington, DC, on May 1. The following day, the party set out to visit, among others, the battlefields at Chancellorsville, Spotsylvania, Bull Run, and Antietam, all culminating with a visit to Gettysburg.[48]

On May 11, Liggett was pleased to welcome his former company commander and mentor from his early days in the 5th Infantry, Maj. Gen. Frank D. Baldwin, now retired. Baldwin remained with the party until May 22, when he returned to Washington. No doubt the two old comrades enjoyed the opportunity to reminisce around the campfire about the "old days" in the Montana

11. Brig. Gen. Hunter Liggett. Courtesy of the Library of Congress.

and Dakota Territories. On May 30, Chief of Staff Leonard Wood drove over to the encampment near Gaines Mill to spend the day observing the exercise. Finally, later that same day, and for several days thereafter, the party had the benefit of insights from a historian from Harvard, Professor R. M. Johnston, regarding the Battle of Bull Run.[49]

Liggett instituted an innovation to the exercises that spring when he scheduled three short staff rides and assigned a student officer to lead each one. The result was obviously beneficial to the student in charge, as well as popular with the student officers, but a subsequent analysis questioned whether it was worth the expenditure of funds and a duplication of effort compared to using expert guidance alone. The class returned to Washington by rail on June 14, and another school term came to an end.[50]

GENERAL LIGGETT

In the middle of the academic year, Liggett traveled briefly to Guantanamo, Cuba, from January 20 through February 3, 1913. Upon his return, he was sick in quarters with typhoid fever from February 10 through 27, no doubt contracted during his visit to Cuba. However, while recuperating, he received some welcome news. On February 12, Liggett reached what for most officers would have been the pinnacle of their careers: he received word that President Taft had nominated him for promotion to the rank of brigadier general in the Regular Army. The appointment became caught up in a fight between the Taft administration and former Confederate general Joseph F. Johnston, now a US senator from Alabama, who opposed the promotion of one of the other nominees. The nomination was finally approved by the Senate effective March 5.[51]

One of the first people to offer their congratulations was Lt. George Marshall. Liggett had just returned from a visit to Fort Sill, Oklahoma, where he had observed field artillery fire exercises, so he was a little late in responding to the letter. "I do not know anyone whose congratulations I value more than I do yours," he wrote, "for I have a very high opinion of your soldierly quality and am very fond of you personally." Ever modest, he continued, "I appreciate the kind sentiments expressed in your letter and hope I shall be able to make good in this grade and I shall not disappoint my friends and especially those in . . . the Army."[52]

At the same time, Liggett received a copy of his efficiency report for the previous year. The panel conducting the review was composed of Maj. Gen. William W. Wotherspoon, president of the Army War College, and brigadier generals Albert L. Mills and William Crozier. All three had good things to say. Wotherspoon called him "one of the most efficient General Staff officers I have known." He also referred to him as a man of "studious habits and wide reading." Crozier echoed Wotherspoon, calling Liggett "an exceptionally studious and able officer [and] qualified for high command." All would welcome him in their command.[53]

The months immediately following his promotion to brigadier general were particularly busy ones for Liggett. On Tuesday, April 1, he served as the judge for a competitive military drill and dress parade as part of the graduation exercises at the Carlisle Indian School. The following week, he was ordered to return to Fort Sill to observe field artillery fire, and two months later, from June 1 through June 14, he led another staff ride. This ride covered the Shenandoah Valley. In addition, Liggett was placed in charge of the troops present at the Gettysburg reunion, and he would remain there on detached service from the War College from June 30 through July 8.[54]

Liggett's scholarship and excellent staff work resulted in his appointment as president of the Army War College, effective July 1, 1913. It was a prestigious and influential assignment and one that he relished. During his term, he would continue to oversee the development of a more professional officer corps, one that would help meet the nation's needs in the coming years.

GETTYSBURG REDUX

Aside from the class work and the staff rides, perhaps the most interesting duty that Liggett performed as president of the War College took place in July 1913 in connection with the fiftieth reunion of the Battle of Gettysburg, which featured the encampment on the battlefield itself by more than fifty thousand surviving Civil War veterans, both blue and gray, many of whom had been at Gettysburg in 1863. Liggett was charged with oversight for the establishment and operation of all aspects of the camp, from tentage to food, and for emergency medical facilities.[55]

Planning for the event began in Gettysburg as early as 1908, when a town meeting attended by about 150 residents appointed a committee of seven prominent citizens to "take the initiative in securing a proper celebration of the 50th anniversary of the battle." The committee had grand ideas for a state and national celebration, a fact the politicians in Harrisburg took note of when approached by the local committee. By the following year, the governor of Pennsylvania had appointed nine men to what was called "The Gettysburg Battle 50th Anniversary Commission." Over the next three years, mass meetings were held in both Gettysburg and Harrisburg as the respective committees coordinated their efforts. Eventually, as the planning went forward, a congressional committee and the Pennsylvania Monuments Commission also weighed in.[56]

The site chosen for the encampment was on the battlefield itself near the "High Water Mark" monument. It encompassed 280 acres, on which were pitched 6,592 tents holding eight men each, all laid out in a grid, with 47.5 miles of company streets lit by five hundred electric arc lamps and thirty-two strategically located fountains dispensing ice water. In addition, there were telephone stations, a temporary post office, ambulances, and aid stations. US Army field kitchens, 173 in all, served 688,000 meals from supper on June 29, for the first arrivals, to breakfast on July 6, when the last of the veterans left for home. While Liggett was in overall command, the actual work was performed under the direction of the chief quartermaster, Maj. James E. Normoyle. In all, the camp accommodated 53,407 veterans, in addition to Liggett's contingent of 124 officers and 1,342 enlisted men, together with cooks, Red Cross volunteers, newspapermen, and honored guests. It was, in short, a massive logistical and diplomatic undertaking by Liggett, who was also on hand to greet and escort the dignitaries.[57]

The days were filled with speeches by prominent state and federal figures, including the president, chief justice, and the secretary of war, in addition to the governors of the various states from which the veterans traveled. At first, Wilson declined the invitation to speak by Pennsylvania governor John Kinley Tener, offering the excuse that Congress was still in session and that it would be inappropriate for him to leave Washington "for any speechmaking occasion." The real reason was the fact that he had a preplanned family vacation in New Hampshire. However, at the very last minute, Wilson decided to give a brief address on July 4. All in all, the president spent approximately one hour at Gettysburg. These exercises took place in a large tent erected adjacent to the camp, which accommodated between ten thousand and fifteen thousand persons at a time.[58]

The real stars of the reunion were the aging veterans themselves, ranging in age from 61 to 112. Despite the blistering heat, they entered into the festivities with gusto and goodwill, including a reenactment of Pickett's Charge. A reporter covering the reunion for the *New York Times* wrote, "The eager zest with which the old soldiers of both armies entered upon the task was almost boyish." Foremost in the minds of the organizers was the comfort and safety of the veterans, so much so that automobiles were banned during the evening so as not to disturb their slumbers. Liggett himself was stopped by an alert sentry as he arrived in camp in his automobile during the evening of June 29 and started down the main road toward his tent. Good-naturedly, the general got out of his car and walked the rest of the way.[59]

By all accounts, the reunion went well, although overall nine veterans died. Eight of them succumbed to natural causes—one of them while waiting in a crowded train station on his way home—and another when his horse bolted. The Red Cross volunteers treated more than four thousand cases of heat exhaustion, dehydration, or overexertion at their several aid stations. The only woman in the encampment was Gen. James Longstreet's widow, Helen, who had arrived at the encampment only to find that she had no accommodations. The camp was open to individual veterans themselves and not their families. Nevertheless, the gallant Liggett made arrangements for her to have her own tent as well as an adjoining one.[60]

Liggett presided over a dinner in a mess tent with his officers on July 5 where everyone was in a festive mood since the reunion had wound down. However, it was estimated that it would take two months to restore the area. In their final report, the commission tendered its "congratulations and appreciation" to Liggett "for his gracious yet dignified discharge of the delicate and exacting duties and obligations there confronting him." He and several other officers were presented with gold medals.[61]

BACK TO BUSINESS

Shortly after the reunion, Liggett received an invitation from his friend Webb Hayes to visit him at his family home, called Spiegel Grove, in Fremont, Ohio. The occasion was the centennial celebration of the successful defense of Fort Stephenson by Maj. George Croghan in August 1813, when attacked by a much superior British force. In declining the invitation, Liggett wrote, "My dear Friend . . . [I] would like very much to come, mainly for the purpose of having a talk with you," but business at the Army War College prevented it.[62]

Part of the business that he referred to was his appointment by Secretary of War Lindley Garrison to head what would come to be called the Liggett Committee. The purpose of the committee was to recommend policies that would improve the effectiveness of the officer corps, in particular with regard to promotions. The US Army had long relied upon a seniority system coupled with promotion based on political connections. Not only did this often result in the promotion of lesser or even unqualified individuals, but it also bred resentment and poor morale among those who had been passed over. The secretary himself favored a system that used examination and promotion boards.

12. Gettysburg, fiftieth reunion (1913). Left to right: General Liggett, Secretary Garrison, and General Wood. Courtesy of the Library of Congress.

While Liggett's committee was unable to gain consensus on the fundamental issue, it did recommend, among other things, that promotions to the rank of brigadier general be made within the various branches of the US Army in proportion to the relative size of each. Garrison adopted this recommendation.[63]

Through it all, Liggett had to prepare for the upcoming school year, which began as any other. In a slight twist, one of the members of the class of 1913–14 was Maj. Gen. John S. O'Ryan of the New York National Guard, the first such officer to have been designated to attend the War College. General O'Ryan would go on to command the 27th Division, a New York National Guard unit, in France during the First World War. He had the distinction of being the only National Guard officer to command a division in France throughout the entire conflict.[64]

In April 1914, as a result of the situation in Mexico, the War Department canceled the balance of the academic year effective April 30, and all student officers were ordered to report to their assigned regiments. There would be no historical and staff rides that year.[65]

In spite of the truncated class schedule, Liggett relished his remaining time spent at the Army War College. It was the culmination of his scholarly journey, much of it self-study, and it added value to his standing and burnished his reputation as a US Army officer. Moreover, he found that teaching by doing, particularly through the staff rides, was a valuable method that benefitted both the teacher and the student. More important, his experience at the War College informed his command style in a way that proved so important when he assumed high command later in France. He proved the adage that "you are never too old to learn."

SIX
The Philippines Again

NEW ASSIGNMENT (TEXAS CITY, TEXAS)

In May 1913, Liggett requested that he be reassigned to a line command, specifically the 5th Infantry Regiment. In any event, after what was more than four years in a staff assignment, it is more than likely that he would have been "Manchued"[1] back to a line command anyway after the current class graduated. In fact, the year before, he had told George C. Marshall he fully expected such a change. "How long I shall remain here, I do not know," he had written, "but probably until summer, in order to see the class through and arrange the course at the College for the next year." He continued, "Then I want to be with troops; having been away four years, which is quite long enough at one time." So Secretary Garrison's announcement of the new assignments in mid-December 1913 came as no surprise. Liggett was to report to Texas City, Texas, sometime during the coming year to command the Fourth Brigade.[2]

In February 1913, during the waning days of the presidency of William Howard Taft, several generals attempted a coup against the Mexican government of Pres. Francisco Madero. The beleaguered president, in turn, asked the help of Gen. Victoriano Huerta, a vicious and ambitious man, who had once served the regime of Porfirio Díaz. Huerta quickly turned against Madero, and within a week, he had assassinated Madero and took the reins of power himself. Given the chronic instability in Mexico, at the direction of the chief of staff, Maj. Gen. Leonard Wood, the US Army began to conduct maneuvers at Texas City in order to test the effectiveness of larger units by consolidating the disparate brigades into so-called mobile army divisions. This was an attempt to modernize, in part, but also was a show of force on the border with Mexico. Under the circumstances, President Wilson continued Taft's exercises, and he steadfastly refused to recognize Huerta.[3]

The coastal area east of Houston near Galveston was chosen as the site for these exercises. It proved somewhat problematic, as it was low and prone to flooding and swarmed with mosquitoes, and it rained constantly. The overall experience of the exercise, though valuable, was one of discomfort and misery for all ranks. Brig. Gen. Clarence R. Edwards, then in command of the 6th Brigade at Texas City, referred to the mosquitoes there as "gray wolves of the air." Another participant wrote of "heat, dust, and alkali water" in the desert southwest along the Rio Grande. "It took . . . months, of engineering and fatigue to make it a living camp," wrote another.[4]

In April 1914, the ever-volatile situation in Mexico took another interesting turn. As a result, the class of 1913–14 at the Army War College was suspended and graduation was moved up to April 30. On April 22, 1914, Liggett's assignment on the general staff and as president of the Army War College abruptly ended.[5]

Earlier in the month, on April 9, local Mexican authorities had seized a US Navy whaleboat and its crew while they were carrying out a routine duty at Tampico. Though the boat and crew were quickly released, tensions between the US and Mexican governments escalated. When it was learned that arms were being shipped from Cuba to Vera Cruz, orders were issued to prevent them from falling into Huerta's hands. As a result, a party of sailors and US Marines seized the customs house and several buildings in Vera Cruz on April 21, and fighting ensued. Meanwhile, Brig. Gen. Frederick Funston and the 5th Infantry Brigade, 2nd Division, which was training near Texas City, Texas, were ordered to proceed to Vera Cruz. This force arrived there on April 27 and relieved the US Navy. It remained there until November 23.[6]

While all that was happening, on April 22, Liggett was first ordered to report to Chicago to await further orders before continuing on to Texas City to take command of the 4th Brigade, 2nd Regular Division. He arrived in Chicago on April 29 and received his orders the same day. By May 4, he telegraphed the War Department that he was in Galveston, Texas, ready to report for duty the following day.[7]

It would be the first time that Liggett had command of a brigade in the field. Up to that point, his experience with a unit of this size had only been theoretical, during his studies at Fort Leavenworth and the Army War College. He was not alone. Col. Robert L. Bullard was already in Texas City. In fact, he had been there since March 2, 1913. He was in command of the 26th Infantry Regiment, as well as in temporary command of the 4th Brigade in the absence of a brigadier general, a position now filled by Liggett. If Colonel

13. 4th Brigade, Texas City, TX (1913). Courtesy of the Library of Congress.

Bullard, who had actively sought promotion, was disappointed that General Liggett, and not he, had taken formal command, he didn't let on. The two would soon come to know each other well and develop a mutual respect.[8]

By the time that Liggett arrived in Texas, many of the troops were bored and restless with having to perform the same training regimen day after day. Morale was low, as many, having been mobilized, were disappointed by the fact that they would not be going to Mexico. At one point, Maj. Gen. William H. Carter, who was in overall command, ordered that the training cease and recreational activities be substituted in their place. Not only did this not help the situation, but it also frustrated officers like Colonel Bullard, who feared that the effectiveness of the previous months of training would soon be undone. Liggett quickly recognized the problem and designed exercises to be conducted during both night and day that were practical applications of tactical study with an eye toward the current situation in Mexico. Bullard found this training to be the "most realistic and useful" he had experienced. Moreover, Liggett took pains to explain the purpose of the exercises to the officers and men. His philosophy was simple: "If the American soldier is made to understand the object of any special course of work, and can see how it can be applied practically in the field," he explained, "he will take up the work and carry it through enthusiastically." Thereafter, Liggett noticed a positive change in attitude among the troops under his command.[9]

On August 20, midway through his assignment in Texas City, Liggett was admitted once again to the Army and Navy General Hospital at Hot Springs, Arkansas, for treatment of another serious flare-up of his rheumatism. From

this point on, his health would be of concern both personally and career-wise. Liggett spent nearly six weeks at Hot Springs as a patient and as a casual following his discharge. Afterward, he returned briefly to Texas City and the 4th Brigade. Perhaps anticipating a change of orders, on October 1, he requested and was granted a leave of absence of one month and fifteen days.[10]

ANOTHER TOUR IN THE PHILIPPINES

In November 1914, Liggett received orders to proceed to the Philippines, there to take command of the provisional infantry brigade then stationed at Fort William McKinley, an eight-thousand-acre post six miles outside of Manila. In total, he would command nearly four thousand officers and enlisted men. Following a short leave to pack, he and Harriet sailed from San Francisco aboard the UST *Logan* on December 5, and they arrived in Manila on January 4, 1915. The couple took several days to get acclimated to Manila and its environs, after which Liggett assumed command of the brigade on January 8.[11]

Sometime after his arrival, Liggett received a copy of his latest efficiency report prepared by Maj. Gen. J. Franklin Bell, which was based on his service at Texas City from May 10 through August 19. As was the case with his previous commanders, General Bell found both his professional zeal and his attention to detail "excellent" and his military bearing "very good." That said, since Liggett had been in Hot Springs for a good portion of his assignment with the 4th Brigade, General Bell was unable to get a full picture. He hedged somewhat in his assessment, thus raising the first hints of some duty limitations. Bell noted Liggett's absence due to illness and went on to carefully say that he had only observed him in camp and not in the field and that Liggett's "efficiency was excellent *while physically fit*" (emphasis added). Although he found Liggett's horsemanship to be "very good," he estimated that his weight was between 210 and 220 pounds. Unfortunately, this guess was made long after Liggett had moved on to his new assignment in the Philippines and was substantially higher than was noted in his previous physical examinations or the one taken a little more than a year later. Perhaps more problematic was Bell's characterization of Liggett's activity as only "fair." No doubt the bookish Liggett led a more sedentary life, but in an army with an increasing emphasis placed on youth and vigor, this spelled trouble. On the positive side, Bell found Liggett to be a "well known officer possessing unusual intelligence," and he recommended him for duty on the general staff at the Army War College or as an attaché. Whether or not Liggett was at all disappointed with the recommendation, it was a moot point since he was by that time right where he wanted to be, serving with the troops in the field.[12]

One person who was looking forward to seeing the general again was 1st Lt. George C. Marshall, still with the 13th Infantry Regiment then stationed at Fort William McKinley. "He should make a fine post commander," he wrote to a friend. "I have known him a long time and have the greatest admiration for his ability and good judgment." Marshall also breathed a great sigh of relief soon after Liggett's arrival, when the latter assigned him to his staff as an aide to, in his words, "prevent my being transferred from Fort McKinley down to the southern end of Batangas Province at Fort Batangas."[13]

This tour of the Philippines was undoubtedly more comfortable than Liggett's first one. For one thing, Harriet would be with him, and for another, the large post just south of Manila had more amenities, and with Manila so close by, there was an opportunity for shopping and cultural activities. They were also able to keep up with the war in Europe through "newspaper accounts," and Liggett was convinced that "it was simply a question of time" before the United States entered the war, especially after the sinking of the *Lusitania* in May of 1915.[14]

A MATTER OF NATIONAL HONOR

Ever since May 1, 1898, when Comm. George Dewey destroyed the Spanish fleet in Manila Bay, the question of what to do about the Philippines became an issue of national importance. At first, President McKinley was not sure whether he wanted to keep the archipelago at all or simply hold on to Manila and its environs as a toehold in the Far East. While the president pondered the question, Dewey asked for troops to hold Manila, and McKinley obliged. Eventually, the president decided to hold on to the entire Philippines, and America committed herself to expending more blood and treasure there. Ultimately, the question became whether it was in our strategic national interest to defend the islands in the event of attack, and if so, how?[15]

Theodore Roosevelt and other powerful men believed that the manifest destiny of the United States extended beyond our shores, and they subscribed to the theories of Alfred Thayer Mahan: that a nation's power and influence were projected worldwide by means of a great naval arm. In order to do that, our fleet needed secure overseas stations to refuel and refit, especially in times of war. The dilemma facing the US military was twofold: how to sustain the fleet and how to reinforce the Philippine garrison. This required a degree of cooperation between the US Army and Navy that simply did not exist, as each had "separate visions" as to the best approach.[16]

The likely opponent in such a future conflict would be Japan, whose growing power in the Western Pacific was cause for concern. Japan had surprised the US and European powers with just how quickly she had overcome the Russian fleet through a surprise attack at Port Arthur in February 1904 and, later, her defeat of the Russian Army at Mukden in 1905. At the same time, on the West Coast, a war scare and serious anti-Japanese sentiments sparked riots and vigilantism.[17]

So serious was the president's concern that Roosevelt dispatched the "Great White Fleet" to sail around the world in order to send a message to Japan and other powers, and his chief of staff tasked the Army War College to address the problem with a plan. As a result, the class of 1907–8 "gamed" a theoretical attack on the Philippines by the orange team (Japan) against the blue team (United States). The students projected a landing in the Lingayen Gulf with seventy thousand to one hundred thousand orange troops, who soon overcame any resistance, including the fortresses guarding Manila Bay, principally Corregidor. The upshot of the exercise was a recommendation that the Philippines be left to their own fate. That course was not acceptable to many in Washington.[18]

By 1911, an initial plan had been approved, but the discussion went on for five years. No surprise—what evolved was a navy-first plan, with the army playing a subordinate role. For the navy, the main question was whether the fleet should have a forward base in Manila Bay or Subic Bay (in addition to a base at Oahu, Hawaii). After considerable back-and-forth, the decision came down to Manila Bay. Therein lay the problem, however, since the army garrison was not large enough to defend Manila, the capital of the Philippines, and at the same time man the forts defending the harbor. As a result, the plan called for an anchorage in Manila Bay and for the army to hold the line in the Bataan Peninsula and fortify the islands at the mouth of Manila Bay, particularly Corregidor. This became known as the "Corregidor-first" plan. Leonard Wood—and later, Douglas MacArthur—were vigorous proponents of this approach. There was, however, an even larger problem with that approach. The Panama Canal did not yet exist. Moreover, there were no plans to split the fleet, and without the means to quickly move it from the Atlantic (where it was most likely to be stationed), the relatively small garrison would more than likely be quickly overcome. That force would, in essence, be expendable. The only "benefit" of such an outcome would be the preservation of national honor.[19]

PHILIPPINE DEFENSE BOARD

In April 1915, the US Army created the Philippine Defense Board and appointed Liggett to head it. The board convened between April 8 and 12 to discuss the continuing question regarding the efficacy of defending Manila Bay and its environs, if not the entire archipelago itself, in the event of war. Liggett and his board concluded that such a defense would be costly and impractical, and they recommended that the present strategy be abandoned. In the words of the Liggett board, the Corregidor-first policy was more symbolic than strategic. They concluded, "In holding [the forts] we are simply defending American sovereignty and dignity to the utmost of our resources, but we are not holding anything of fundamental strategic importance from the standpoint of the main naval campaign."[20]

Liggett must have known, if only from his recent assignments to the general staff and particularly at the Army War College, that he had weighed in on a long-standing dispute. This position created a firestorm back in the States, where a review board rejected Liggett's recommendations, a decision supported in an assessment by the Army War College. Both argued that it was essential to hold the Bataan Peninsula.[21]

THE DAILY ROUTINE

During May 1915, the inspector general conducted the annual review of Fort William McKinley and the troops. Liggett accompanied his brigade in the field for the part of the inspection that took place on May 24 and 25. In June, he led the provisional brigade on a march to Camp John Hay near Baguio in northern Luzon. Situated approximately five thousand feet above sea level, the site was a popular retreat for diplomats and US Army officers,

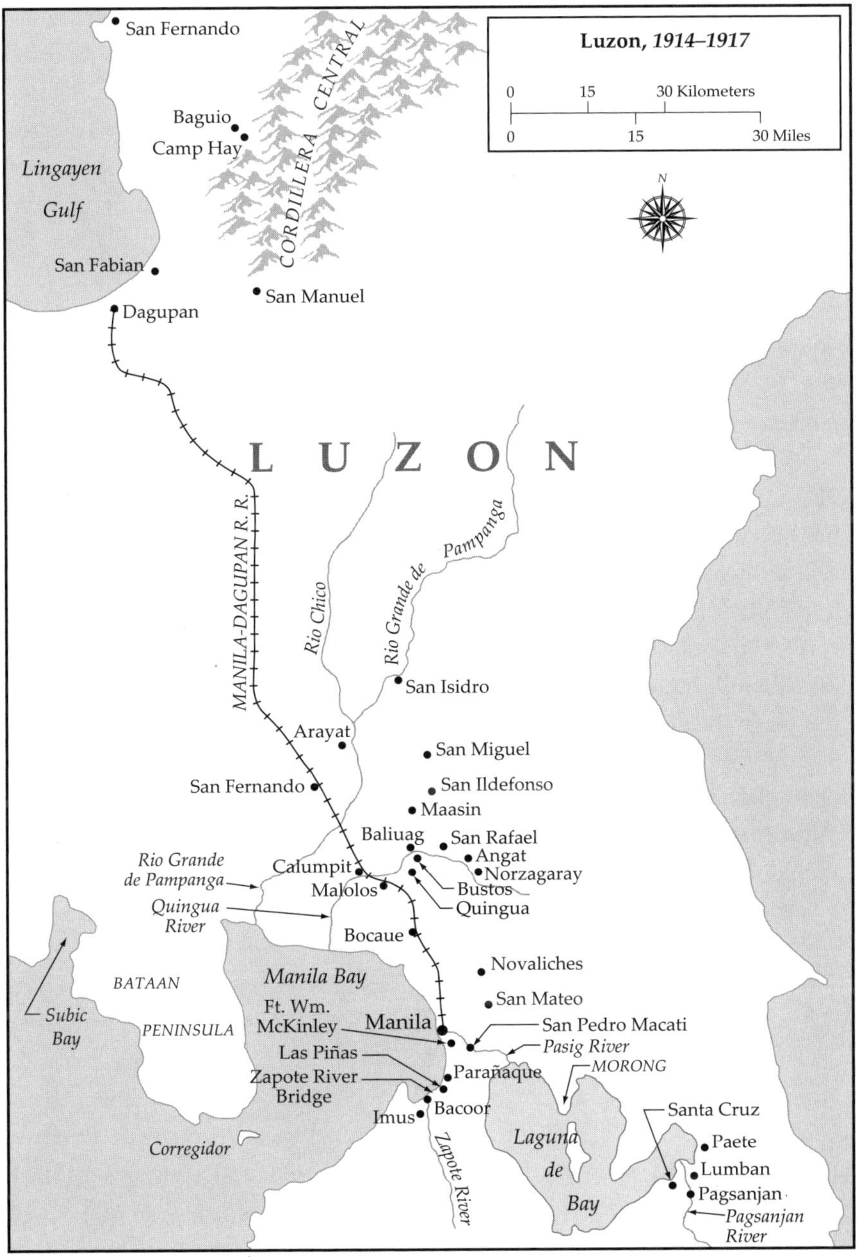

Map 3. Luzon, Philippines (1914–17)

as the cooler mountain air provided a welcome relief from the sticky summer humidity of Manila. The brigade returned later that month. Liggett reported for his annual physical examination on December 17, where the surgeon noted that his weight was 202 pounds, just two pounds higher than his 1912 exam, and that his "figure and general appearance" were "good." On December 22, Liggett took to the field once again, as he led the provisional brigade on another march to Camp Hay. George Marshall served as acting adjutant for the expedition. The party returned to Manila on January 1, 1916.[22]

Upon his return to Manila, Liggett received a copy of his efficiency report for the calendar year 1915, prepared by the department commander, Maj. Gen. Thomas H. Barry. Overall, the report commended Liggett's fitness to command in virtually every category, save one—physical fitness. Barry pulled no punches: although he listed Liggett as six-foot-one and two hundred pounds (based on his recent physical examination), he went on to report that his subordinate failed "to keep himself in suitable physical condition for hard field service." As to his marching ability, Barry was even more blunt, describing it as "poor" and Liggett as being "too fat and soft." This assessment would continue to dog Liggett. In the event of war, perhaps inconsistently, Barry found that Liggett was best suited for duty with troops and found him to be an "excellent and well qualified officer." With the possibility of American participation in the ongoing European conflict growing likelier every day, this report should have been another reminder for Liggett to get in shape.[23]

General Barry also filed a second efficiency report, dated April 15, 1916, coincident with his relinquishing command of the Philippine Department to Liggett. It is, for all intents and purposes, word for word the same report as filed in January.[24]

The following year, Gen. John J. Pershing and Secretary Newton D. Baker, who had access to each general officer's personnel file, would have seen Barry's assessment that Liggett was "too fat" and not in "suitable physical condition" in both reports, and that was undoubtedly a significant factor in their hesitation to retain Liggett in command of his division—or, for that matter, any division—in France in spite of his well-deserved reputation as a military scholar. Without question, at this time, Liggett battled his weight and would do so for the balance of his career. However, from an objective standard, at just over six feet tall, two hundred pounds might be considered somewhat overweight, but it alone is hardly disqualifying. Nevertheless, and despite the fact that he had passed all his physical examinations, his general appearance was characterized as "stout" in two of them, and as Liggett would discover later on in France, in Pershing's mind, appearances were important.

FORESHADOWING

Beginning on January 13, 1916, Liggett conducted a two-week staff ride from Manila all the way "up the central valley of Luzon to the Lingayen Gulf and back." He turned to Marshall to help with the planning, and the younger man also accompanied the group as Liggett's aide-de-camp. The stated purpose of the exercise was to formulate a defense for a hypothetical Japanese attack on the Philippines. The subtext was Liggett's pushback against the rejection of his report's premise and to demonstrate that if a defense of the islands was called for, rather than holding out on the defensive, awaiting relief, it would be better for a combined force of American and Filipino troops to take an initial stand against an enemy landing at the beaches. He would nonetheless continue to swim against the tide. Other similar staff rides would follow, but as it turned out, this one presaged the actual invasion of the Philippines, when the main Japanese force came ashore in the Lingayen Gulf on the morning of December 22, 1941.[25]

In 1925, several years following his retirement, Liggett still held firm to his earlier assessment. "It soon became apparent," he opined, "that the true defense of [Luzon], as of every other island, was primarily a function of Sea Power, and that an effective defense of the Philippines required a first class naval base at Guam."[26]

PHILIPPINE DEPARTMENT

Liggett assumed overall command of the Department of the Philippines on April 15, 1916. He moved his headquarters to Manila, and he would remain in that post until the United States entered into the war in Europe. As department commander, Liggett toured the various subordinate commands, including, in May 1916, a return to Mindanao. There, he told Webb C. Hayes, he found that Zamboanga was "so much improved that you would not recognize it." Later on, he went to Davao, where he "found everything progressing there and the people treated me like they would the returning Grand Poobah." The *presidente* of the subdistrict was a fellow whom he had once jailed for "carabao stealing" but had been found innocent at trial. "Now," he told his old friend, "he is quite wealthy and a shining light." He added that the man had showed "the good effects of discipline." Liggett also visited the islands of Cebu and Iloilo, where he found that "progress has been wonderful."[27]

On October 14, 1916, Liggett went to China on an inspection tour and returned to Manila on November 10. He must have anticipated a change in command, and on November 15, he requested that he retain command of the Philippine Department until April 15, 1917, "for the purpose of seeing the completion of the Field Training planned in this Department; and to carry through certain plans for the stationing of troops on Luzon." The War Department granted the extension.[28]

Liggett achieved another milestone in his career while in the Philippines: he was promoted to major general in the Regular Army on March 6, 1917. Maj. Gen. Frederick Funston died suddenly of a heart attack, in San Antonio on February 19, 1917, at the age of fifty-one, which created a vacancy that President Wilson quickly filled with his nomination of Liggett. On March 6, Liggett received a telegram from Maj. Gen. Hugh Scott indicating that he had been nominated to be a major general. He had an ally in the governor general of the Philippines, Burton Harrison, a Wilson appointee, who had sent an unsolicited cable to the adjutant general two weeks before, urging Liggett's appointment "in recognition of his services [in the] international situation." On March 22, Liggett cabled acceptance of his appointment.[29]

Liggett was the beneficiary of a paradigm shift in promotions within the higher ranks, where seniority had lost much of its importance, as Brig. Gen. Clarence R. Edwards also soon found out. Edwards was at that time in command of the US Army units defending the Panama Canal. As the most senior brigadier general, Edwards fully expected that he would be selected for promotion. He was obviously disappointed but sent his colleague a cable congratulating him on his promotion. Liggett's reply to his friend was at once gracious and demonstrated his sense of humor: "Your cablegram was particularly gratifying, since logically your being at the head of the list entitled you to this promotion. . . . I always knew you were a good sport and big enough to look at things in a broad way, and as I am old enough to be your grandfather I shan't stand in your way very long."[30]

Liggett also received congratulations from Webb Hayes. After thanking his friend, he asked what he had been up to for the past year. "I hope you are well and just as full of 'ginger' as in former days out here," he wrote. Alluding to their earlier voyage together, he added playfully, "We won't have any more '*Immanuense*' trips anyway!"[31]

By May 14, Liggett was back in San Francisco, ready to take command of the Western Department of the Army, which he assumed the following day. That same day, he took his oath of office as a major general.[32]

SEVEN

World War I, Opening Rounds

A WORLD AT WAR

Shortly before he died, Chancellor Otto von Bismarck was heard to remark, "One day the great European war will come out of some damned foolish thing in the Balkans." Once again, history had proved the "Iron Chancellor" correct. Since August of 1914, all of Europe, and a good part of the Middle East, had been at war. Virtually landlocked and in danger of being cut off from foodstuffs and vital materials, Germany fought back with a campaign of unrestricted submarine warfare in an attempt to put England and her Allies in the same position. The North Atlantic became the graveyard for millions of tons of vital shipping. German U-boats didn't only sink the shipping of the combatants; their campaign was extended to neutrals like the United States. A convoy system adopted by the Allies helped offset the losses. Under pressure from repeated warnings to stop sinking US vessels, Germany temporarily suspended the unrestricted attacks—but soon resumed them. The final straw for the United States, which had admittedly been leaning more and more toward support for England and the Allies, was the sinking of the freighter *Aztec* on April 1, 1917. By April 6, the president had asked for, and Congress approved, a declaration of war.[1]

SUNSETTER

As commander of the Western Department, Liggett spent much of that spring visiting potential "training areas and camp sites" to be used by National Army draftees throughout the far west, from San Diego to Washington State. Secretary of War Newton D. Baker had delegated the final selection of these sites, called cantonments, to the department commanders.[2]

On September 15, 1917, Major General Liggett was given command of the 41st Division, a National Guard unit drawing broadly from the Northwest, including the states of Washington, Oregon, Idaho, Montana, and the Dakotas, as well as New Mexico, Colorado, Wyoming, and the District of Columbia. It was appropriately enough called the Sunset Division, and the assignment could well have proven to be the sunset of Liggett's career. The division initially assembled at Camp Fremont near Palo Alto, California, but it was soon transferred to Camp Greene near Charlotte, North Carolina.[3]

Joining Liggett at Camp Fremont was Col. Malin Craig. They had developed a good working relationship during their time at the Army War College, and when Craig heard that Liggett had been assigned to command the 41st Division, he requested an assignment there as the latter's chief of staff. Liggett approved, as he recognized the younger man to be an intelligent and efficient officer. What Liggett did not know, and would come to find out in France, was the fact that in addition to his fine soldierly qualities, Craig also had a dark side. He could be narrow-minded, petty, and mean-spirited, traits that manifested themselves in his interactions with other officers, where he was often "quick to censure" those more senior, particularly Maj. Gen. Clarence R. Edwards. Another colleague, Maj. Gen. Charles Pelot Summerall, one of the more successful American Expeditionary Forces (AEF) commanders and a difficult man himself, referred to Craig as having "a sadistic mind for injuring others." Nevertheless, Liggett, whose upbeat personality most often made allowances for the personal foibles of others, trusted Craig in most regards, and they continued to work well together. They could be considered an odd couple of sorts—Liggett was studious, patient, thoughtful, and willing to give his subordinates the benefit of the doubt, as well as room to learn their jobs just as he was having to do, while Craig was intelligent, decisive, often caustic, and willing to see to it that Liggett's orders were carried out. What's more, Craig stood in good stead with the so-called Leavenworth Crowd at Chaumont.[4]

Malin Craig was born in St. Louis, Missouri, on August 5, 1875, the son of a career US Army officer. He spent his early years growing up on military posts throughout the American West. Following three years at what became Georgetown University, Craig enrolled at West Point, graduating in 1898, just in time for service in Cuba during the Spanish American War. Throughout his early career, he served in responsible positions both at home and abroad, particularly in the Philippines. Craig would cap his long career as a chief of staff.[5]

While at Camp Fremont, Liggett, who was by now battling a weight problem, had the "good fortune" (although some might say otherwise) to find a cook among the ranks of the 41st Division. It had come to his attention that a

14. Maj. Gen. Malin Craig. Courtesy of the Library of Congress.

Greek immigrant, a naturalized citizen and candy maker from Seattle, knew a thing or two about gourmet cooking, and the next thing the recruit knew, he had been assigned to division headquarters and would accompany the general to France as his personal chef. This also proved to be an astute political move, as Liggett's special mess enjoyed a reputation within the AEF as being one of the best in France and was frequented by visiting general officers, both French and American, including Pershing himself.[6]

Liggett spent all of one day at Camp Greene before he received new orders. Like many senior officers, he was detached for brief observation duty with the

Allied forces in France and Belgium. In essence, this was an audition in order to help Pershing determine their fitness to command a division. Liggett and Colonel Craig, along with thirteen similarly situated general officers and the 102nd Field Artillery Regiment of the 26th ("Yankee") Division, all sailed for Europe from Hoboken, New Jersey, aboard the SS *Finland*. The ship pulled away from the pier just before noon September 23, 1917, and joined a convoy that included the transports *Antilles*, *Henderson*, and *Lenape*, as well as the cruiser USS *San Diego*, which provided an escort. After several rough days at sea, the men settled into a normal routine of physical training and ship's drills. The *Finland* arrived without incident at St. Nazaire on October 5, and the troops disembarked the following day.[7]

Liggett reported immediately to General Pershing's headquarters in Paris, from which he, along with Colonel Craig and an aide, were immediately dispatched to Gen. Sir Hubert Gough's Fifth British Army headquarters, located just north of Ypres in Belgium. He spent the first night there, at which time he sat in on a staff meeting detailing the day's events. The British Army was in the midst of a protracted effort to seize Passchendaele Ridge in what would be later referred to as the Third Battle of Ypres.[8]

The following day, Liggett and Craig drove to Elverdinge, Belgium, where they spent the next week at the headquarters of Maj. Gen. Sir Geoffrey Fielding of the Guards Division. There, amid daily rain, Liggett got a firsthand look at the deep, ubiquitous, and glutinous mud of Flanders, and he experienced several night bombings. Liggett spent several days at Bethune visiting the British First Army Corps commanded by Gen. Sir Arthur Holland. This was followed by a visit to the 41st British Division near Loos, where he studied supply, camouflage, and training methods. All in all, Liggett called his time spent in the British sector a "delightful and an invaluable experience." He was particularly struck by the "dogged cheerfulness" of the British soldier.[9]

Liggett then took a turn with the French. He and Craig drove to the Houthulst Forest, also in Belgium, and the headquarters of Gen. Adolfe Marie Messimy, whose division was part of the French First Army. Messimy was a former minister of war. There, Liggett observed a wide variety of France's weaponry in use as well as its aviators.[10]

Liggett returned to Chaumont in early November, then took a trip to Paris in the company of Pershing and several other general officers on November 4. It was important to Pershing that potential division commanders view the front lines firsthand, after which he would receive feedback from their respective hosts. As an example, General Fielding of the Guards offered a written assessment of Liggett to Pershing, stating (incorrectly, as it turned out) that he was "very much too old to command a Division in the field."[11]

Liggett's experience at the Allied front simply reinforced the principles of modern warfare espoused by the Army War College, articulated in an August 1910 report prepared by the general staff for the US Army chief of staff. Submitted at the conclusion of his student year, the report, in part, emphasized the changing role of a senior commander, given the size of the modern battlefield and the range of the new weaponry: "The leadership of troops no longer depends on personal example; it must be assumed at a distance, gradually increasing in time and space." His own words, written soon after the war, echoed a key premise of the earlier report. "The first thing I determined to my own satisfaction at the front was that a general officer has nothing to learn in the front line," Liggett wrote, "[and that] he should know every inch of his ground and know it well, but in modern war on the scale that it was fought in France, the nearer one gets to the first line, the less one sees." He added the observation that "the perspective is smothered in the close-up."[12]

A CLOSE CALL

On November 10, 1917, Pershing cabled Secretary of War Newton D. Baker, to whom he reiterated his view regarding the need for vigorous and fit division commanders in France, calling it an "imposition on the Allies" even to send unfit candidates over as observers. "Of the major generals now in Europe," he wrote, "[the] following [are] considered unfit: Clements, James Parker, . . . and probably Hunter Liggett of whom will report later." This hesitation on Pershing's part no doubt reflected the fact that Liggett had a well-deserved reputation as a good soldier and as an officer who was "level-headed, imperturbable in crisis, a student of military history, unselfish, and loyal." In hindsight, it is difficult to see why Pershing expressed doubt at all. Liggett was certainly no threat to his authority, and by all accounts, he was, hands down, the most qualified of the candidates, a fact recognized by his fellow officers, such as major generals Frank D. Baldwin (at this time retired) and Robert L. Bullard.[13]

There is no doubt that later on during his career, Liggett gained a substantial amount of weight; however, this has been somewhat exaggerated over the years, with some historians placing his weight in the range of a grossly obese three hundred pounds. This simply does not square with the reality. According to his physical examination made on December 17, 1915, Liggett stood 72.5 inches tall and weighed 202 pounds. By modern standards, he would have had a body mass index of twenty-seven, indicating that he was overweight but certainly not obese. Though possible, it is highly unlikely that he would have gained one hundred pounds in fewer than two years. Moreover, a photograph taken in March 1918 in conversation with Major General Edwards, who was approximately the same height and never described as obese, shows Liggett to be slightly stockier with a somewhat larger girth than his colleague, indicating that his weight was distributed more disproportionately in his upper body. Moreover, Liggett's mustache and jowls did not enhance his appearance. More than likely it was a combination of Gen. Thomas H. Barry's assessment in 1916 ("too fat and soft"), implying a lack of stamina, and Liggett's age that gave Pershing pause.[14]

On November 20, Liggett was ordered to report to Bordeaux and from there to return to the United States to join his division. These orders were quickly countermanded when it was determined that he would not be able to rejoin his division in time, as its departure was imminent.[15]

Meanwhile, on November 15, Liggett had written a letter to Webb C. Hayes, now a successful businessman, who was traveling in Europe with his wife. Sometime earlier, he had met the Hayes for dinner in the Latin Quarter in Paris. He was as much in the dark about his own situation as that of his division. "There is absolutely no news here," he wrote. "Nobody knows anything, or if they do, they won't tell." His frustration evident, he added, "I am trying to get settled temporarily in a billet, but for how long I cannot tell."[16]

The 41st Division sailed for France without Liggett. By December 15, leading elements of the division began to arrive, although Liggett was not immediately aware of it. On December 18, he took the time to send a short note to Webb Hayes, who was in Italy touring the Italian front. Both of them were still in the dark as to their respective statuses—Liggett as to the whereabouts of his division and Hayes as to a commission. "I do not suppose you have heard anything from Washington," Liggett wrote. "I hear nothing and am still awaiting the arrival of our people when of course we shall go to them at once." Liggett added, "We hear all sort of rumors and believe a minimum of these." Nevertheless, Liggett traveled to Paris the following day so that at the very least he would be close enough to greet the troops when the 41st Division finally did arrive. Word finally reached him that his division had been directed to proceed to the small village of La Courtine, and he joined it there on Christmas Eve.[17]

The 41st Division was not slated to play an active role in the upcoming fight, as shortly after its arrival, it was designated as a depot division—that is,

15. Maj. Gen. John J. Pershing and Lt. Col. James G. Harbord, Washington, DC (1917). Courtesy of the Library of Congress.

one that would be broken up into smaller parts and used to strengthen other divisions, its officers and noncoms used to replace casualties. Liggett was in the unenviable position of presiding over the dissolution of his own command.[18]

FIRST ARMY CORPS

All the while, Pershing continued to purge the AEF of older, less energetic officers, replacing them with ones whom he felt would be up to the task of commanding a division under the demanding conditions of modern warfare. The grounds for relief were euphemistically referred to as "physical inefficiency." One division commander who had been favorably passed on was heard to remark that "the official life of every high commander in the AEF hung by a thread." Liggett was well aware that his physical appearance would be a critical factor in whether he retained his command, and he worked hard to demonstrate to Pershing that he was fit. On December 18, 1917, Brig. Gen. James G. Harbord, Pershing's chief of staff, noted the following observation in his diary: "Liggett, who stands well with the Army, has a tremendous waist measurement which promises poorly for activity, though to do him justice I see him walking every morning trying to walk it off, a very discouraging task, once it has arrived."[19]

On January 15, 1918, Liggett was summoned to AEF Headquarters at Chaumont. Surely he was already disappointed with his assignment, given the decision to designate his division as a replacement one so soon after its arrival in France. Moreover, he had been told by his sources that an order for his relief had already been "drawn up and a successor selected." His sources were correct. According to Harbord, authority for Liggett's relief had already come "unsought" from the War Department in mid-December. Accordingly, as Liggett entered general headquarters (GHQ), he was likely expecting the worst, but he was pleasantly surprised when Pershing offered him command of the First Corps, AEF ("I Corps"), effective January 20, 1918. Liggett relinquished command of the 41st Division on January 17, and he established his corps headquarters at Neufchâteau on January 20.[20]

Liggett's selection was a close call—closer, no doubt, than he knew or ever let on. Early in December, when Liggett and Craig were getting ready to sail home, Pershing, who had sought authority from the War Department to retain Liggett and to send Gen. Richard M. Blatchford home in his stead, discovered just in time that the cablegram had never been sent. In fact, it was still sitting in the code room. Harbord, who had been in a position to know, later reminisced that "the Army might have lost a Lieutenant General and successful Army Commander . . . if another hour had elapsed with the cablegram undelivered." Years later, with his characteristic low-key sense of humor, Liggett would write, tongue in cheek, "I never have inquired and the report [of my relief] continues to be only hearsay to me."[21]

PREPARING FOR WAR

Initially, I Corps consisted of the first four divisions to form in France—the 1st, 2nd, 26th, and 42nd—as well as the 32nd in reserve and Liggett's old 41st as a replacement division. As the war progressed and more divisions arrived in France, the makeup of the corps would change in accordance with the French system. As such, divisions would be interchangeable from time to time as the situation demanded, though the corps headquarters staff, as well as certain support units (e.g., corps artillery), would remain constant. The first four divisions would come to be called "Pioneer" divisions, or the "Old Reliables," since they had served in France the longest. Moreover, by the time the war had ended, they would collectively suffer 30 percent of the casualties experienced by the approximately twenty-eight American divisions that saw some service on the continent. At this time, these four were at various stages in the three-step training process, with the 1st Division the furthest along.[22]

During this training period, although some divisions served with the British Army, the bulk of the American divisions were under the tactical control of the French Army while Liggett retained administrative control. The latter involved areas like supply and some training in the American mode, and Liggett spent much of his days going from unit to unit, observing the training process and familiarizing himself with the officers under his command. He also listened to countless gripes about a lack of clothing and equipment, as the Services of Supply had a long way to go to keep up.[23]

Things were particularly tough on the enlisted men. During what has been described as the worst European winter in decades, they were billeted for the most part in unheated, vermin-infested lofts in small villages whose streets were lined with piles of raw manure. Short of coats, gas masks, gloves, and galoshes, they suffered greatly. In addition, the deep, glutinous mud was more than a nuisance. Everyone looked forward to the coming of spring.[24]

The Americans began their training in Lorraine, a relatively quiet region in northeastern France, under the watchful eye of their French tutors, battle-hardened veterans of three and a half years of war. That is not to say that there was no enemy activity but merely that it was in general limited to raids, patrols, and intermittent shelling by both sides. As a result, the Americans began to experience their first casualties. After a month or two of physical conditioning and weapons training, during the next phase, the Americans were actually inserted into the active lines side by side with a comparable French unit for four to six weeks. In the final phase, the Yanks were given a sector of their own under overall French command.[25]

MICROMANAGEMENT

Pershing had great difficulty relinquishing command—any command—as he felt the need to be in charge of every situation. Moreover, he was particularly interested in the 1st Division, and he saw to it that it was assigned the best officers and had a priority on equipment, like trucks. As a result, the division was often referred to as "Pershing's Own." Even after assigning Liggett to command I Corps, Pershing had established a "private and special line" between his headquarters at Chaumont and that of Gen. Robert Bullard's 1st Division, thus undermining Liggett's authority. If the latter was irked (which was very likely), he did not show it. However, if, from time to time, the performance of General Bullard's division failed to meet Liggett's high standards, he did not hesitate to give him a "hard bump" regardless of the source of the orders.[26]

A VISIT FROM COLONEL HAYES

Shortly after the United States declared war on Germany, Webb Hayes, then sixty-one years of age, sought an active commission in the US Army. Even with the support from old comrades in arms, like former chief of staff Samuel B. M. Young, his application seemed to be stalled within the bureaucracy. He had traveled to Europe on his own, no doubt hoping that Pershing would take notice. On February 1, 1918, Hayes appeared unannounced at Liggett's headquarters at Neufchâteau shortly after breakfast and asked his old friend for an endorsement. The latter readily obliged. "I am of the opinion that his eager desire for service now should meet with every encouragement," he wrote, adding, "He is fit in every sense and would, if given [the] opportunity, prove of great value especially on duty with the Lines of Communication [later, Services of Supply] where his energy and business sense would, in my judgment, prove very valuable." Hayes ultimately received his commission and served in various administrative capacities in both France and Italy.[27]

On March 2, Hayes, not yet commissioned, was back at Liggett's I Corps headquarters. He wanted to see the front lines, in particular the 1st Division at Gondrecourt, which was still under Liggett's command. In an effort to control the flow of information, Pershing had instituted a strict policy that all visitors to the front lines be cleared at GHQ—that is, by him. With no permit in hand, Hayes insisted upon seeing Liggett, whose staff kept him at bay, explaining to him that his friend could not issue such a permit even if he wanted to. Fortunately, Liggett was temporarily out of the office. It seems that GHQ, not knowing what to do with Hayes, passed him along to Liggett's headquarters, trusting that either Malin Craig or the general himself would fully comply with Pershing's directive.[28]

Several days later, Liggett wrote to Hayes apologizing for the fact that he had been out of the office and had missed him. He also took the time to confirm Craig's actions and to explain the situation at length: "What he told you about my authority . . . is absolutely correct. I could not have given it. The whole business now . . . is done at Chaumont for everyone not on duty, and officers who want to go up there are obliged to show their orders from GHQ here on the way." He hoped his friend understood and ended the letter with a solicitous word about his wife, who was still traveling with him. "I hope Mrs. Hayes is not in Paris during any of the Hun visitations," he wrote, "as bombing at night seems to be a nerve-wracking affair."[29]

THE EDWARDS PROBLEM

A comparison of the personalities and command styles of Liggett and Pershing is a study in contrasts. The latter was a micromanager and had a tendency to do too many things, much of which should have been delegated to staff or subordinates. As one historian wrote, Pershing "wore too many hats." As a result, he did not always think things through. As a commander, he was not loved by his troops, and he led by fear and censure. He placed personal loyalty first and foremost and rewarded it with promotion. Pershing had a staff full of ambitious younger officers willing to do his bidding without question. In spite of his flaws, Pershing, at least initially, enjoyed the full support of both President Wilson and Secretary Baker.[30]

Unlike Pershing, Hunter Liggett was blessed with a temperament that seemed well suited to dealing with the many different problems that face any commander of high rank, particularly when it came to his interactions with fellow officers, especially Allies, both above and below him in a chain of command replete with thin-skinned bullies, pompous prigs, and martinets. Robert Bullard, himself testy and thin-skinned, knew Liggett well, particularly from their days in Texas. He described the latter's personality: "Liggett had the valuable faculty of seeing what was important and what was not; and he did not waste his time or attention on what was not going to count. Faster and with less concern (yet without offending) than any other that I know, he could dismiss trifles or unimportant things; he just good-humouredly but effectively passed over them without notice, no matter who brought them up."

His dealings with Maj. Gen. Clarence R. Edwards were proof positive of Bullard's assessment. All throughout his tour in France, Liggett was caught between his willingness to work with Edwards and the unwavering prejudice against the man, driven by not only Pershing and his staff but even Liggett's own staff, led by Malin Craig. So bad was it that at one point, Liggett ordered his staff to desist and to leave Edwards alone.[31]

As a subordinate, General Edwards could well and truly try the patience of any commanding officer, including Liggett. He was blunt, opinionated, and too often intemperate in his speech. Edwards was considered a "political" general, given his friendship with Taft and other important men, many from his native Ohio. Yet for all his faults, he was a superb administrator, one who could get things done whether through channels or, as he often did, in less conventional ways, such as with a letter or a phone call to a friend. He was solicitous of the welfare of his troops, who reciprocated with a devotion to a degree that, in the words of Maj. Gen. James G. Harbord, "no general officer of [Harbord's] acquaintance" experienced. They affectionately referred to him as "Daddy," a nickname that he relished. The importance of this relationship of a commander with his troops, especially to the morale of a division, is something that Liggett recognized.[32]

The old US Army had many such men within the officer corps but not many of his high standing. What truly set Edwards apart was the fact that, for reasons we will probably never know for sure, he had at some point in his career incurred the enmity of John J. Pershing. Perhaps it was simply the fact that he viewed Edwards as a potential rival. In any event, Pershing made it his mission to purge the AEF of Edwards (as he had already done with so many other less energetic officers) no matter what, and he had imbued his subordinates with the same zeal. Edwards's relief proved to be a tough nut indeed. Maj. Gen. Hugh A. Drum, who served as First Army chief of staff under both Pershing and Liggett, referred to the former's enduring "vindictiveness" toward Edwards. Admittedly, Edwards had a high learning curve when it came to tactics, but Pershing raised the bar so high that it was a miracle that Edwards lasted as long as he did. At one point, after listening to Pershing suggest ill health as grounds for Edwards's relief, Liggett pointed to the excellent

16. Generals Clarence R. Edwards and Hunter Liggett. Courtesy of the National Archives and Records Administration.

"spirit and discipline" of the Yankee Division. Pershing would have none of it, and two days later, he chided Liggett for his patient approach. "You will be all right if you can make anything out of Edwards," he told him sarcastically. Liggett chose to ignore Pershing, as it was in his nature for Liggett to give his subordinates an opportunity to learn and grow in their assignments.[33]

Edwards also had the unfortunate habit of commenting unfavorably, often publically, about certain fellow officers, many of them of higher rank. As a close confidante of the good-natured President Taft, he may have felt immune, but the AEF under Pershing was something else. Edwards failed to realize that Liggett's support was essential to his survival. During the initial stage of the training, both Edwards and Liggett had headquarters in Neufchâteau, so each could observe the other. In late January 1918, Edwards sent a long letter to his wife, Bessie, that he titled "Memorandum of the News," in which he offered the following observation about Liggett: "He is very nice, considerate, and the selection was made, I fancy, on account of seniority and age. Unfortunately his staff are in command. I marvel at the way he has aged and fallen off." Edwards continued with a further, very prescient observation: "He has Lieut. Colonel Malin Craig as chief of staff, who between you and the post, is commanding the corps, and it is fraught with a good many hazards and possibilities of friction as he likes to make quick decisions and to interfere. But there is no use borrowing trouble and we will get along as well as possible."[34]

Edwards's assessment of the situation was only partly correct. He was right to be concerned about his own relationship with Craig. However, he misread the relationship of Liggett with his chief of staff. Liggett looked at the big picture and expected Craig to fill in the details, which he was only too happy and able to do. Liggett generally couched his orders to his subordinate commanders more diplomatically, suggesting certain courses of action, and when that method failed, Craig stood ready to enforce those orders. If the latter sometimes crossed certain bounds, as with Edwards, Liggett simply reined him in. They made a very effective team, but Liggett was definitely in charge.

SCHOOL'S OUT

In April 1918, the continuing pressure of the German spring offensive forced some major changes. The 1st Division, which had completed all three phases of its training, was quickly inserted into the French line near Cantigny. It would soon go on the attack there and win a very costly victory but one that Pershing badly needed to strengthen his hand with the Allies. At the same time, the 26th Division, which had not yet undergone its so-called open warfare training, replaced the 1st Division and an adjoining French division, and it was given responsibility for the entire Toul sector. Even in the alleged quiet sectors, like Toul, the Germans were determined to bloody the noses of the brash Americans as they had in small raids against the 1st Division in November 1917 and the following March.[35]

Such was the case at Apremont in early April, as the 104th Infantry Regiment of the Yankee Division beat back a determined German attack in three

Map 4. Northeastern France and Germany (1917–19)

days of fierce fighting. The Yankees even came to the relief of the French units next to them, and the regiment was ultimately awarded the Croix de Guerre. It was the first time an American unit had been decorated by a foreign country.

Seicheprey was a different story. On April 20, the Germans launched a massive raid with nearly three thousand troops, many of whom were specially trained and equipped, to overrun two companies of New England Guardsmen from the 102nd Infantry Regiment in an effort to seize prisoners. While casualties were heavy on both sides, no ground was lost. However, the Germans made off with more than 180 prisoners. Pershing was livid and blamed Edwards for what he sarcastically referred to as an "affair." Liggett referred to it as a "check," and Gen. Fenelon Passaga (French XXXII Corps) saw it for what it really was: an "incident" from which the division must "profit by its lessons." Years later, even Pershing's attitude softened somewhat.[36]

AISNE-MARNE OFFENSIVE

Starting in March 1918, the Germans launched a series of major attacks commencing in Flanders and moving east. Each drive was met with limited success, creating several salients, or deep pockets, in the Allied line. One such attack, which opened on the French in May, stretched in an arc from Soissons down to Château-Thierry on the Marne and then back up, ending at Reims. The attack on the French line near the Marne continued unabated, to the point that Paris itself was threatened. The French were overwhelmed and called upon the US Army. Pershing sent in Maj. Gen. Omar Bundy's 2nd Division, which included a brigade each of soldiers and marines. In late June, after a month of tough fighting, the German drive was slowed as the marines pushed them out of Belleau Wood while the US Army displayed its mettle near Vaux.[37]

By early July, the Allies had formulated a plan to push the Germans from the Marne salient. As part of that drive, Liggett's I Corps was composed of the 26th Division and the French 167th Division, led by the very capable General Schmidt. The 2nd Division remained in the sector, also under Liggett's tactical command. Liggett established his headquarters in La Ferté-sous-Jouarre, a large market town on the Marne. He ostensibly enjoyed all aspects of a corps command for the first time, and in fact, he was the first senior officer to do so since the war with Spain. Liggett also had the honor of commanding French troops for the first time since the American Revolution. Yet at times, he must have felt like a glorified division commander, since Gen. Jean Marie Joseph Degoutte (French Sixth Army) was a constant presence at corps headquarters, offering advice and vigorously pressing the attack. It would be a learning experience for all, including Liggett, but an important test of independent command for future American divisions.[38]

On July 4, he met with Brig. Gen. William Lassiter, his chief of the corps artillery, who had insisted that the chain of command for division artillery run through him. Liggett had not fully formed any opinion on the subject at that time, and he had no idea what policy, if any, had been formulated at GHQ. Thus, at a critical stage prior to an impending offensive, this important issue was still up in the air. On July 13, in anticipation of an imminent German attack, Brig. Gen. Albert J. Bowley, the 2nd Division artillery commander, prepared a plan to place his guns farther forward so as to be more effective.

Both generals Degoutte and Liggett objected. Liggett told Bowley that the function of artillery was to defend the second line of resistance and that it should be placed far enough back so as to avoid capture in the event of an enemy breakthrough. However, as a result of the offensive, Liggett's view as to the use of artillery would evolve.[39]

On the eve of the offensive, when an understandably nervous General Edwards asked for advice, Liggett told him not to bunch his troops in the front line, as they would be vulnerable to artillery, and to be careful not to outrun the day's objective but to stop and wait for further orders. Liggett was learning his lessons, too. His views on this point would soon evolve, and he would later tell Pershing that it was better to give his commanders some initiative to continue the drive beyond the objective, if the situation warranted, so as not to allow the enemy breathing room to shore up his defenses. However, that conclusion would come months and many casualties later, in the midst of the battle in the Argonne Forest.[40]

However, before the Allies could launch their counteroffensive on July 18, the German Army showed that it could muster at least one last thrust. Between July 15 and 17, it attempted to expand the salient and force a crossing of the Marne near Château-Thierry. Liggett's 26th Division withstood the attempt, as did elements of the 28th Division, National Guardsmen from Pennsylvania. However, it was Col. Ulysses Grant McAlexander's 38th Infantry Regiment, part of the 3rd Division, that stopped the Germans cold and earned the glory and the sobriquet "Rock of the Marne." The Germans never did recover the initiative and remained on the defensive for the balance of the war.[41]

On July 18, on the eve of the Allied counteroffensive, Pershing issued an order for Edwards's relief and a transfer to the Italian front, only to suspend it the following day. Even so, Brig. Gen. André Brewster, the AEF inspector general, later showed up at Liggett's headquarters during the attack, asking about unverified rumors concerning Edwards. Brewster asked Liggett for a written memo that could be used to support Pershing's desire to relieve Edwards. As he had consistently done in the past, Liggett pointedly refused. "I will not pull Pershing's chestnuts out of the fire," he had told his aide at one point.[42]

Liggett's I Corps kicked off the drive on July 18. The men of the 52nd Brigade of the 26th ("Yankee") Division fought bravely and succeeded in achieving their initial objectives but not without casualties. Two days later, when the drive continued with the entire division fully engaged, some elements became bogged down in a wooded area, while others were slowed by the inability of the French 167th Division on their left to keep pace. Liggett suggested to Edwards that he should keep moving and bypass the resistance in the woods. Edwards chose not to follow the advice, thus further slowing the drive and frustrating Liggett, who was under pressure from General Degoutte to keep it going at all costs. His frustration no doubt got the better of him when Edwards, concerned with mounting casualties, asked for yet another delay so as to bring his artillery forward. Liggett summarily denied the request. Perhaps Liggett's view of a less active role for artillery was a factor in his decision, but more than likely, Edwards had cried wolf one time too many.[43]

Once again, a valuable lesson was lost in the heat of battle, one that savvy commanders like Maj. Gen. John A. Lejeune, a marine, would employ to great effect and one that Liggett would later come to appreciate—that is, the need to coordinate infantry and artillery. From top to bottom, commanders were learning lessons. Edwards actually had that one right.[44]

Initially, the plan had called for the 26th Division to shrink its front by half as it guided slightly left, all the time moving forward on the attack. This would have been a difficult maneuver for an experienced regular division, let alone a National Guard division in battle for the first time. A lack of good liaison was a continuing problem throughout the AEF during the war, and with the fog of war, by July 21, neither Edwards nor his staff could say with certainty just where the elements of Brig. Gen. Charles Cole's 52nd Brigade were located. The problem was further compounded when Liggett and Degoutte realized that as the front line shrunk with the maneuver, the French 167th Division, which was having a difficult time maintaining the drive to begin with, would be pinched out. Accordingly, Degoutte told Liggett to have Cole's brigade take over General Schmidt's sector, and Liggett in turn told Craig to draft the order. Thus an already confused situation became much worse as Cole's brigade lost cohesion—and worse, there was the real likelihood a large gap would be created. Liggett soon recognized the problem and, in his words, "suspended" the order after it had been at least partially complied with. Fortunately, General Schmidt was finally able to move forward, and he did so on his own initiative, thus averting the worst scenario. In effect, Schmidt's division and Brig. Gen. George Shelton's 51st Brigade pinched out Cole's 52nd Brigade.[45]

It took a couple of days to sort out Cole's brigade, which was intermingled with the French. Meanwhile, the 51st Brigade, with some assistance from the nearby 28th Division, tackled Epieds and Trugny Wood. Pershing and his staff at Chaumont quickly blamed Edwards for the mess, but in reality, much of the blame lay with Liggett and Degoutte, whose expectations exceeded the ability of the division to perform the difficult maneuver in its very first battle, having been in combat for several days and suffered heavy casualties. Much later, upon reflection, Liggett assessed the circumstances as inevitable given the change in axis that called for "troop leading of a high order." Moreover, calling the "movement as a whole . . . creditable," he opined that "units were bound to go astray in the necessary changes of direction, especially at night." However, that is not to say that Liggett let Edwards off the hook. Taking him aside out of the hearing of others, he admonished him quite firmly. "General Edwards," he told him, "the trouble with you is that you never obey your orders or make your officers obey theirs, intruding your own judgment or allowing your officers to exercise their ideas when only one thing is called for—exact obedience." In addition, he strongly suggested that Edwards relieve some officers, and he told Chaumont that the division needed to "reconstitute itself" and could use a period of rigorous training. At one point, there was even talk of breaking the division up and assigning eight thousand men to the 42nd Division as replacements.[46]

The bulk of the Yankee Division was relieved by the 42nd ("Rainbow") Division, another National Guard unit. However, the Yankee engineers and artillery remained in the field—as they were attached to that division, and later to the 4th Division—for the next phase of the attack. This included a difficult multiday fight at Sergy. As each new division assumed responsibility for the continued attack, Liggett gave its commanders the same advice: "Don't bunch your troops in the front line, and do not attack machine gun nests directly." He might as well have been talking to the wall, as heavy casualties continued to mount, especially in the 42nd Division, prompting General Degoutte to comment, "Americans are too careless and prodigal of men." Nevertheless, he pressed Liggett to continue the attack.[47]

Poor liaison also continued to be a serious problem, and like Edwards, Maj. Gen. George H. Cameron, the 4th Division commander, could not tell Liggett precisely where all his units were, and he "did not seem to have things especially well in hand." Despite these continuing issues, the drive ended successfully at the Vesle River on August 4.[48]

At some point during the drive, Liggett and his entire staff came down with dysentery. The general, who from time to time throughout his career had suffered such bouts, weathered it better than his younger colleagues. They blamed the problem on the abundance of "dead horses, men, and flies." All this was true. Sgt. Robert Forbush of the 101st Engineers wrote that his head cold was "not quite bad enough to hold out the awful stench of the dead horses and men." He added, "On top of that the water was bad with so many dead bodies soaking into the earth." In addition, sanitary discipline had broken down to the point that Col. Ralph Porter, the Yankee Division surgeon, had to issue an order prohibiting what he called "promiscuous defecation."[49]

Shortly after the conclusion of the drive, General Cameron approached Liggett and suggested that he relieve Brig. Gen. Benjamin Poore, the 7th Brigade commander, as Cameron felt that he was too cautious and had not performed satisfactorily during the last drive. Liggett was "disappointed" to hear this about his old colleague from the Army War College and Fort William McKinley, where Poore had commanded the 8th Infantry Regiment, and he was reluctant to order his relief. Perhaps thinking back to his own close call, as well as the Edwards situation, he told his aide that it was not so clear-cut, as "there were considerations, such as past history and accomplishments and the difficulty of finding as good [a] man to take his place." Liggett declined to relieve Poore, who would ultimately justify Liggett's faith in him during the fighting in the Meuse-Argonne.[50]

ST. MIHIEL

On August 20, 1918, after recovering from a mild flare-up of his rheumatism the week before, Liggett moved his headquarters to Saizerais, and by early September, his I Corps was composed of the 2nd, 5th, 82nd, and 90th Divisions, with the 78th Division as a reserve. Final preparations were underway for the initial battle to be fought under Pershing's direction by the US First Army, which had been activated on August 13. The town of St. Mihiel was the focus. The initial objective, which had been in the planning stages for months, was to reduce the triangular salient, which was approximately two hundred square miles in area (with its apex at the town of St. Mihiel), and capture the German troops that had been occupying it since 1914. The plan also had the larger goal of driving on to the German city of Metz. Pershing and his staff had settled on Metz as an objective from an early date since it was a vital communications center and rail hub, as well as a gateway to the important coal and iron mines near Briey. Liggett and other graduates of Leavenworth or the War College were very familiar with Metz and the Lorraine countryside, having studied the Franco-Prussian War, and could now put that knowledge to good use.[51]

On August 30, without any prior discussion, Mar. Ferdinand Foch visited Pershing at his headquarters in Ligny-en-Barrois with a change of plan. In light of recent gains, he and Fd. Mar. Sir Douglas Haig proposed that Pershing abandon the St. Mihiel attack scheduled for September 10 and instead join with them in the Argonne and elsewhere on the Western Front, as they sensed a weakening of the German effort that they wanted to exploit. Part of the new plan would involve the parceling out of various American units to both the British and the French for the final drive. Pershing was surprised and somewhat stunned, and he expressed his reservations. After all, the First Army was no more than two weeks old and on the verge of carrying out its first major attack, one that had been months in the planning. Foch gave Pershing some time to mull things over, and after speaking with Gen. Henri Pétain, Pershing met again with Foch on September 2. Pershing was adamant that the St. Mihiel attack go forward, albeit with some modification—chiefly, after a two-day delay and without the continuation of the drive to Metz. In addition, he agreed to join the general attack in the Argonne two weeks later. This decision to proceed with both attacks as planned would not only seriously tax his staff but would also have serious consequences later on in the Argonne.[52]

Also on August 30, at a conference with Pershing at Ligny-en-Barrois, Liggett reviewed the plans and the role that his corps would play in the upcoming battle. At that time, he suggested a modification of the plan. In brief, the 82nd Division, which was located on the right flank nearest to the Moselle River, was slated to merely conduct a demonstration, while the 90th Division would drive toward Thiaucourt. However, Liggett knew that the Germans had "dominating artillery" on ridges north of Pont-à-Mousson near Vittonville that could well disrupt the main attack, and he suggested that the 82nd Division be given a more active role in that regard. The French Army group commander was not in favor of Liggett's idea, as there were not enough French troops on their right to move forward in tandem. Pershing agreed. Although his suggestion was not accepted, nevertheless, it was evidence of Liggett's grasp of the larger picture.[53]

During the lead-up to the attack, there was the usual confusion and nervousness among Liggett's division commanders, who were leading their troops in a major battle for the first time. For Liggett and his staff, this was a repeat of the Aisne-Marne Offensive, only now he had to deal with more than one inexperienced division commander. In his typical patient style, he calmly made his points. As late as August 24, it appeared to him that Maj. Gen. William P. Burnham of the 82nd Division "did not know what to do" when the Germans fired on his field kitchens. Moreover, he observed the troops under Burnham's command were "undisciplined."[54]

Maj. Gen. Henry T. Allen of the 90th Division was a courageous dandy and former cavalryman who appeared much too frequently at corps headquarters—so often, in fact, that Liggett had to give him a gentle hint. "Allen," he told him, "you have on a new pair of boots every time you come to see me." Despite being told by Liggett not to put too many battalions in the outpost line, Allen continued to work around the order as his division rehearsed for the attack. He argued to Liggett that he wanted to expose the maximum number of troops to the front in the short time remaining. Liggett was adamant that he could have no more than four and told Craig to issue the order. Four days later, Allen appeared at Liggett's headquarters, still arguing his position, and the general seemed to waiver, if only halfheartedly. Allen left with the impression that Liggett had approved. Craig told Liggett after Allen left that he felt that he had been undercut. The general quickly recognized the need to support his chief of staff, but at the same time, he saw some merit in Allen's argument. He immediately sent a letter to Allen that on the one hand reinforced his chief of staff's order limiting the front line to just four battalions but on the other allowed Allen to substitute whole units in the line from time to time at his discretion.[55]

At this time, Liggett also visited the headquarters of Maj. Gen. John E. McMahon of the 5th Division, who did not appear "very brisk and alert and [seemed] a bit bewildered" and who nervously asked a lot of "fool questions," including what to do with his artillery if the Germans attacked.[56]

The attack was preceded by a massive sustained artillery bombardment starting at 1:00 a.m. on September 12, tapering off several hours later. In all, 550,000 Americans, along with 110,000 French soldiers, were assembled for the battle. Liggett's I Corps occupied the far right of the line on the south face of the salient. To its left was the 4th Army Corps under Maj. Gen. Joseph Dickman. On the northwest face of the salient was the 5th Army Corps under Maj. Gen. George Cameron, which was made up of the 26th Division and assisted by elements of the 4th Division. The French II Colonial Corps occupied the apex, pushing east from there.[57]

Liggett sent his divisions forward at 5:00 a.m. Unknown to the Americans at the time was the fact that the Germans had already decided to abandon the salient in order to shorten their lines and that, by sheer coincidence, they were literally in the process of withdrawal. As a result, the Allies pressed forward against lighter resistance than anticipated. The gap was closed at Vignuelles early the following morning when the 26th Division, after a dramatic nighttime march, joined hands with the 1st Division, thus bagging a large number of German prisoners and substantial equipment.[58]

Touted at that time as a significant American victory, in hindsight, the attack at St. Mihiel could well be considered a case of overreach. On the plus side, it was significant since it enlarged the American footprint on the Western Front in a large-scale action. The attack deprived the German Army of a foothold on the Meuse south of Verdun and freed up a vital French rail line. Finally, at least in the short run, it posed a threat to the Germans in Metz, and moreover, casualties were remarkably light—in fact, less than expected. Yet the fact remains that it was an attack against an enemy already in the process of withdrawing from the salient. More important, it placed added pressure upon the planners, like George C. Marshall, to turn quickly from one front to another. Time alone would have been a factor, but the French road net was unable to efficiently support the movement. Worse, it forced Pershing to use some untested divisions, and their commanders, in the last and single most important fight of the war. Given the apparent ease of the effort at St. Mihiel, some, like Douglas MacArthur, were disappointed that the attack was not continued toward the important and well-fortified city of Metz as originally planned. But that was not part of Pershing's bargain with Foch. Besides, the reality was that the US Army was not really ready, something that Liggett was quick to recognize. "The possibility of taking Metz and the rest of it, had the battle been fought on the original plan, existed, in my opinion, only on the supposition that our army was a well-oiled, fully-coordinated machine," observed Liggett, "which it was not as yet."[59]

Despite the success of the attack, as Liggett noted, much work was still needed to fine-tune the US Army. For one, liaison continued to be an issue. As an example, General Allen was initially unable to locate his patrols when asked to do so by Liggett, though by the end of the day, Allen had established liaison with the 5th Division and delivered a map to Liggett showing the location of his units. There also needed to be some adjustments in command. After a visit to the 5th Division headquarters, Liggett felt that General McMahon appeared "somewhat shaky" but, consistent with his practice, was willing to give him a chance to prove himself. McMahon, who did not demonstrate any improvement, would later be relieved by Pershing upon Liggett's recommendation. St. Mihiel was a testing time for senior commanders. Allen demonstrated marked progress in Liggett's eyes, while McMahon did not.[60]

EIGHT
World War I, Coup de Grace

THE MEUSE-ARGONNE

In keeping with his agreement with Mar. Ferdinand Foch, John J. Pershing and his staff quickly turned their attention to the forthcoming Allied attack. The American sector encompassed the Argonne Forest on the west to the east side of the Meuse north of Verdun. The Germans had made a considerable effort to fortify what was already difficult terrain for any attacker, from deep woods, high ridges, and ravines to dark valleys with winding streams. Several days after the attack had begun, Lt. Col. Pierpont L. Stackpole made the following observation: "The Argonne country they are going through is certainly the limit—ravines, sharp banks, heavy timber, dense brush, and all the obstacles the Germans have been able to construct during four years of occupancy."[1]

The main fortifications were set in three lines of wire, concrete bunkers, and strategically sited machine guns, not to mention artillery well versed in the techniques taught by Col. Georg Bruchmüller. It was referred to collectively as the Hindenburg Line, with each succeeding defensive line named for one of the Valkyries: Giselher, Kriemhilde, and Freya. On paper, the initial advantage in troops lay with the 1,200,000 men of Pershing's First Army; however, this advantage was offset in part by the terrain and man-made obstacles. In addition, many of the American divisions were either new to France or only partially trained. Pershing's agreement with Foch had come with a price tag, and the doughboys would now bear the cost.[2]

The US First Army was aligned with four corps abreast, from left to right: Liggett's I Corps, followed by V Corps (Maj. Gen. George H. Cameron) and III Corps (Maj. Gen. Robert L. Bullard)—all of them American—together with the French XVII Corps (Maj. Gen. Henri Claudel), which was a mix of both French and American divisions. The primary responsibility for the latter lay in securing the heights east of the Meuse so as to protect the right flank of the main American attack.[3]

Part of Liggett's responsibilities involved dealing with the delicate or inflated egos of his division commanders. He had excellent people skills and was known for a low-key, nonconfrontational manner. On the eve of the big offensive, Liggett had asked Malin Craig to send Gen. Peter Traub a personal letter under his signature, advising him that he had received reports from several sources indicating some "slackness of discipline" in the 35th Division. Instead of looking at the note as a timely heads up, Traub took the matter personally, expressing his hurt feelings in a letter to Liggett. The latter immediately followed up with another letter, no doubt couching the advice more diplomatically.[4]

The American attack commenced on the morning of September 26, following a tremendous artillery barrage all up and down the line. Pershing had designated a series of phase lines, or objectives, for the first day and each succeeding day. Progress was uneven. All the divisions achieved some gains toward reaching their objectives—that is, all except Cameron's V Corps, which had stalled in its attempt to overcome fierce enemy resistance at Montfaucon. Instead of simply bypassing the impediment and taking advantage of the gains, all the other divisions held their positions, thus enabling the enemy to shore up its defenses and to reinforce its lines. Liggett considered this operational decision to be a mistake and would later tell Pershing so.[5]

At the time of the attack, I Corps was aligned from left to right as follows: 77th, 28th, and 35th Divisions, with the 92nd Division in reserve. In order to quell any nervous anticipation as he waited for the first reports to filter back, Liggett sat alone in a corner of his headquarters at Rarécourt with two decks of cards, calmly playing double solitaire as, in his words, an "anodyne" to keep him from "nail biting or pacing the floor until [his] nerves [were] shot."[6]

For the next week, however, as the attack progressed, Liggett and his staff were out among his divisions, gathering information as well as patiently advising and encouraging the commanders. The situation Liggett found was not altogether encouraging. In the face of the glaring failures of his division commanders, he masked his frustration, knowing full well that he had no effective control of his own corps. For Liggett himself, failure was never an option.[7]

Maj. Gen. Robert Alexander's 77th Division was having difficulty piercing the dense Argonne Forest, in part because the French division to its left could not or would not keep up and in part because of well-placed machine gun nests but in large measure due to poor liaison. Alexander told Liggett that his division was experiencing machine gun fire from the rear. Liggett told him that he needed to keep some trailing companies behind to mop up any German machine gun nests that had been bypassed.[8]

It was a similar story with Maj. Gen. Charles H. Muir's veteran 28th Division, which was pushing up the narrow valley of the Aire River assisted by a paltry few Renault tanks. Muir appeared to be "nervous and without resource," and when asked by Liggett, his staff could not locate all of their units. The problems stemmed from the usual lack of liaison, compounded by breaks in the communication wire to forward units. Perhaps worst of all, the division appeared disorganized, with many stragglers, which was an indication of a poor command. As with Alexander, Liggett also told Muir to make sure that he organized a mop-up force so as not to slow down the main advance.[9]

However, the worst case by far was Maj. Gen. Peter Traub's 35th Division, which simply lost cohesion. For one thing, traffic in his sector was a nightmare, as his engineers had failed to fill a large crater in the main road. For another, his artillery was too far behind the attack to provide effective support, despite a specific admonition from Liggett. Moreover, neither Traub nor his staff could tell precisely where his units were. Traub was clearly out of his depth, and by leaving his headquarters at a critical juncture with so many parts in play in order to find his own front lines, he actually blinded himself to the whole picture. Finally, Traub, on Craig's advice, ordered a limited withdrawal, thus giving up what ground he had gained at such a large price. Compounding the problem was the fact that the movement took place during daylight and invited a costly counterattack. Liggett admonished Traub, telling him that had he known beforehand, he never would have permitted the withdrawal. Moreover, despite the fact that the division would be relieved shortly, he strongly suggested that Traub retake those positions promptly or the division "would never be any good again."[10]

On a visit to General Alexander's headquarters on September 28, Liggett received a report that German troops were using the cry of "Kamerad" as a ruse to feign surrender, only to then open fire upon or to toss a grenade toward unsuspecting doughboys. The report also said that the enemy was giving the command of "fall back" in English as yet another ruse in order to sow confusion. As a result, Alexander's men took no prisoners following a particularly tough fight at Abri St. Louis. Liggett was incensed and supported the actions of the doughboys, telling his aide that under the circumstances, such actions called for summary execution, particularly of the officers. In point of fact, throughout the war, the cry of "Kamerad" with hands raised was commonly used by German machine gunners after they had run out of ammunition.[11]

That same story would repeat itself all across the American sector. Many infantrymen, seeing so many of their fellows cut down, took it upon themselves to shoot instead of accepting the proffered surrender. Typical was Robert D. Burrows of the 102nd Infantry, who explained the situation to his family in New London, Connecticut: "We captured a machine gunner and he said, 'Kamerad,' but a revolver bullet finished him. We never take a machine gunner prisoner. If you saw the American dead, which I have, you would know why."[12]

TIME-OUT

On October 1, Pershing called a halt to rest and regroup. Bloodied and exhausted, the American Expeditionary Forces (AEF) had suffered nearly twenty-six thousand casualties during the initial phase, including stragglers and others missing. During this pause, new divisions relieved the old. In I Corps, the battered 35th Division was replaced by the 1st Division, commanded by Maj. Gen. Charles P. Summerall, who ran a much tighter ship than Traub.[13]

Meanwhile, Pershing called upon Liggett at his headquarters during the early evening of October 3, ostensibly to discuss the continuation of the offensive. At that time, he told Liggett verbally to continue his attacks on his own initiative and not to stop until stopped by the Germans. Liggett concurred and told the commander in chief that the past practice of halting when the objective was reached simply destroyed momentum and gave the enemy time to "bring up reinforcements and draw out guns."[14]

Then Pershing shifted topics and told Liggett that now that the Second Army would soon be activated, he intended to turn the First Army over to him, adding that "it might not happen for some time." Obviously pleased, Liggett told Pershing that "he would do his best."[15]

SECOND PHASE

Pershing resumed the offensive at 5:25 a.m. on October 4, and the doughboys struggled forward with only modest gains. Much of the high ground at Cunel and Romagne still remained in German hands, and east of the Meuse, the 29th and 33rd Divisions found the going tougher than anticipated. On the plus side, Blanc Mont was secured by the 2nd Division, but the ridge behind it offered stubborn resistance.[16]

Liggett pushed Alexander's New Yorkers hard, and the general in turn pushed his men "in his own imperious bull-headed way." One of those was Maj. Charles Whittlesey, who, with an augmented battalion, advanced deep into the Argonne Forest beyond the German lines, with limited support from the French on their left and none by the 28th Division on their right. Thus with flanks exposed, the inevitable result was five days of living hell. Surrounded by the enemy, Whittlesey and his rapidly dwindling "Lost Battalion" heroically held off repeated attacks until finally relieved on October 7.[17]

For that matter, Liggett pushed all his commanders hard, but more important, in order to break the stalemate and after consulting with First Army staff, he applied his own initiative with a bold flanking maneuver. Summerall's 1st Division had made a significant penetration of the German lines, which Liggett exploited by using one brigade from the 82nd Division, his reserve, as his other divisions continued the attack. By October 10, Liggett's gambit had succeeded in breaking the stubborn German resistance. With that plan, Liggett "demonstrated his flair for tactics," wrote historian Edward M. Coffman. The Argonne Forest had been cleared. In time, George B. Duncan's

17. Lt. Gen. Hunter Liggett. Courtesy of the National Archives and Records Administration.

82nd Division replaced the 28th Division, and it quickly took Cornay and Chatel-Chéhéry. At about the same time, the 1st Division was transferred to the V Corps, replaced by the 78th Division led by the hard-driving James H. McRae.[18]

LETTING GO

By orders dated October 13, 1918, Pershing officially relinquished command of the First US Army to Liggett, as he would then have two American armies under his overall command. It was the moment that Liggett had prepared for his entire career. Three days later, he was promoted to the rank of lieutenant general on an emergency basis.[19]

Liggett arrived at his new headquarters at Souilly on October 12 in order to facilitate a smooth transition and to familiarize himself with Pershing's staff, which would now be his own. Yet General Pershing was not ready to let go of the First US Army; he couldn't help himself. He had planned a resumption of the attack to begin October 14, and he was on hand at First Army headquarters to see it commence. Liggett was initially deferential to the commander in chief, going so far as to tell the various corps commanders that he visited that he had no formal orders and that they should carry out Pershing's plan. However, Pershing returned the following day, and to Liggett's consternation, further orders were issued over Pershing's signature. On October 15, Liggett diplomatically addressed the situation. "Give First Army a directive," he told the commander in chief, "and I will do all that is humanly possible to carry it out." Pershing ignored that plea; it was the same the next day, with Pershing still "butting into details, with numerous changes of mind." Liggett's aide called the situation an "extraordinary spectacle." Finally, on October 17, when there was still no change, the usually patient Liggett had had enough, and he told Pershing to "go away and forget it." The commander in chief finally got the message.[20]

At First Army headquarters, Liggett continued to command with a light touch. George C. Marshall recalled that Liggett never attended the daily staff meetings where orders were finalized and formulated for issuance to corps commanders. Rather, he conveyed his directions through his chief of staff, Brig. Gen. Hugh A. Drum. Thus younger officers had the opportunity to exercise their judgment and learn while doing. On the other hand, Liggett frequently discussed the progress of a given operation with Marshall and others, never failing to impart some lesson in the process.[21]

THE MILK OF HUMAN KINDNESS

By all accounts, Brig. Gen. Michael J. Lenihan was a brave and capable officer, although at times indecisive. A graduate of West Point (class of 1887), Lenihan was well liked by his men, who referred to him as "General Mike," and by his colleagues for his wealth of stories. He had recently been "strongly recommended" for division command by his own division commander, Maj. Gen. Charles Menoher. He was in command of the 83rd Brigade of the 42nd Division, and one of his two regiments was the 165th Infantry, otherwise known as the "Fighting 69th New York" of Civil War fame.[22]

The 83rd Brigade had taken enormous casualties in its repeated attacks, across open fields, upon the well-defended German positions near the towns of St. Georges and Landres-et-St. Georges. These defenses included well-sited machine guns and deep, chest-high rows of barbed wire—little wonder, as the German line formed part of the much-vaunted Kriemhilde Stellung. In fact, two of the 83rd Brigade's three battalions were virtually decimated, and the exhausted survivors stared helplessly in sadness and horror for days at the bodies of their fallen buddies, still entangled in the German wire, unable to retrieve them.[23]

On October 15, impatient with the lack of forward movement, the V Corps Commander General Summerall personally visited the headquarters of the 42nd Division as well as the 83rd Brigade and its regiments. He summarily relieved Lenihan and other brigade officers. By all accounts, the relief was impulsive and unjustified. Moreover, it sent the brigade morale into a tailspin. Fr. Francis Duffy, the division chaplain and certainly no friend of the corps commander, wrote that the men referred to him derisively as "Von Summeralz." Years later, however, in justifying his decision to relieve Lenihan, Summerall wrote that he had observed the latter to be "confused and completely unstrung."[24]

Lenihan demanded a formal inquiry, which was conducted by Col. S. Field Dallam, the V Corps inspector general. Colonel Dallam recommended that Lenihan be reinstated; however, Summerall refused to accept the findings. Liggett carefully considered the situation and his options. Since the relief came from below, he overruled Summerall. So as not to have it be seen as a total rebuke to Summerall, he restored Lenihan to duty but gave him command of the 153rd Brigade of the 77th Division.[25]

LIGGETT'S TURN

Once in full command, Liggett immediately paused any further attacks for two weeks in order to regroup and realign his forces, which now included the main

American effort on both sides of the Meuse River. During this time, he took the opportunity to visit the various fighting divisions. Pershing was impatient to see some progress, but Liggett held firm, agreeing only to relatively small "local operations." Besides, he could confidently point to having reached a consensus with the French commander, Gen. Paul Maistre. Moreover, troop strength had been greatly reduced by an increase in casualties and by another enemy—influenza. Liggett's patience and determination won out. Originally scheduled for October 28, the final phase was postponed until November 1. After consultation with General Maistre, Liggett agreed to a further one-day delay so that a coordinated attack could take place on November 2.[26]

Liggett was actively involved in the planning and coordination of his corps commanders. As a preliminary matter, on October 25 Liggett and Drum met with Gen. Henri Gouraud, the tough, one-armed commander of the French Fourth Army, in order to coordinate the details of the forthcoming attack. The meeting did not go well at first, as Gouraud, who was used to Pershing's "endless quibbling discussions," even about "nonessentials," thought that Liggett was cut from the same bolt of cloth as his predecessor. However, Liggett's quiet firmness and gracious manner soon won the Frenchman over. The meeting ended on a high note, with both men sharing a cigar. Once again, the contrast between Liggett and Pershing could not have been clearer.[27]

Coincidently, Liggett received official notice of his promotion to lieutenant general on November 1, though effective as of October 16. Pershing continued to hold firmly to his belief that victory on the Western Front would ultimately be achieved by concentrating an overwhelming mass of infantrymen, with their marksmanship skills, at the point of attack, however, Liggett's thinking was not as rigid and continued to evolve. While his divisions rested and were refit, Liggett's mind was not idle. He had now reached the pinnacle of his career, something he had prepared for virtually his entire adult life. For one thing, Liggett had become convinced that many casualties had resulted from a lack of effective artillery support. It was not that the American artillery units performed poorly; rather, it was the failure of most division commanders to coordinate infantry and artillery. He agreed with savvy commanders like major generals Charles Summerall and John A. Lejeune, who made sure that their artillery was within effective range even if it meant briefly halting an attack. In addition, Liggett felt that more artillery should be made available to commanders instead of sitting idle in corps reserve. Finally, he authorized air support on enemy targets during an infantry attack, not just on rear areas, as in the past. He kept all of that in mind as he planned the next objectives, and he issued orders accordingly. Liggett continued to learn and to adapt.[28]

As further evidence, Liggett took the time to plan the implementation of the offensive. The previous flanking maneuver had worked so well with the 82nd Division that he used it on a much larger scale, this time with the full participation of the French Fourth Army on the left. On the right, the American I and V Corps operated in tandem, part of the former holding, while the balance of that corps and V Corps pressed the attack. The Germans, fearing an envelopment, quickly withdrew just as Liggett had predicted.[29]

EXIT CLARENCE EDWARDS

For some time, AEF planners had assumed that the war would extend well into 1919, however, given the renewed Allied efforts, by mid-October, there was a feeling that it could well end much sooner. For Pershing, it was now or never to renew his effort to relieve General Edwards. Accordingly, he sought and received permission from Secretary Newton D. Baker to do so. On October 20, he issued the order, couching it in the form of a letter about Edwards's value to the war effort training troops back home, wisely masking his true purpose by issuing similar orders for several other generals, including Omar Bundy and George Cameron. In short, it was, in Hugh Drum's words, the culmination of the "vindictiveness" of Pershing and his staff toward Edwards. Summerall blamed Malin Craig for his role in the relief, saying that his "false charges . . . blighted the career of an able officer." Outrage was felt throughout New England and lingered on for many years. It was also felt within National Guard circles.[30]

It is clear that Pershing went around Liggett, who had consistently opposed the idea. In spite of the fact that he was well aware of Edwards's shortcomings, he recognized that Edwards enjoyed the love and affection of his officers and men and feared that the morale of the division would plummet with his departure. In fact, in March of the following year, Liggett had a long conversation with Maj. Gen. André Brewster, the AEF inspector general, a "by the book," "no nonsense" officer. Brewster confided to Liggett that in July 1918, just prior to the Aisne-Marne Offensive, the staff at general headquarters (GHQ) had been determined to relieve Edwards for "incompetency and tactical blunders" without first conferring with Liggett. Brewster had asked the staff for specifics, but the staff was unable to give them. Moreover, when Brewster found out that Liggett objected to any such relief in the midst of a battle, he had adamantly opposed such an order, and it was rescinded. Later, in October, once again in the midst of an offensive and again without Liggett's blessing—under the exact same circumstances—the relief was ultimately accomplished. Once again, Liggett was not in agreement with the timing of Edwards's relief, telling Brewster that it was a "mistake" and "*if it was to be done at all*, it should have been done much sooner" (emphasis added). Liggett would later remark to his aide that Edwards had done "the best he knew how" during the Aisne-Marne Offensive.[31]

On October 25, Liggett replied to a letter from Edwards dated the same day that, among other things, congratulated him on his promotion. "I regret very much that I missed seeing you the other day," he wrote, "I intended to come to your P. C. and have a talk with you but I have been so busy since coming to this place [Souilly] that I have not had a moment to go anywhere east of the Meuse." He went on to thank Edwards for his congratulations, and he added, "I am sorry that you are leaving us and would certainly have liked to have seen you before your going, but there is little chance of that now. I hope you have good luck and get back quickly." It is apparent that Liggett had not been informed in advance of Pershing's decision: "I did not know until I was told that orders had been issued, about the relief of several general officers here who are going back to the States."[32]

With the departure of General Edwards, Yankee Division morale and combat effectiveness plummeted.[33]

THE SEDAN AFFAIR

The closing days of the war were marred by an incident that could well have ended tragically. Fortunately, as it turned out, the situation concluded with only bruised egos and lasting enmity. It began with yet another instance of Pershing's meddling. As late as October 29, Pershing was back at First Army headquarters acting as if he was still in command. Liggett told him to give him a directive but to leave the army command to him. Pershing did not get the message. In early November, as American troops were closing in on the Meuse and the city of Sedan on the opposite bank, Pershing got the notion that Americans, not the French, should liberate Sedan. While the heights overlooking the city were important, the city per se was not a significant strategic objective. Yet it symbolized the humiliation that French forces endured both during the Franco-Prussian War (1870–71), when the Germans seized the city in September 1870, and again in 1914. Logically, courtesy would dictate that the French should enjoy the privilege of liberating it, if only to redeem their sacred honor. That did not seem to register with Pershing.[34]

On November 3, Pershing had a brief contretemps over an issue of command with Gen. Paul Maistre, commander of the French Centre Army Group, which included Gen. Henri Gouraud's Fourth French Army, which was situated on the left flank of the US First Army. Maistre apologized to Pershing, who was left with the impression that the French general would defer to the Americans should they drive closer to Sedan earlier than the French did. Pershing himself recounted that Maistre "offered no objection" to his suggestion to that effect and "on the contrary warmly approved." At some point shortly thereafter, Pershing met with Liggett and "talked excitedly about taking Sedan," no doubt in light of his conversation with Maistre. Liggett did not approve, and in fact, with his keen sense of history, he agreed with General Gouraud that it was not a good idea, as the French had already designated a specific unit to fulfill that mission. Accordingly, Liggett shifted his corps boundary with the French a little to the east to accommodate them. For Liggett, the issue was closed.[35]

Nevertheless, despite Liggett's opposition, on November 5, Pershing sent Col. Fox Connor with the message to Liggett's headquarters. There, he expected to find Hugh A. Drum, who continued to serve as First Army chief of staff, to tell him that it was Pershing's desire that the US First Army should have the "honor" of entering Sedan first and moreover that there was some urgency in this. Liggett was not at his headquarters at the time; for the previous several days, he and his aide had been visiting various corps headquarters on the rapidly advancing American front. Nevertheless, the commander in chief had no problem taking advantage of Liggett's absence. Drum was not present when Connor arrived, but Colonel Marshall, the assistant chief of staff, was.

As a result, Marshall drafted a short, two-paragraph order over Liggett's name directed to both corps commanders. Citing Pershing's desire, he went on to state, "He has every confidence that the troops of the I Corps, assisted on their right by the V Corps, will enable him to realize this desire." Allied politics aside, the order seemed clear enough—that is, that Joseph Dickman's corps would play the leading role with Summerall's corps in support. Marshall held the draft until Drum returned a short time later. Inexplicably, Drum added patently ambiguous language to the second paragraph to the effect that "boundaries will not be considered as binding." The order was signed by Drum, countersigned by Colonel Marshall, and then telegraphed to Dickman and Summerall. Just to make sure he had made his point, Pershing himself followed up with a visit to both I Corps and V Corps headquarters on the evening of November 6 to deliver the same message.[36]

At that time, the 42nd and 77th Divisions (part of Dickman's I Corps) were on the left of the American line adjacent to the French, and the 1st Division (part of Summerall's V Corps) was just to their right. Brig. Gen. Frank Parker, the 1st Division commander, with General Summerall's apparent blessing, took that order and literally ran with it during the night of November 6, sending five columns right through the rear areas occupied by the 77th and 42nd Divisions and into the French sector. This action very nearly created a friendly fire disaster when men from the latter found strange troops in their rear intermingled with their own and, in the words of General Dickman, "thoroughly tying up their communications and supplies and interfering most seriously with the tactical dispositions."[37]

On the humorous side, Brig. Gen. Douglas MacArthur, formerly of the 84th Brigade (42nd Division) and recently appointed division commander, with his unorthodox cap that resembled that of a German officer, was "captured" by First Army troops but quickly released as soon as the mistake was discovered. MacArthur had a good laugh over the whole thing.[38]

General Liggett returned to his headquarters at Souilly on November 7, and for whatever reason, neither Marshall nor Drum saw fit to bring the memo to his immediate attention. They made only vague references to the "eagerness . . . to get to Sedan and the reluctance of the French to have them [do so]."[39]

The incident finally came to Liggett's attention the following day, when he began to receive frantic telephone calls from the French, irate that American troops were in their sector and interfering with French operations, coupled with the threat that they were prepared to fire on the interlopers if the situation was not immediately sorted out. Liggett was "furious," stating, "It was the only occasion in the war when I lost my temper completely." He was upset with not only the thought of his troops seizing Sedan before the French but also the fact that it was an incredibly stupid maneuver, or, in his words, a "military atrocity." After a brief explanation from Colonel Marshall, Liggett, memo in hand, told Drum point-blank that it was "the source of trouble." He then issued immediate orders for General Summerall to recall his troops to his own area. Summerall later described Liggett's communication that day as "violent criticism." Liggett then rushed pell-mell for Dickman's headquarters to calm the roiling waters there.[40]

If Dickman calmed down somewhat after Liggett spoke with him and his staff, he was not mollified, and for months afterward, every chance he got, he persisted in his request for an investigation and insisted that charges be brought against both Parker and Summerall. Liggett understood Dickman's point, but it was late in the game, and in actuality, nobody got hurt. So he let the matter drop. Besides, he had also met with both Parker and Summerall, and he believed that at least the latter had learned his lesson. Nevertheless, Liggett never felt the same about either of them, particularly Summerall, whom he had considered an officer of superior caliber.[41]

And just what did Pershing think of the whole matter? Liggett soon found out. When Pershing visited his headquarters at Souilly on November 8, he told Liggett that he thought that the interdivision rivalry was amusing. In essence, "Drop it," said the commander in chief. Anyone other than Liggett might have pressed the point, but his burst of anger passed quickly, and he remained focused on the offensive. Yet when all was said and done, Liggett never wavered in his firm conviction that the whole incident was caused by Pershing's meddling.[42]

ARMISTICE

From the time that Liggett resumed the offensive on November 2, the First Army made sure-and-steady progress without letup. To command an army in time of war, however brief the tenure, was the culmination of all his study and hard work during his long career. Throughout those final days, he lost neither his focus nor his humble demeanor. He offered advice and suggestions to his subordinate commanders—and where warranted, a clear, firm order. Liggett dealt with road congestion, stragglers, and Pershing's continued meddling, among many other issues.

Ultimate victory was assured when the armistice took effect on November 11. At that moment there was total silence, something that was so foreign to the exhausted troops that they paused to absorb it. The pause soon gave way to a spontaneous, collective cheer all along the four-hundred-mile front. As the damp chill of evening set in, open campfires were lit on both sides of the line for the first time in years, creating a flickering outline of the front line as far as the eye could see in both directions. Like a massive Fourth of July fireworks display, the night sky was punctuated by colorful bursts of signal rockets in a spontaneous feu de joie. Although still frowned upon, former enemies mingled, cautiously at first, then more freely in many places, exchanging greetings, food, cigarettes, and souvenirs. Years later Liggett himself recalled that moment "when the infernal uproar which had been continuous for a long time suddenly gave way to a silence which was stunning."[43]

A PRESIDENTIAL VISIT

Pres. Thomas Woodrow Wilson sailed to France aboard the SS *George Washington* on December 5, 1918, and he and his party arrived at Brest eight days later. Once ashore, the president traveled extensively throughout France, England, and Italy, where he was welcomed by throngs of enthusiastic citizens eager to get a glimpse of the author of the "Fourteen Points." The president was elated with the public acclamation, which he naively believed represented the attitude of the more pragmatic European politicians like Lloyd George and Georges Clemenceau, who viewed him as an idealistic interloper.[44]

One of the items on the presidential agenda was a visit to a representative American division on Christmas Day. The 26th ("Yankee") Division was selected on the basis that it had seen "the longest period of service in France." The plan for the day's events involved drive-by inspections, a review at Humes of a composite or provisional division (made up of various units from all the divisions in the area, including the 26th Division), and a visit to an enlisted billet, all capped off by, at Wilson's request, a simple Christmas dinner at noon with a small enlisted contingent, eaten out of mess kits.[45]

On the day itself, most Yankee Division units stood in formation all day along the various roads and lanes in the division area, in mud and sleet, waiting in vain for the president and Pershing to pass by. Wilson did briefly inspect a billet in Mandres-la-Côte, and he attended the review at Humes, where Liggett had a brief conversation with the president while standing next to him on the reviewing stand. Wilson turned to him and said that he "was pleased that the war was ended and in the way it was ended." Liggett responded that "he had no doubt . . . if it had continued two weeks longer, [the Allies] could have destroyed the German army, [but] that would have involved the loss of many more of [their] own men, and he was glad [they] had been spared that loss." Wilson was pleased with Liggett's comments.[46]

The highlight of the day, Christmas Dinner with the troops, never came off. Wilson later agreed to a much smaller affair with several dozen officers in attendance, in a division hospital on the outskirts of the small village of Montigny-le-Roi. Major General Summerall was in attendance. He had met the president on several previous occasions in Washington and at West Point, and he tried to say a word to him as he entered the building. To his surprise,

Wilson passed by without even a nod of recognition. So too, with the mayor of Montigny-le-Roi, who asked Wilson to sign the guest book. At first, the president curtly refused. After the mayor insisted, Wilson signed the book "with very bad grace." Inside the hall, the president appeared bored throughout the dinner. A short time later, after he had eaten, Wilson rose, flashed his trademark smile, waved, and said "good-bye" and nothing else.[47]

A SHORT RESPITE

After the initial euphoria following the armistice had worn off, the doughboys wanted to go home—the sooner the better. The main problem was the fact that there were then approximately two million men serving in France. It had taken most of a year and a half to get them there, but that would not work in the reverse. More and larger vessels would be needed, as well as a suitable deepwater port. To that end, Brest was chosen, and an effort was made to improve the facilities at Camp Pontanezen just on its outskirts. Eventually, that facility was able to process approximately sixty thousand men at a time, and as a result, most of the troops came home through there. Even so, it would take more than six months to process the bulk of the men.[48]

In the meantime, a serious effort was made to occupy the soldiers' time, as idleness can quickly undermine effectiveness and morale. In addition to drill, recreational and educational opportunities were afforded, and long-overdue leaves were granted on a staggered basis. In spite of these measures, discipline became lax in some units, morale did suffer, and there were increasing incidents involving drinking. Two men from the 101st Engineers, obviously intoxicated, tried to punch Maj. Gen. Henry C. Hale, their new division commander, before vigilant military police stepped in.[49]

For Liggett, there was also a physical and emotional letdown after the intense stress of the previous year. On January 4, he contracted a case of bronchitis that kept him confined to his quarters for a week. He took the time to travel to Chaumont on January 14 to participate in a ceremony where he and nine other American generals were named by Mar. Henri Pétain as commanders in the French Legion of Honor. This was followed by lunch with General Pershing. During lunch, without mentioning his bronchitis, he asked for leave to visit Nice so that he might enjoy a brief respite from his arduous schedule. His request was granted without hesitation.[50]

Liggett and his party set out from Bar-sur-Aube on January 20 for what turned out to be a busy driving tour with stops that included Avignon, Monte

Carlo, Nice, and finally Cannes, where they stayed at the Hotel Carlton. They even took a short trip into Italy. Relaxed and reenergized, Liggett returned to Bar-sur-Aube on January 29.[51]

MARKING TIME

On February 9, Liggett attended one of many memorial services held throughout the AEF for the late president Theodore Roosevelt, who had died suddenly of a pulmonary embolism on January 6, 1919, at the age of sixty-one. Three days later, Liggett drove to Chaumont to attend a decoration ceremony, at which he accepted Belgium's highest honor, the Order of Leopold, conferred by Lt. Gen. Aloïs Biebuyck. The ceremony had originally been scheduled for February 10 but had to be postponed when the Belgian general had been unable to attend.[52]

Always the student of history, Liggett took time off to visit the site of Alisia (now Alise-Sainte-Reine), the stronghold of the young Gallic chieftain Vercingetorix, who was defeated by Julius Caesar after a siege in September of 52 BCE. He had been subsequently transported to Rome, where the proud warrior was made to "pass under the yoke" prior to his execution in 46 BCE.[53]

In late February or early March, Liggett responded to a congratulatory letter from General Drum's wife, dated January 28, who at the same time must have asked about her husband's situation. If Liggett harbored any lingering pique with his chief of staff over the Sedan affair, it was not at all evident in his gracious response. "He is a remarkable Chief of Staff," he told her. Liggett went on to praise Drum at some length and to reassure his wife: "It isn't any small job to successfully do the work of that office for an army of a million men or more, and he has done it about as nearly perfectly as anybody in the world could, since the Army was organized. You have every reason to be proud of him. He is in splendid health and the strain he has been through does not seem to have affected him at all. We are of course comparatively on easy street now. I think I have been exceedingly fortunate in having him as Chief of Staff." On a more personal note, he added, "I am of the opinion that quite frequently he gets a little homesick. He does not say much about it, but I know perfectly well he is mighty anxious to get home."[54]

On March 1, 1919, Liggett moved his quarters to *La Pipiere*, a château situated on a hill just southeast of Bar-sur-Aube. His days were filled with formal ceremonies, inspections, and farewell parties as units disbanded and made their way home. From time to time, he was called upon to make, in his

18. Legion of Honor ceremony, Chaumont, France (January 14, 1919). Liggett at far left. Courtesy of the Library of Congress.

aide's words, "short felicitous speeches." Among other things, Liggett was concerned about a shortage of lumber that resulted in an inability to build adequate facilities for his troops, who, eager to get home, continued to show definite signs of lax discipline and, in some cases, low morale.[55]

Liggett left Bar-sur-Aube by special train at midnight March 23, bound for Chaumont. At a ceremony there later that afternoon, he was finally awarded the Distinguished Service Medal "for exceptionally meritorious and distinguished services as Commander of the First Army of the American Expeditionary Forces." The award had first been announced on December 4, 1918, but for one reason or another, the ceremony had been delayed.[56]

ARMY OF OCCUPATION

After the fighting was over, much thought was given to the postwar occupation of parts of Germany, at least until she signed a formal peace treaty. Accordingly, a Third Army, the so-called American Army of Occupation on the Rhine, three corps strong, was created utilizing a mix of both experienced and more recently arrived divisions, all of which had been under Liggett's command at one time or another. Initially, the command was given to Maj. Gen. Joseph Dickman; however, in time, Pershing became dissatisfied with his performance. Dickman had a reputation as a loud, profane man, and he simply could not leave the Sedan affair alone, still stewing about generals Parker and Summerall. There were also some reports that he had developed too close a relationship with the German authorities at the expense of relations with our French allies. Accordingly, on March 20, 1919, Pershing met Liggett at Bar-sur-Aube and asked him to take over the command of the Third Army. Liggett was ready to go home and told Pershing so. Moreover, he was genuinely concerned about Dickman's postwar chances for maintaining his rank in light of his proposed relief. Pershing was not persuaded.[57]

In the end, good soldier that he was, Liggett accepted the assignment. The official orders appointing Liggett to the command were dated April 19; however, through a mix-up at GHQ, they were not transmitted to Liggett, and he only saw them for the first time when he appeared at Chaumont on April 28 and picked them up. Two days prior, Liggett drove to Paris, where he paid his respects that afternoon to Secretary of War Newton D. Baker, then staying at the Hôtel de Crillon. They discussed various divisions in the Third Army, which Baker had recently visited with Pershing, and the secretary was impressed with what he had seen. At one point, the subject of Liggett's future plans must have come up, as he asked Baker if he could be assigned to the Western Department headquartered in San Francisco when he returned to the United States. He and Harriet had fallen in love with the Bay Area during their brief stay there prior to his sailing to France. Baker told Liggett that it should not be a problem.[58]

Liggett started for Coblenz, Germany, at 10:30 a.m. on Wednesday, April 30. His entourage included two cars and a truck to carry the luggage. He and his party arrived there on May 2, having driven through a late spring snowstorm, bypassing Metz due to riots. He spent the next week at the Coblenzer Hof while Stackpole searched for more suitable quarters and ultimately found a home on the banks of the Rhine. Liggett would take formal command of the Third Army on May 2 until it, too, was disbanded on July 2, 1919, after the signing of the peace treaty.[59]

As an astute observer, Liggett soon realized that all was not what it seemed. Touted as a powerful force, poised to strike immediately if Germany broke the terms of the armistice, the army of occupation was definitely not that. In fact, the reality was that it was merely marking time until Germany signed a peace treaty. Moreover, Liggett was repeatedly reminded that he was under strict orders that there would be no forward movement of the Third Army in the absence of a direct order from Pershing. Pershing's order, in turn, could only be based on an order from President Wilson. Finally, the Third Army was not fully operational, since it was lacking much of its artillery and support troops.[60]

Liggett blamed this lack of preparedness on a want of seriousness on the part of Pershing and his staff. Nevertheless, he was given the responsibility for leading the American forces in the event that Germany balked at the peace terms, so Liggett prepared a detailed plan of action. It should have come as no surprise to anyone that knew him that he was ready as the deadline approached, and Foch transmitted preliminary orders through Pershing to advance. On June 19, Liggett called Maj. Gen. John L. Hines (III Corps) and his chief of staff, Brig. Gen. Campbell King, to his headquarters and handed them a detailed memorandum that covered the disposition of American forces, as well as the likely places to expect an attack by the German Army and how to meet it. In Lieutenant Colonel Stackpole's words, Liggett had "thought the advance through all the way to Berlin." Calling upon his wealth of military knowledge, Liggett the teacher explained his plan in detail to Hines and King, offering at the same time a lucid disquisition on Napoleon's successful Jena Campaign in October 1806 that covered much of the same ground.[61]

If Liggett knew the score, so did the doughboys, and it was hard to keep them razor sharp when it became increasingly obvious that there would likely be no imminent forward movement. Idle soldiers can quickly become a fractious and disgruntled lot, especially those assigned to the Third Army. For one thing, they were aware that some units would be going home soon, some of which had arrived in France later than they did. Discipline became a problem. Liggett received reports of "restlessness and resultant drunkenness" in the 2nd Division and failure to observe military courtesies by both officers and enlisted men, as well as news that troops in the 42nd Division were "badly demoralized" and of "rowdyism" in general.[62]

Harassment of the German population became commonplace, some of it minor like the practice of "hat knocking" civilians when they did not doff their hats in the presence of the American flag and public intoxication. On a more serious note, there was a reported incident where an elderly German couple was assaulted on the street by four doughboys. The men were quickly rounded up by the military police. On May 18, a Sunday afternoon, Liggett himself was a witness to the indiscipline when he attended a review scheduled just prior to the start of a baseball game at Coblenz. The general and his party were heckled from the grandstand with shouts of "The war is over!," "Clear the field!," and "Cut out the review!" Liggett ignored the taunts, but upon further reflection, he felt that he should have cleared the grandstand and also that it was not right to have scheduled the inspection at the same time and place.[63]

On May 15, Marshal Foch, accompanied by Gen. Charles Mangin and a large staff, paid an official call on Liggett at his headquarters at Coblenz. As the marshal's steamer *Bismarck* landed, a nineteen-gun salute was fired by a flotilla of French gunboats. This was followed by a luncheon and a visit to the fortress of Ehrenbreitstein, situated on the east bank of the Rhine opposite Coblenz, along with the usual inspections. However, much of the afternoon and evening, interrupted only by dinner, was taken up with lengthy discussions regarding contingency plans to be implemented in the event that the Germans rejected the terms of the proposed treaty. Pershing telephoned Liggett that evening asking for an update on the meetings. Foch and his party left the following morning after breakfast.[64]

Eight days later, Gen. Sir William Robertson, commander of the British Army of Occupation, along with his staff paid a similar visit to Liggett at Coblenz. Once again, there were inspections and a visit to the fortress Ehrenbreitstein. The two commanders discussed plans for a forward movement in the event that the treaty was rejected. Robertson and his staff left following a luncheon.[65]

An awkward moment occurred during dinner at the officers' mess on May 26, when someone asked Liggett what he thought about Brig. Gen. Frank Parker. Liggett replied, "Well, he obeys orders." General Summerall, who was within earshot, and for whom the remark was obviously intended, promptly snapped, "Yes, he always obeys orders." Four days later, Liggett attended a Decoration Day service at an American Cemetery nearby in France.[66]

Finally, after some last-minute balking regarding the requirement that Germany acknowledge its "guilt," a humiliated German government agreed to sign the peace treaty that included crushing reparations. Accordingly, on May 28, the Hall of Mirrors at the Palace of Versailles was the solemn scene for the formal signing ceremony. Liggett had received a last-minute invitation to attend the ceremony but declined to do so. Clemenceau was ecstatic, but more astute observers saw it as the first step toward an inevitable conflict with Germany in the future.[67]

Meanwhile, more accolades came Liggett's way. On June 10, the Italian government conferred on him the title of Grand Officer in the Order of

Sts. Maurice and Lazarus. Earlier in the day, Liggett entertained Gen. Jean Marie Joseph Degoutte, with whom he had become acquainted from his earliest days in France. As a corps commander, Degoutte had been in overall command of many American divisions during their training and during the Aisne-Marne Offensive. After an inspection tour of the Coblenz area, the Frenchman left "depressed" at the lack of devastation there in comparison with Northern France and Belgium. He also remarked that the armistice came a month too soon, as a total victory would have resulted in the complete surrender of Germany. This was a view shared by many American officers as well, including Liggett.[68]

GOING HOME

With the reduction of the occupation force all but a fait accompli, Liggett traveled to Chaumont on July 1 in order to ask for relief from his duties in Germany so that he could return home. There he spoke with Gen. James G. Harbord, who indicated that Pershing had anticipated Liggett's request and that he agreed. Liggett's successor to a much smaller occupation force would be Maj. Gen. Henry T. Allen. The general spent the next several days in Paris attending ceremonies and saying his good-byes, which included a luncheon with Pershing and a visit to Lafayette's Tomb. Liggett and Stackpole left Paris on July 9 and arrived in Brest two days later. They had booked passage on the SS *Aquitania* with a scheduled departure on Sunday, July 13.[69]

Aboard the *Aquitania* were elements of the 5th Infantry Division, as well as a number of staff and field-grade officers, including General Dickman. In

19. Lt. Col. Pierpont L. Stackpole. Courtesy of the George C. Marshall Foundation.

his conversations with Liggett, it was apparent that although Dickman was still fuming about generals Parker and Summerall, he had thought better of filing formal charges. That was progress, as earlier in the year, Liggett had told Dickman that it was not in his "self-interest" to push the protest. In addition, Dickman told Liggett that he was puzzled by his relief from command of the Third Army, since Pershing had written to him to say that his performance was "entirely satisfactory." He speculated (incorrectly) "that it was Chief of Staff Peyton C. March's doing."[70]

Also aboard the ship was the well-known American poet Ella Wheeler Wilcox, who was traveling home in the company of her close friends, Mr. and Mrs. W. H. Ritter. For months, she had been doing war work in England and France under the auspices of the Red Cross and had exhausted herself—so much so that she was carried aboard on a stretcher while the ship was in Southampton. On the second day out from Brest, Mr. Ritter approached the general and asked if he would pay a call on Wilcox, a widow, who, he explained, was terminally ill with cancer but unaware of the gravity of her situation. Liggett visited with Wilcox, and what is more, he called upon fellow officers to do the same. Liggett's kind gesture was totally lost upon his aide, who cynically noted in his diary that "these ladies [Wilcox and Mrs. Ritter] appear eager for attention and can't stand the idea of no notoriety for [the] seven days of their voyage."[71]

The voyage passed otherwise uneventfully, and the ship landed in New York City on July 20.[72]

NINE
Final Command and Retirement

HAIL THE CONQUERING HERO

The SS *Aquitania* docked at New York City at noon on Sunday, July 20, 1919. Maj. Gen. David Shanks, commander of the port of embarkation, met Liggett at the gangplank and escorted him to Harriet, who was waiting with the expectant throng there to greet their returning doughboys. From there, the couple went to the Hotel Belmont. While in New York, Liggett received his orders assigning him to command the Western Department. He and Harriet were certainly pleased with that news, which meant a return to San Francisco. On Tuesday, Liggett made a courtesy call on Maj. Gen. Thomas H. Barry, his former department commander in the Philippines, now on Governors Island. Other than that, the couple had time to catch up and to see the sights.[1]

On Wednesday, it was back to business, as Liggett and his aide traveled to Washington. For the next two days he made the rounds, meeting with Secretary of War Newton D. Baker and chief of staff Maj. Gen. Peyton C. March. He described both visits as "cordial." Next, he saw the chief quartermaster, who promised to make much-needed improvements to Fort Mason in San Francisco, which would be under Liggett's command. He also took time to visit with retired chief of staff Lt. Gen. Samuel B. M. Young, still governor of the United States Soldier's Home in Washington. Liggett even stopped in at the Army War College and, finally, paid a call on some members of Congress from California. After this whirlwind tour, he was back in New York on July 25, where he had a chance to catch his breath for several days before returning to Washington on Wednesday, July 30.[2]

In the meantime, Liggett accepted the invitation of city officials to visit Reading, Pennsylvania, on his way back to Washington, DC. His last visit to his old hometown was fifteen years prior, and it would give him an opportunity to see old friends and relatives. In addition, he planned a stop in nearby Birdsboro, where he had spent much of his youth. Two days of festivities were originally planned, including a large parade. However, the second day's events were canceled after Liggett received new orders from General March to proceed without delay once again to Washington on Tuesday, July 29. Nevertheless, in anticipation of the visit, Liggett's birthplace was "brilliantly decorated," and all city residents were asked to display their flags as a tribute to their local hero.[3]

Accordingly, early Monday morning, July 28, the general and Mrs. Liggett, accompanied by the general's chief of staff, Lt. Col. Pierpont L. Stackpole, boarded a train in New York bound for Reading. Along the way, a hometown delegation met them in Allentown and traveled the rest of the way with them, and the train slowed down at Fleetwood so that people lining the tracks could get a glimpse of the general. At Reading, a large crowd had already gathered at the Outer Station to greet them upon arrival. The Liggetts entered a waiting car, and a six-car procession then followed to the Berkshire Hotel for a luncheon at 1:00 p.m. Right after lunch, Mayor Edward Filbert drove the couple to 145 South Sixth Street to show the general his birthplace. Liggett, who had moved to Birdsboro as a young boy, was, not surprisingly, unable to confirm it. "All I'm sure of is that I am a Berkscountian," he said. However, some older relatives in the group did confirm the location.[4]

The parade followed early that same afternoon, starting from Fourth and Washington Streets, with Liggett and the grand marshal riding in a "gaily decorated" open car. Everything but the weather cooperated. By one account, the temperature soared to a sultry one hundred degrees, accompanied by periodic drenching downpours. Despite the weather, upward of forty thousand residents lined the parade route, including many veterans from the 42nd ("Rainbow") and 28th ("Keystone") Divisions. When the parade reached Fifth and Penn Streets, Liggett stepped out of the car and joined Harriet, who had been presented with a large bouquet of American roses, and other dignitaries on the reviewing stand at Penn Square.[5]

During a formal ceremony, several presentations were made to the general, including an announcement that the local Veterans of Foreign Wars (VFW) post had been renamed in his honor. With characteristic humility, Liggett requested that the post be named "Liggett-Willets," so as to "preserve part of the former name." As the crowd disbursed, several hundred persons, mostly veterans, lingered in the "driving rain," clamoring for a speech. Normally not given to such speeches, Liggett could not refuse, especially when he saw many of the men in uniform, and in an impromptu talk, his voice at times almost breaking with emotion, he spoke to them: "I see that many of you boys [who] were over there in France with me have come home again. A few of the lads who went overseas with you are yet to come back. They'll be back soon. But there are some—a great many too—who will never come back. They will stay there always. But if you fellows who did return were as glad to get back as I am, I know you are very happy. I wish you all the luck in the world, and I'm sorry I can't say any more." The men loudly shouted their approval as he departed.[6]

Liggett was then driven to City Park, where he addressed a group of four hundred schoolchildren who had assembled there in the rain. "Obey your teachers and parents like I did not," he advised them playfully. Afterward, he took the time to visit privately with his friends and relatives. Later that evening, there was another dinner, also at the Berkshire Hotel, followed by a reception where there were more honors for him. With the stress of the day, and having been soaked to the skin, Liggett suffered a severe attack of lumbago, most likely related to his recurring rheumatism. Not wanting to disappoint, he told his hosts that he would "stick it out," but as a precaution, a doctor was called.[7]

Then Lieutenant Colonel Stackpole and the Liggetts headed east for a brief tour of his boyhood home at Birdsboro, accompanied by Mayor Filbert and a city detective by the name of George E. Kemp, who no doubt drove. Harriet was eager to see her husband's boyhood haunts, including his home at 233 North Furnace Street, now a retail store, and Hill Hollow, which she had heard so much about. Along the way, the general stopped the car at St. Michael's Cemetery near Birdsboro, where he made his way through an overgrown graveyard and, in a spontaneous gesture, laid Harriett's bouquet of roses on the "battered" grave of his old mentor Professor Henry C. Hunter. Liggett returned to his car, and there, in the twilight, he told a small group, "It was my old teacher. He gave me my chance in life, and I owe him very, very much. My Christian name came from him." At 10:30 p.m., about two thousand townspeople gathered at the Friendship Fire Company to welcome him. The general made a brief speech and shook hands with the townspeople as they filed past. Finally, at midnight, Liggett said good-bye to Harriet, who returned to the Berkshire Hotel to spend the night before heading to New York the following day. The couple planned to meet there after his business at the War Department was finished.[8]

The day got even longer. By 2:30 a.m. Tuesday, Liggett's party had reached the outskirts of Philadelphia but were unable to find the Reading Railroad Terminal. An alert Philadelphia policeman saw the car stopped beneath the elevated tracks and went over to inquire. As luck would have it, the policeman, a veteran who had served in France, quickly recognized General Liggett, saluted, and before anyone could say another word, got into the car and guided it to the station in West Philadelphia, where Stackpole and Liggett boarded a 3:20 a.m. train for Washington. Mayor Filbert and Detective Kemp returned to Reading, which they reached at 6:30 a.m.[9]

Liggett sent an open letter to the citizens of Reading, thanking them for the fine reception. In it, he lauded the Pennsylvania troops that had been under his command for doing their duty. With his characteristic modesty, he shifted the honors accorded him to his soldiers: "I wish that for a moment I might think I deserved these honors as a personal tribute. I accept this gracious welcome rather as a tribute to the American soldiers I have had the privilege of directing during the Great War." Liggett's acknowledgment of the doughboy's role was sincere, and he would repeat it time and again. "The American soldier is the best in the world," he proclaimed, "and my army, I think, was the greatest fighting unit ever put together."[10]

Shortly after the reception in Reading, his friend Albert Burkholder sent him a congratulatory note to which Liggett replied. "I am very glad you are pleased with my remarks," he told him. "I am not much on speeches and prefer to listen to others who can do that sort of thing much better than I can." Liggett went on to thank Burkholder for his laudatory comments on his career and to share his philosophy about work: "Throughout, the one idea of doing the very best you can all the time has predominated, I think, both our lives."[11]

A LITTLE DUSTUP WITH THE COMMANDER IN CHIEF

Unlike Hunter Liggett, in toting up John ("Black Jack") Pershing's attributes, modesty would not be likely to make the list. As the mission of the First Army wound down, Liggett drafted a final report on its operations and accomplishments. A copy reached the desk of General Pershing, which triggered a terse response when he read it over. In short, Pershing felt that some portions of the report did not always reflect favorably upon him or adequately cover the period of his command. By the time word of Pershing's displeasure reached Liggett in August 1919, he had been back in the United States for a month. Pershing delegated the unpleasant task of this reply to Col. George C. Marshall, who wrote his friend from Paris with as much tact as he could muster: "General Pershing has just read the report of the Commanding General, 1st Army, and he is not entirely satisfied with that portion of it dealing with the period during which he personally commanded the 1st Army. He proposes re-drafting this portion of the report." Marshall was also directed to contact Brig. Gen. Hugh A. Drum, First Army chief of staff, to recall all copies of the report (presumably including Liggett's) and to sound Liggett out about his "desires" to divide the report with Pershing as coauthor.

Never one to leave well enough alone when he could weigh in, Pershing appears to have told Marshall himself to send a mass mailing, addressed to all the recipients, demanding the return of the draft report, rather than simply trusting Drum to do so. The normally careful Marshall, not sure of Liggett's exact whereabouts, sent the letter in care of the War Department in hopes that it would arrive in a timely fashion. The problem came to a head when, by an oversight on Marshall's part, Liggett was inadvertently included on the distribution list for the generic form letter, which, as fate would have it, was delivered first.[12]

This unwelcome communiqué undoubtedly triggered a very prompt and angry response from Liggett—one of his rare flashes of temper. For more than a year, Liggett had played the loyal subordinate to Pershing, his junior. It was just another example of Pershing's meddling—this time with a twist, as it was personal—and it must have brought back memories of the previous year. As will be recalled, Pershing had reluctantly turned over the reins of command in the Argonne, but while Liggett was briefly away from his headquarters, the commander in chief had been responsible for setting in motion the infamous Sedan order. Not only did the affair cause long-standing bad feeling among some AEF commanders, like generals Charles P. Summerall and Joseph Dickman, but it had also very nearly created an unfortunate rift with the French. Had it not been for Liggett's timely return and, more important, providential intervention, that situation could well have been worse. While the wording of Liggett's response to the form letter is not known, it certainly got Marshall's attention.

Marshall immediately cabled Liggett, his tone apologetic: "Form letter requesting return of First Army Report of Operations was sent to you through error. I signed it without noting name of addressee. Please ignore form letter and hold your copy pending corrections of portion referring to General Pershing's period of command of First Army." This may have ended the matter for the time being, but Liggett would remember. The revised report of operations would not be published for another five years.[13]

LAST COMMAND

Secretary Baker was as good as his word, and Liggett was assigned to command the Western Department (later designated as the IX Corps Area). He and Harriet soon settled into their quarters at Fort Mason in San Francisco, California. That Christmas, the Liggett's spent the holiday at the home of their friends Col. and Mrs. Beecher Ray in Los Angeles. Harriet had planned to do so the year before but postponed the visit due to the influenza epidemic.[14]

Certainly, Liggett's new assignment was not as demanding as his duties with the AEF, but it had its moments. On September 19, 1919, what began as a small brush fire set by a careless landowner in Mill Valley was whipped by strong winds and suddenly turned into a large stubborn inferno that spread quickly to nearby southern Sausalito, consuming several homes in its path. The fire also touched Muir Woods. The following day, despite the valiant efforts of local volunteer fire companies, aided by area residents, the fire continued to burn out of control. The desperate Sausalito mayor, E. G. Coughlin, called the mayor of San Francisco, James Rolph, who dispatched the fire tug *Dennis T. Sullivan* and a large contingent of firemen and equipment. General Liggett also received a call for assistance, and he sent more than six hundred soldiers to Mill Valley from various installations throughout the Bay Area in order to battle the blaze, including a convoy with firefighting equipment, commissary supplies, and an ambulance. Liggett also dispatched his aide-de-camp, Lt. Col. Joseph C. Hatie, to keep him apprised of the situation. Neighbors helped neighbors save their personal belongings, and although there was considerable property damage, including the destruction of many homes, no lives were lost. Liggett and his soldiers drew high praise from Mayor Coughlin.[15]

THE WOBBLIES

In the immediate aftermath of the war, the undercurrent of discontent, for the most part patriotically dormant in 1917 and 1918, began to bubble up in the form of a nascent but vocal anarchist movement and more active union activity. The years 1919 and 1920 were marked by race riots, strikes, and other violent clashes. In February 1919, in Seattle, Washington, a massive general strike paralyzed the city, including the busy shipyards, for the better part of a week. In New England, telephone workers struck, as did members of the Boston Police Department. The latter catapulted Gov. Calvin Coolidge onto the national scene and eventually the White House. Overall, the year 1919 saw three thousand strikes involving four million workers. In addition, the Russian

Revolution in 1917 and Lenin's call for world revolution fed a "Red Scare" in the United States that colored all such activities for many years.[16]

On June 2, 1919, anarchists bombed the home of Atty. Gen. A. Mitchell Palmer in Washington, DC, and targets in six other cities. Fortunately, Palmer escaped injury; not so lucky was a night watchman in New York. By far, the worst incident of terror occurred the following year, when at noon on September 16, 1920, terrorists set off a bomb on Wall Street, killing thirty-eight people and wounding dozens of passersby. People were understandably nervous and on edge, and the situation was ripe for overreaction by citizens in the form of vigilantism. The same was true of their government, which was already marked by its strict censorship and other policies restricting dissent that had been enacted during the war, in particular the Espionage Act of 1917 and the Sedition Act of 1918.[17]

The most vocal and demonstrative, and arguably the most controversial, of the unions was the Industrial Workers of the World (IWW), most often referred to as the "Wobblies." The union was particularly active among miners, lumbermen, and mill workers throughout the West. Their leader was William "Big Bill" Haywood. Members of the union engaged in demonstrations and some acts of physical violence, but more often than not, they were the objects of violence, some official and some by vigilantes. Antiunion sentiment ran high, and the activities of these organizations, particularly the IWW, were considered anti-American and often lumped together with those of the anarchists, communists, socialists, and radicals in general.[18]

Washington State was the locus of considerable union activity as well as being a hotbed of antiunion sentiment. After the brutal beating of forty Wobblies by vigilantes in Everett, Washington, in November 1916, a violent affray followed that resulted in several deaths on both sides. In Centralia, the IWW hall had been repeatedly vandalized and local officials had turned a blind eye.[19]

November 11, 1919, was the first anniversary of the armistice, and hundreds of towns and cities all across the United States staged parades and other observances. One was held in Centralia, Washington, and among the scheduled participants was a contingent of the VFW. Given past incidents in town and the fact that there were strong signs that violence toward the IWW would likely recur during the parade, a number of union members stood watch over their meeting hall. At least two of them—including Wesley Everest, himself a veteran—expecting the worst, had armed themselves with pistols.[20]

When the VFW contingent reached the union hall, it halted, and urged on by their leaders, the men stormed the building. In the confused fight that followed both in the hall and outside, shots were fired, and four VFW members were killed and one wounded. Overwhelmed, the Wobblies retreated, and the contents of the hall were burned in the street. In the ensuing confusion, two separate antiunion vigilante groups joined the pursuit, killing one of their own in a gun battle after each mistook the other group for union members. Wesley Everest, wearing his Army uniform, was cornered and surrendered after a short flight, and he and the others were taken to the jail. That night, the jail was broken into by yet more vigilantes, and Everest was taken to a nearby bridge, where he was castrated and hanged, his body riddled with bullets. No one was ever caught and prosecuted for the crime.[21]

Ten IWW members were accused of complicity in the killings and were put on trial. In hopes of obtaining an impartial jury, the venue was moved to nearby Montesano, Washington, and scheduled to begin the following February. Concerned with the possibility of further violence, Gov. Louis F. Hart of Washington asked General Liggett to send federal troops for the duration of the trial "as a purely precautionary measure." Liggett authorized the dispatch of a regiment. After a six-week trial, two men were acquitted, and the remaining defendants were sentenced to terms ranging from twenty-five to forty years. Centralia erected a statue to the fallen Legionnaires in 1924.[22]

ALL GLORY IS FLEETING

As was the case in the past after large conflicts were over, Congress moved quickly to reduce the size of the US Army. This caused some concern on the part of many experienced officers, Liggett among them. In the interim, he spoke out for higher quotas at West Point for enlisted men from the Western Department who wished to enroll there. The quotas were soon raised from twenty men to thirty as a direct response.[23]

By June 30, 1920, he had reverted to his permanent rank of major general, his higher rank having been attained during the war on an emergency basis. Only Pershing retained his rank. That same year, Liggett received an honorary degree from the University of California. In time, he would receive many awards for his service in France. In addition to the Distinguished Service Medal ("for exceptionally meritorious and distinguished services"), Liggett was awarded the Croix de Guerre with palm, as well as the Legion of Honor (commander) from France, the Order of Leopold (grand officer) from

Belgium, the Order of Sts. Maurice and Lazarus (grand officer) from Italy, and the Panamanian Medal of La Solidaridad (second class).[24]

FADING AWAY

Liggett reached the mandatory retirement age of sixty-four on March 21, 1921. At an understated ceremony at his headquarters, without pomp or pageant and attended only by close friends and the officers in his command, a telegram from the War Department was read, noting that he had been relieved of command and that he would be succeeded by Brig. Gen. Richard M. Blatchford, coincidently, the selfsame general who was sent home from France instead of Liggett. The ceremony was quintessential Liggett, and he returned briefly to Birdsboro for a visit prior to returning to San Francisco. Not one to sit idle, on May 1921, he was named chairman of the Central Committee of Relief of Disabled Veterans in San Francisco.[25]

Shortly thereafter, Liggett was briefly returned to active duty and appointed to a special embassy to Peru to participate in ceremonies there marking the centennial of Peruvian independence. He would represent the US Army. The delegation arrived in Callao on July 22 aboard one of three American battleships. The Peruvian government made a private residence available to the Americans during their stay. While in Peru, Liggett was presented with a commemorative medal and was awarded the Order of the Sun of Peru. He returned with the delegation in early August.[26]

The general was philosophical about his retirement. "Yes, I've had my share of the excitement," he admitted. "I guess I can afford to take it easy." As for those younger men coming up behind, he did not begrudge them at all, saying, "I'll give the young fellows a chance to store up memories, and I hope they have as many as I when they reach my age."[27]

After decades of reading history, Liggett finally decided to write on the subject. In 1925, he published *Commanding an American Army: Recollections of the World War*, which chronicled his experiences in France leading the doughboys. Later on, between April and July 1927, he wrote a series of seven articles for the *Saturday Evening Post*, which he consolidated and eventually released in book form that same year, titled *A.E.F.: Ten Years Ago in France*. Years afterward, he was asked why he had spent so much time writing these memoirs. Perhaps thinking back to the contretemps over the preparation of the Report of Operations of the First Army, Liggett good-naturedly quipped, "I shouldn't have written those memoirs. Jack Pershing's the man who should have done it, but I knew he was too damn lazy."[28]

Neither did the general forget the veterans, and he took an active role at the local American Legion post. In April, a month after his retirement, Liggett showed up unannounced at the local post, dressed in blue overalls, and asked if he could help in the construction of the new club rooms. For the better part of two hours, no one seemed to recognize the elderly, white-haired man quietly sawing boards and driving nails. Finally, it dawned on a fellow worker just who the mystery man was. Obviously surprised, he asked, "Why General, how long have you been here?" Liggett's response was not recorded. No doubt he smiled and graciously made light of the question.[29]

Hunter Liggett was also an "ardent advocate for preparedness." Like many senior officers that had served in France with the AEF, Liggett believed that the fact that America had been woefully unprepared cost the lives of many a doughboy. "America's unpreparedness in the last war and in other wars was frightful and criminal," he was quoted as saying.[30]

MORE OF THE SAME

In April 1924, Liggett wrote a short letter to George Marshall, thanking him for sending copies of the report and asking to be remembered to General Pershing. He became somewhat philosophical. "Hope you are well and happy," he told the younger man, "I know you are busy and one must be so to be very, very happy." True to his own advice, he told Marshall that he had volunteered his time and labor building another clubhouse, this one for enlisted servicemen located on the Embarcadero. He also served as vice president of the Association of Graduates of the United States Military Academy from 1928 to 1932.[31]

During the spring of 1929, Liggett's editor friend, Albert Burkholder, wrote and asked him for a signed photograph, which he intended to present to the Liggett post of the VFW in Reading. The general obliged but could not resist a little self-deprecating humor. "I am sending you my photograph taken in 1919," he wrote. "I sometimes think, however, no one should have his photograph taken after the age of 45 has been reached."[32]

The effort to restore Liggett's rank as a lieutenant general was a surprisingly long one. As early as 1921, soon after he had retired, the reinstatement was favored by Secretary of War John Weeks. Yet only Pershing's rank as general of the armies was made permanent—not Peyton March, Tasker Bliss, Robert L. Bullard, nor Liggett were so favored at that time. After years of talk, such a bill was finally introduced by Sen. Hiram Johnson of California on February 17, 1928, and approved unanimously by the Senate military

20. Letterman General Hospital, San Francisco, CA. Courtesy of the Library of Congress.

committee on April 9. In introducing the measure, Johnson said that the victory in the Argonne was a "great triumph . . . in large measure due to [Liggett's] ability and genius." On June 21, 1930, by act of Congress, signed by Pres. Herbert Hoover, Liggett was at last restored to the rank of lieutenant general on the retired list. He was most certainly pleased, as were his supporters, who had worked hard to make it happen. Justice was finally done.[33]

During their later years, the Liggetts lived in a home at 2760 Scott Street, a gift from the city of San Francisco, which had also presented the general with a gold-mounted ceremonial sword.[34]

FADING AWAY

As the years passed, Liggett's health deteriorated. Finally, on January 17, 1935, following a vacation to Hawaii with Harriet, he checked himself into Letterman General Hospital at the Presidio, where he spent the balance of the year virtually bedridden. His heart was failing. Eventually Harriet, herself in frail health, would move into Letterman to be with her husband during his long stay. On July 24, he had surgery on an enlarged prostate in order to relieve a urinary blockage.[35]

Nothing seemed to stem the inexorable ebbing of his vitality. By October, there were further complications. Yet game to the end, he told a good friend, "I am going to get up soon." For two weeks in mid-December, he drifted in and out of consciousness, and finally, on December 28, he lapsed into an irreversible coma. The general died at 7:45 a.m. on Monday, December 30, with Harriet at his bedside.[36]

On Wednesday, Liggett's body, dressed at his request in his olive drab World War uniform, his chest adorned with his many decorations, was taken from the mortuary to the rotunda of the San Francisco City Hall, where the general's remains lay in state from noon until noon the following day. An Episcopal funeral service took place at Grace Cathedral on Thursday, where Maj. Gen. Paul B. Malone eulogized the general. Liggett was, he said, "a living Rock of Gibraltar—an inspiration to the greatest American army ever assembled."[37]

Burial followed at the Presidio National Cemetery. There, at the Lombard Street gate, in the midst of a cold "driving rainstorm," the funeral cortege halted. The casket was transferred to a caisson and draped with a flag while a fifteen-gun salute was fired by the guns at Fort Scott. The procession, with muffled drums and muted trumpets, advanced slowly to the gravesite, and a horse, with boots reversed in the stirrups, followed the general's remains. The procession passed between an honor guard of 1,400 men from the 30th ("San Francisco's Own") Infantry and the 6th Coast Artillery, standing at present arms. At the grave, a canvas shelter was erected to protect Harriet and those involved in the ceremony; however, the hundreds of other mourners took what little shelter they could find beneath nearby trees. The military service was brief, with another fifteen-gun salute, followed by three volleys, and ending as "Taps" was sounded. Throughout, Harriet was distraught, and she was overheard to lament, "Why did they let you go before me?"[38]

In the meantime, as word of Liggett's death spread, tributes continued to flow from those who knew him best. When asked to comment on Liggett's death, General Pershing, who was in Tucson, Arizona, at the time, said, "I am deeply grieved at the passing of General Liggett . . . He was an accomplished soldier and an outstanding leader in the A. E. F . . . and left the stamp of his high character on every unit he ever led. Of fine loyalty and excellent military judgment, he had my entire confidence. . . . History will give Hunter Liggett a high place among the great soldiers who have served the Republic." He added later that "in peace or war the country felt confident of the accomplishment of any object entrusted to him, and he will be remembered as one upon whom, in large measure, the dependability of the American Army rested in its most gigantic struggle."[39]

Mayor Angelo Rossi spoke for all San Franciscans: "One of San Francisco's most distinguished citizens and one of the world's most noted and beloved soldiers is gone from our midst. A timely gentleman, who bore his honors modestly and took part in our civic life with unselfish steadfastness, General Liggett will be sorely missed by his fellow citizens." It was a reciprocal sentiment for Hunter and Harriett. "I have seen much of the world," he once said, "and . . . I want San Francisco in place of all the other cities I have seen."[40]

Gen. Malin Craig, who had served as Liggett's chief of staff throughout much of the war, offered the following tribute: "General Liggett was a real leader. He commanded not only the respect and esteem of all the men under him, but also their genuine affection. With the exception of General Pershing, General Liggett did more to bring about our victory in the World War than any other American officer."[41]

After her husband's death, Harriet Lane Liggett was unable to maintain the family home on Scott Street due to limited finances and her own failing health, and she moved to the Richelieu Hotel on Van Ness and Geary Streets. In March of 1938, Congress passed a bill authorizing a $1,200.00 a year pension for her and ten other widows of prominent military officers, only to have it vetoed by President Roosevelt. Although that would have afforded her some financial relief, Harriet's health continued to deteriorate, and on April 13, 1939, she entered Letterman General Hospital, where she died on April 28 at the age of seventy-seven. Like her husband, she, too, died of heart failure. She was buried at the Presidio beside her husband just as the world was ready to erupt into another global war.[42]

Epilogue

SIC TRANSIT GLORIA MUNDI

NEARLY FORGOTTEN

Shortly after Liggett's death, a group of influential residents of Reading, Pennsylvania, including veterans and some state and local politicians, formed the National Liggett Memorial Commission. In March of 1936, the group brought a proposal before the mayor and city council to erect a memorial boulder or band shell dedicated to the general's memory in City Park. In the past, the city had already honored both Pres. William McKinley and cavalryman David M. Gregg with statues and had prominently displayed an anchor from the battleship *Maine* as a memorial to those lost in that tragedy. Nevertheless, the proposal was rejected.[1]

In May 1937, when the Army and Navy Club of San Francisco offered Reading a duplicate of the bronze plaque it had commissioned containing a bas-relief of General Liggett, the offer was also refused following a secret meeting between some members of the Reading City Council. The donors, unaware of the vote the previous year, were incredulous; so were many citizens of Reading, particularly its veterans. Yet the local politics had changed since the end of the Great War, as the mayor and four of the five members of the city council were members of the Socialist Party. Each of them was firmly opposed to war in general and to the looming conflict in Europe. Mayor J. Henry Stump was quite clear in his sentiments. "In rejecting the plaque," he explained, "the Socialist members of city council were simply reaffirming their anti-war principles and their party's stand against war."[2]

The anti-war sentiment wasn't unique to Reading; it was part of rather a modest but vocal national movement called "America First." The aviator Charles Lindbergh was a very prominent participant, as was then student Kingman Brewster.[3]

Not surprisingly, the following day, when word of the decision became public, both the Community Memorial and the YMCA of the Borough of Birdsboro immediately spoke up and indicated a willingness to accept the honor. In the interim, the lone Republican councilman, Frederick A. Muhlenberg, continued his efforts to reverse the decision and to have the vote taken in an open forum. The result of the revote was the same as before. No doubt feeling some pressure, Mayor Stump pushed back with a personal attack. He said that Liggett, once he became an adult, "paid no attention to the city and county of his birth, paying but one visit to it late in life." He ungraciously added that "the real war heroes are not the generals, but the privates." The former, he opined "are back far enough [from the front line] to be safe."[4]

At this point, officials in Berks County stepped in, suggesting the county courthouse as a possible venue. The Reserve Officers Association passed a resolution condemning the actions of the mayor and council. The resolution read in part that it was "a fallacy that war can be abolished by ignoring it" and that the city council did not "represent the true consensus of opinion of the citizens of Reading."[5]

The county commissioners voted unanimously on May 19 to accept the offer, and the plaque was sent to the Gregg Post No. 12 of the American Legion in Reading. Soon after and with little fanfare, it was bolted to the wall on the first floor of the courthouse on September 13, in advance of the dedication ceremony, which took place twelve days later. Although space in the first-floor corridor was limited, about 150 citizens attended the twenty-minute ceremony. After an invocation, Judge Paul N. Schaeffer delivered some brief remarks. He told the assemblage, "This refusal to receive the plaque is doing injury to our fair city that is incalculable." In truth, he told them, "we should be proud to receive this plaque." Moreover, he said, "we must recognize the debt we owe to the men from private to general, who are willing to give their all so that this nation might live."[6]

Forty-seven years later, on Sunday, December 30, 1984, the forty-ninth anniversary of Liggett's death, the Pennsylvania Historical and Museum Commission dedicated a historical marker in front of his birthplace at 145 South Sixth Street, Reading. Present for the ceremony were two surviving doughboys from the 28th Division.[7]

THE PERSHING LEGACY

In large measure, the American Expeditionary Forces (AEF) was a creation of John J. Pershing. He chose the principal participants, and while most were very intelligent, almost all of them to a man were loyal first and foremost to him. Pershing quickly purged the command of older officers, many well respected, like Maj. Gen. William L. Sibert. He could also be vindictive, as is apparent with his yearlong campaign to relieve Major General Edwards. Not only did he send Edwards home roughly two weeks before the armistice; at the same time, he blocked all his decorations and awards, both French and American. Although Edwards would belatedly receive them, he was the only senior commander to go home without any decorations. Those close to Pershing got the message early on: "Stick with me and you will be rewarded; cross me and you will be summarily dismissed." He and Maj. Gen. Peyton C. March, the chief of staff, constantly dueled over the extent of their respective authority, even to the ridiculous point of the wearing of the Sam Browne belt, which March had banned for all officers returning from France. Protective of his legacy, he admonished Liggett regarding the preparation of the report of First Army operations, recalling all copies and then taking nearly five years to produce his version.

Pershing's circle was tight, and few dared to openly challenge him. It has been said that "history is written by the victors"—so, too, the history of the AEF.

Despite Pershing's shortcomings, his lasting legacy is the imprint he and his protégés left on the US Army. During the First World War, the integration of the formally educated officers into the collective was not as seamless as some would have liked. This would become quite clear during the First World War in France, where Pershing surrounded himself with younger officers who had received training at Fort Leavenworth or the Army War College—or both. Some resentment shown by older officers was to be expected in a conservative organization like the US Army. However, the arrogant meddling of certain members of the GHQ staff with the command of the various divisions even drew the ire of Robert L. Bullard and Charles P. Summerall, both of whom had combat experience and schooling at the Army War College. Both came to recognize the value of such schooling, but each had sharp words about the manner of its application by Pershing's staff, whom were often referred to as the "Leavenworth clique" or the "Chaumont crowd." Summerall summed the situation up with his observation that "there was an impassable gulf between GHQ and the troops. GHQ knew little of the real conditions or difficulties and was always ready to sacrifice anyone who might be blamed."[8]

In the end, the Leavenworth clique won out in principle, but in practice, the rough edges were smoothed out in the implementation by men like Summerall and George C. Marshall, who were able to bring their influence and experience to bear on the postwar US Army. The US Army was much better off for it. Speaking to a class at the Army War College in April 1933, Maj. Gen. James G. Harbord, then retired, discussed the high value of a West Point education and the multiplier effect, when such an officer "in mature life" has been "further standardized by the Service Schools and Army War College." This is a sentiment that Liggett could certainly have echoed, and what is more, he could take justifiable pride in the role he played in the growth of the War College and the careers of many of its graduates.[9]

NO FAT ABOVE THE COLLAR

Hunter Liggett was proud to be a soldier, and he was determined to be the best soldier that he could be. In fact, everything else, even his marriage, took a back seat to his duty. In addition to a lifelong course of self-study, he also took advantage of the nascent US Army schools not only to make himself better but also to improve the profession itself. A colleague who had served with Liggett was unstinting in his praise: "No officer with whom I have been associated in the service has so profoundly impressed me with his zeal for the study of his profession, the depth and accuracy of his knowledge of the literature of it, and his practical familiarity with all its details. His frank, straightforward and generous character in addition to his perfect mastery of his profession gave him unusual influence for good among enlisted men as well as officers." These attributes were not lost on the higher ranks of the US Army or, for that matter, civilians in and out of government, whom he had met and impressed and who were in a position to help advance his career.[10]

For the first two decades of his long career, Liggett's experience was nearly indistinguishable from that of all his colleagues in the post–Civil War era. Though he was of an older generation of officers who too often "played the game" either through influence or by sheer longevity (and sometimes both) to advance in rank, Liggett broke with that stereotype. What set him apart was his personal effort to improve himself as an officer, and that did not go unnoticed. The real turning point came when he audited the course at Fort Leavenworth, which in turn led to his appointment to the general staff and ultimately to the Army War College. From there, his career took off, and what is more, he was then in a position throughout the remainder of his career to influence future leaders like George C. Marshall.

If he had one disappointment, it was the fact that he had virtually no experience leading troops in battle despite his service in Cuba and the Philippines. In the end, it did not matter, as he was the beneficiary of the Root reforms, which he himself helped foster, and he ultimately went on to lead more than a million men in the Meuse-Argonne, the largest single battle that American forces had fought to that date.[11]

He was by all accounts quiet and modest and much more accepting of others, flaws and all, than Pershing who led by fear or the promise of reward. When asked to compare the two men, a former doughboy quipped, "Believe me, when Pershing came around everybody snapped to attention. Even the clocks had to stop until he was out of sight. But when Liggett showed up he would say, 'All right, boys, go on with whatever you're doing.'" He was always a teacher at heart and, at the same time, one who never stopped being a student. Even as a senior commander, Liggett was able to learn valuable lessons. A prime example was his use of a flanking maneuver by the 82nd Division to help to clear the Argonne Forest. He was also willing to engage in self-reflection, as was the case with his disappointment that the same flanking maneuver did not achieve a more dramatic result. Years later, in a letter to Hugh A. Drum, he came to accept the fact that the "difficulties were great" and that the demands that he had placed on the "comparatively green" 82nd Division exceeded its capabilities. The division "did well under all the circumstances," he wrote.[12]

Liggett recognized that the constant criticism of other officers did not make for effective leadership, yet his quiet demeanor masked the fact that he was made of sterner stuff. He had a fierce inner determination to succeed at whatever task he was given, something he proved on Little Porcupine Creek as a junior officer fresh from West Point. It was that quest to improve himself and the US Army that he would impart on a new generation of senior officers as president of the Army War College, and it was this same quiet determination that challenged Pershing in the Meuse-Argonne sector and secured the ultimate victory there.

Where Pershing commanded by fear and censure, Liggett was willing to allow his subordinates to grow into their jobs while suggesting certain courses of action. Where Pershing was feared, Liggett enjoyed the respect, and often affection, of his subordinates. Liggett was a modest man and a student of military history at a time when many officers of his age and background still relied upon a combination of pull and seniority to get ahead. He was thoughtful and supportive of his subordinates, yet unafraid to speak frankly and forcefully to his superiors when necessary. A colleague referred to him as a "fine, able, [and] modest soul."[13] More recently, historian Edward Lengel described Liggett as follows: "opinionated but tactful, independent but loyal, and confident without being self-centered. He was both smart and levelheaded." Yet for all his success, he left a very small footprint.[14]

Through it all, Liggett remained a good and decent man who never lost touch with his humanity and that of his friends and fellow soldiers. One of those comrades in arms, George C. Marshall, wrote to Harriet Liggett a little more than two years after her husband's death, while she was a resident of the Richelieu Hotel. He wrote, "[Liggett] was a grand man, one of the finest characters, and absolutely the sweetest, I have ever known."[15]

ABBREVIATIONS

ACP	File #5228-ACP-1892, 1st Lieutenant Hunter Liggett, 5th US Infantry, NARA RG94
BHC	Berks History Center, Reading, PA
CRE	Clarence Ransom Edwards Papers, Massachusetts Historical Society, Boston, MA
GCML	George C. Marshall Library, Lexington, VA
MHI	Military History Institute, Carlisle, PA
NARA	National Archives and Records Administration
RBHL	Rutherford B. Hayes Presidential Library, Spiegel Grove, Fremont, OH
RG	Record Group
USMA	United States Military Academy, West Point, NY
USMC	Gray Research Center, United States Marine Corps History Division, Quantico, VA

NOTES

PREFACE

1 Sheryl Timberman, email message to author, June 21, 2016.

2 Pierpont Langley Stackpole, *Diary of Lieutenant Colonel P. L. Stackpole, A.D.C. to General Liggett, January 25, 1918 to August 3, 1919*, GCML; Robert H. Ferrell, ed., *In the Company of Generals: The World War I Diary of Pierpont L. Stackpole* (Columbia: University of Missouri Press, 2009); Hunter Liggett, *A.E.F.: Ten Years Ago in France* (Cranbury, NJ: Scholar's Bookshelf, 2005), 313–14 ("admirable companion"); Everett S. Stackpole, *History and Genealogy of the Stackpole Family* (Lewiston, ME: Press of *Journal*, 1899), 163; Michael E. Shay, *Sky Pilots: The Yankee Division Chaplains in World War I* (Columbia: University of Missouri Press, 2014), 12–13.

3 Charles Francis King, "General Hunter Liggett," master's thesis, University of Oklahoma, 1964.

4 Allan R. Millett, *The General: Robert L. Bullard and Officership in the United States Army 1881–1925* (Westport, CT: Greenwood, 1975), 487; Ferrell, *In the Company of Generals*, 193 ("no papers").

CHAPTER ONE

1 Obituary, *Reading Eagle*, September 27, 1887; Mrs. Nathaniel Perkins to Cyrus T. Fox, February 22, 1923, BHC; "Tombstone Inscriptions," St. Paul's Methodist Episcopal Church, Geigertown, PA, BHC. As further confirmation that he was the son of James and Ann Liggett, he is buried with their daughter Ann. "Cemetery Inscriptions," Elverson (PA) Methodist Church, BHC; 1850 US Census, Pennsylvania, Berks, Robeson Township (Series M432, Roll 754, Page 410B).

The census record dated September 6, 1850, indicates that the couple had married within that year. 1850 US Census, Pennsylvania, West Nantmeal Township, Chester County (Series M432, Roll 765, Page 200B). The census record lists George's occupation, and that of his son Charles, in 1850 as "shoemaker."

2 1850 US Census, Pennsylvania, Berks, Robeson Township (Series M432, Roll 754, Page 410B); Cyrus T. Fox, ed., *Reading and Berks County Pennsylvania: A History*, vol. 2 (New York: Lewis Historical Publishing, 1925), 168–69; *Reading Directory and City Register for 1856–57: Containing the Names, Occupations and Residences of Housekeepers and Voters Residing within the Limits, Alphabetically Arranged* (Reading, PA: J. Knabb, 1856), 59; "Cemetery Inscriptions," Elverson (PA) Methodist Church,

BHC. The typed record gives Margaret's date of death as "1853," some four years before Liggett's birth. The stone itself correctly lists the date as "1857."

3 *Reading Directory, 1856–57*, 59. The Directory lists an Ann and Hannah Liggett as "tailoresses" with a shop at 108 South 4th Street, BHC; 1860 US Census, Pennsylvania, West Nantmeal, Chester County (Series M653, Roll 1091, Page 428); Obituary, *Reading Eagle*, September 27, 1887; 1860 US Census, Pennsylvania, West Nantmeal, Chester County (Series M653, Roll 1091, Page 433).

4 1860 US Census, Pennsylvania, Robeson Township, Berks County (Series M653, Roll 1076, Page 342) ("Ann Liggett"); Fox, *Reading and Berks County*, 168–69; *Dictionary of American Biography, Supplement One, to December 31, 1935* (New York: Scribner, 1944), 494–95; Obituary, *Reading Eagle*, September 27, 1887; *Harrisburg Telegraph*, July 29, 1919, p. 16. When Liggett later accepted an appointment to West Point in 1875, James's occupation was listed as "Merchant–Shoe Dealer" of "moderate" means. *Circumstances of the Parents of Cadets*, vol. 1 *(1842–1879)*, Special Collections and Archives, USMA.

5 Fox, *Reading and Berks County*, 168–69; Obituary, *Birdsboro Dispatch*, January 3, 1936; *Reading Eagle*, December 30, 1935, p. 1; 1870 US Census, Pennsylvania, Berks County, Robeson Township (Series M593, Roll 1308, Page 282B); *Reading News-Times*, July 24, 1919, p. 3 ("bureaucracy").

6 *Reading Eagle*, July 6, 1975 ("kindly baker").

7 *Hunter Liggett, Lieutenant General, US Army*, Nomination to Fort Leavenworth Hall of Fame (six-page typescript, n.p., n.d.) ("two uncles"), MHI; Perkins to Fox, February 22, 1923 ("John Hunter"), BHC.

8 *Circumstances of the Parents of Cadets*, vol. 1 *(1842–1879)*, USMA ("six competitors including self"); *Reading Eagle* (undated article), BHC ("14 were prepared to take the test"); *Birdsboro Dispatch*, January 3, 1936; Bruce A. Hoffman, ed., *Forge and Foundry: An Historic View of Birdsboro, Berks County, Pennsylvania* (n.p., 1976), 27.

9 *Reading Eagle* (undated article), BHC; *Reading News-Times*, July 24, 1919, p. 3 ("Algebra, etc.").

10 Mark A. Smith, "The Politics of Military Professionalism: The Engineer Company and the Political Activities of the Antebellum U.S. Army Corps of Engineers," *Journal of Military History* 80, no. 2 (April 2016): 357; Stephen E. Ambrose, *Duty, Honor, Country: A History of West Point* (Baltimore: Johns Hopkins University Press, 1999), 10–23; John Adams to Thomas Jefferson, August 20, 1821, in Lester J. Cappon, ed., *The Adams-Jefferson Letters: The Complete Correspondence between Thomas Jefferson and Abigail and John Adams* (Chapel Hill: University of North Carolina Press, 1987), 573–74*n*45; Nathaniel Philbrick, *Valiant Ambition: George Washington, Benedict Arnold, and the Fate of the American Revolution* (New York: Viking, 2016), 262 ("most important"); Charles P. Summerall, *The Way of Duty, Honor, Country: The Memoir of General Charles Pelot Summerall* (Lexington: University Press of Kentucky, 2010), 222–23 ("Engineering"). It should be noted that a small garrison known as the "Corps of Artillerists and Engineers" had occupied West Point from the early days of the Republic, and that classes were held there to train young officers known as "cadets."

11 Rory M. McGovern, "The School of Experience: George W. Goethals and the U.S. Army, 1876–1907," *Journal of Military History* 81, no. 2 (April 2017): 400 ("rigid curriculum"); Ambrose, *Duty, Honor, Country*, 131, 174 ("fight for rank"); Edward M. Coffman, *The Old Army: A Portrait of the American Army in Peacetime, 1784–1898* (New York: Oxford University Press, 1988), 66.

12 Ambrose, *Duty, Honor, Country*, 224–26; Summerall, *The Way of Duty*, 14 ("ordeal"); Geoffrey Perret, *Eisenhower* (New York: Random House, 1999), 46–47.

13 *Official Register of the Officers and Cadets of the U.S. Military Academy, West Point, N. Y., June, 1876* (West Point, NY, 1876), 17; Ambrose, *Duty, Honor, Country*, 227–28 ("sense of isolation").

14 Ambrose, *Duty, Honor, Country*, 74 ("200 demerits").

15 *Official Register (1876)*, 17; *Register of Delinquencies*, p. 54, USMA.

16 *Official Register (1877)*, 18; Liggett, *Ten Years Ago*, 291 ("love of maps").

17 *Register of Delinquencies*, p. 187, USMA.

18 "Funeral of Gen. Custer," *New York Times*, October 11, 1877.

19 "Funeral of Gen. Custer."

20 *Official Register (1878)*, 15; *Hunter Liggett, Lieutenant General, US Army*, Nomination to Fort Leavenworth Hall of Fame (six-page typescript, n.p., n.d.), MHI; *Register of Delinquencies*, p. 187, USMA.

21 Liggett, *Ten Years Ago*, 285.

22 Gina Reardon-Gaddis, "Catherine Amole Liggett," St. Peter's UCC Cemetery, Knauertown, PA, *Find a Grave Memorial* #24601460, September 1, 2007, BHC.

23 General Orders No. 7, June 13, 1878, *Post Orders*, vol. 9, *July 1, 1875–July 3, 1880*, p. 340, USMA; General Orders No. 10, July 29, 1878, *Post Orders*, vol. 9, *July 1, 1875–July 3, 1880*, p. 348, USMA. Shortly after Liggett's appointment as a sergeant, a classmate and newly appointed cadet lieutenant, Lorenzo L. C. Brooks, was reduced to the ranks for "abuse of office" when he gave an "unauthorized order resulting in interference and molestation" of another cadet. While this freed up another lieutenancy, it is unclear whether Liggett, who was promoted to lieutenant several weeks later, succeeded to that position since another classmate was also promoted at that same time. Special Orders No. 47, July 2, 1878, *Post Orders*, vol. 9, *July 1, 1875–July 3, 1880*, p. 344, USMA.

24 *Official Register (1879)*, 27, 32; Summerall, *The Way of Duty*, 222–23 ("emphasis on engineering"); *Register of Delinquencies*, p. 469, USMA.

25 "West Point Graduates," *New York Times*, June 13, 1879.

26 "West Point Graduates."

27 "West Point Graduates." Liggett would later echo these words at the end of his long career: "No matter how much the machinery of war may be developed," he observed, "in the final analysis it is the *man* we must understand. Man, with all his strength and all his weaknesses, always has been and always will be the basic element, and it is the knowledge of his psychology that we must master when we consider how his best efforts may be developed in war." Hunter Liggett, *Commanding an American Army: Recollections of the World War* (Boston: Houghton Mifflin, 1925), 160–61 (emphasis in the original).

28 "The Army and the Navy," *New York Times*, July 9, 1879; George W. Cullum, *Biographical Register of the Officers and Graduates of the U.S. Military Academy at West Point, New York, from Its Establishment, in 1802, to 1890*, vol. 3, 3rd ed. (Boston: Houghton Mifflin, 1891), 321; Coffman, *The Old Army*, 62 ("three-month leave"). Liggett signed and dated the acknowledgement of receipt of his commission and oath of office in Birdsboro, Pennsylvania. Hunter Liggett to Adjutant General, July 9, 1879, ACP; Oath of Office, July 8, 1879, ACP; Fox, *Reading and Berks County*, 168–69.

Fox is incorrect when he states that James was elected in 1877. Other sources indicate that he served two terms from 1879 through 1883. *Dictionary of American Biography, Supplement One*, 494–95; 1880 US Census, Pennsylvania, Berks County, Birdsboro (Series T9, Roll 1100, Page 259D).

CHAPTER TWO

1 Post Return, Fort Keogh, Montana Territory, October 1879, Returns from US Military Posts, 1800–1916, NARA 94.2.2 (hereafter cited as Post Return); Post Return, Cantonment at Tongue River, Montana Territory, September 1876; Statement of the Military Service of Hunter Liggett, War Department, Washington, DC, March 5, 1936, BHC; 1880 US Census, Montana Territory, Custer County, Fort Keogh (Series T9, Roll 742, Page 74A); Robert Wooster, *Nelson Miles and the Twilight of the Frontier Army* (Lincoln: University of Nebraska Press, 1993), 94–95, 113–14; Robert M. Utley, *Frontier Regulars: The United States Army and the Indian, 1866–1891* (Lincoln: University of Nebraska Press, 1984), 288.

2 Alice Blackwood Baldwin, *Memoirs of the Late Frank D. Baldwin, Major General, U. S. A.* (Los Angeles, CA: Wetzel Publishing, 1929), 12–13, 189.

3 Nelson A. Miles, Report, September 1879, *Annual Report of the Secretary of War for the Year 1879* (Washington, DC: GPO, 1879), 1:74 (hereafter cited as *Annual Report*).

4 It is not possible to determine either Liggett's precise route to Fort Keogh or his means of getting there. I have assumed that he took his full three-month leave following his graduation from West Point. That being the case, he would have begun his journey no earlier than September 13, somewhat late in the season. I have used a *New York Times* reporter's journey, taken just three-months earlier, as a logical guide. "Montana's Rapid Growth," *New York Times*, June 23, 1879.

However, there were alternatives, such as a rough overland route from Bismarck and Fort Abraham Lincoln to Fort Keogh, which was used year-round by the military and travelers but especially during the seven or eight months of the year when navigation on the rivers was not possible. Another factor that could make the steamboat trip impractical was if the water in the Missouri and Yellowstone Rivers was low. In that case, the journey from Bismarck to Miles City, which would normally take eight days, could then take as long as fifteen to twenty days. With the extension of the Northern Pacific from Bismarck to Miles City, it was anticipated that the same trip would take fifteen hours over a more direct route. When Liggett arrived at Miles City, Northern Pacific survey crews were already in the field plotting the route.

5 "Montana's Rapid Growth."

6 "Montana's Rapid Growth."

7 Baldwin, *Memoirs*, 8–10 ("Miles City"); "Montana's Rapid Growth" ("700 inhabitants"); Wooster, *Nelson Miles*, 124 ("frontier rough element"); "Cowboys' Customs," *New York Times*, October 21, 1883 ("firing their pistols").

8 "Montana's Rapid Growth" ("courthouse"); Baldwin, *Memoirs*, 8–10 ("churches").

9 Edmund Morris, *Theodore Rex* (New York: Random House, 2001), 79 ("brave peacock"); Michael E. Shay, *Henry Ware Lawton: Union Infantryman, Frontier Soldier, Charismatic Warrior* (Columbia: University of Missouri Press, 2016), 136 ("Lawton on Miles").

10 Wooster, *Nelson Miles*, 2–4.

11 Post Return, Fort Keogh, January 1880; Emma Ovenshine (1867–1927) is listed in the 1880 Census as "Sallie" age thirteen. It is obvious that the census taker

mistakenly switched the names of mother and daughter. 1880 US Census, Montana Territory, Custer County, Fort Keogh (Series T9, Roll 742, Page 75D); Michael E. Shay, *Revered Commander Maligned General: The Life of Clarence Ransom Edwards, 1859–1931* (Columbia: University of Missouri Press, 2011), 26, 50–51, 80.

12 Liggett, *Ten Years Ago*, 260 ("Baldwin"); Baldwin, *Memoirs*, vii ("energy and resourcefulness"); 1880 US Census, Montana Territory, Custer County, Fort Keogh (Series T9, Roll 742, Pages 74B, 75D); Edward M. Coffman, *The War to End All Wars: The American Military Experience in World War I* (Madison: University of Wisconsin Press, 1986), 249 ("no equal").

13 A US Army horse required fourteen pounds of hay and twelve pounds of grain (a mixture of oats and corn or barley) per day. Erna Risch, *Quartermaster Support of the Army: A History of the Corps 1775–1939* (Washington, DC: Center of Military History, 1989), 379.

14 Don Rickey Jr., *Forty Miles a Day on Beans and Hay: The Enlisted Soldier Fighting the Indian Wars* (Norman: University of Oklahoma Press, 1973), 244–45 ("endurance of fit infantry"); Alfred H. Terry, Report, October 6, 1882, *Annual Report* 1882, 1:84.

15 Nathaniel Philbrick, *The Last Stand: Custer, Sitting Bull, and the Battle of the Little Bighorn* (New York: Penguin, 2010), xvii, 29–30.

16 Cullum, *Biographical Register*, 3:321; Robert M. Utley, *The Lance and the Shield: The Life and Times of Sitting Bull* (New York: Henry Holt, 1993), 167–68 ("disarm and dismount").

17 D. W. Meinig, *The Shaping of America: A Geographical Perspective on 500 Years of History*, vol. 3, *Transcontinental America, 1850–1915* (New Haven, CT: Yale University Press, 1998), 158–59 ("picket-line").

18 In what was undoubtedly a "shakedown" detail, 2nd Lieutenant Liggett, along with one private from Company G assigned to look out for him, accompanied Company K, led by 2nd Lt. Oscar Long, to Fort Abraham Lincoln, Dakota Territory on December 2, 1879, for unspecified detached service. He returned to Fort Keogh on February 28, 1880. Post Return, Fort Keogh, December 1879, and January and February 1880; Cullum, *Biographical Register*, 3:321.

19 Liggett, *Ten Years Ago*, 259 ("on their mettle").

20 Alfred H. Terry, Report to Adjutant General, October 4, 1880, *Annual Report* 1880, 1:63; Post Return, Fort Keogh, March 1880.

21 Record of Events, Post Return, Fort Keogh, March 1880; Alfred H. Terry to Nelson A. Miles, May 29, 1880, published as General Orders No. 3, District of the Yellowstone, June 14, 1880, reprinted in full in the *Helena Herald*, July 1, 1880, p. 1; Alfred H. Terry, Report to Adjutant General, October 4, 1880, *Annual Report* 1880, 1:62–63; Nelson A. Miles, Report, September 21, 1880, *Annual Report* 1880, 1:75.

22 Michael A. Leeson, ed., *A History of Montana. 1739–1885: A History of Its Discovery and Settlement* (Chicago: Warner & Beers, 1885), 536 ("Little Porcupine Creek"); Alfred H. Terry to Nelson A. Miles, May 29, 1880, published as General Orders No. 3, District of the Yellowstone, June 14, 1880, reprinted in full in the *Helena Herald*, July 1, 1880, p. 1; "Gen. Liggett, 78, War Hero, Indian Fighter, Is Dead," *Chicago Tribune*, December 31, 1935, p. 5; Record of Events, Post Return, Fort Keogh, March and April 1880; Alfred H. Terry, Report to Adjutant General, October 4, 1880, *Annual Report* 1880, 1:62–63; Nelson A. Miles, Report, September 21, 1880, *Annual Report* 1880, 1:75; Statement of the Military Service of Hunter Liggett. There are

slight discrepancies among the various sources as to the date of the encounter (e.g. post return [March 8] and the reports of Terry [March 9] and Miles [March 10]). I have used March 9 as that is also used in Liggett's record of service.

23 Post Return, Fort Keogh, June 1880; Alfred H. Terry, Report to Adjutant General, October 4, 1880, *Annual Report* 1880, 1:64–65.

24 Hunter Liggett to "My Dear General [Godfrey]," September 23, 1921 ("bull dog"), MHI. While Liggett's specific route or itinerary for the Bighorn scout is not known, at some point, either coming or going, it took him to the Little Bighorn battle site, as it is on a more or less direct line west from Fort Keogh to the Bighorn Mountains. Moreover, he distinctly mentions touring the battlefield with Philo Clark, who the post returns indicate was on that same expedition and who died just four years later. Finally, although leaves for officers were fairly liberally granted, it is highly unlikely that a relatively new second lieutenant would be in a position to obtain one for that purpose alone.

1st Lt. William Philo Clark (1845–84) was a graduate of West Point (1868) and an aide and scout of General George Crook (1876), who died in Washington, DC, while serving on the staff of General Phil Sheridan. He was the author of the definitive work on Indian sign language titled *The Indian Sign Language*. Statement of the Military Service of Hunter Liggett; Post Return, Fort Keogh, June through September 1880.

25 "A Fight with Stage Robbers," *New York Times*, May 28, 1886 ("driver killed"); "Four Horse Thieves Hanged," *New York Times*, June 12, 1886 ("vigilantes").

26 Post Return, Fort Keogh, October 1880. The most celebrated attempted US Army payroll robbery in the Montana Territory took place on May 14, 1884, near Glendive. Maj. Charles Henry Whipple, a US Army paymaster, with a sergeant as a guard, was carrying thirty thousand dollars from Glendive to Fort Buford via stagecoach when seven masked men attempted a robbery. Sergeant Conrad of the 7th Cavalry was killed and the stage driver was wounded. However, in the ruckus, Whipple managed to slip out of the coach and escape into the underbrush with the payroll intact. The local sheriff caught up with the robbers, who fled after a gun battle. Maj. J. Franklin Bell and Company F, 7th Cavalry, were dispatched from Fort Buford to aid in the pursuit. It is not known if the highwaymen were ever caught. However, an arrest was made of a local horse dealer who had aided the would-be thieves. Whipple ended his distinguished military career as paymaster general of the US Army. Alfred H. Terry, Report, October 6, 1884, *Annual Report* 1884, 1:111–12; "Resisting Arrest by Sheriff," *New York Times*, May 22, 1884; "Charles Henry Whipple (General)," Whipple Website, http://whipple.org, accessed December 2016.

27 Record of Events, Post Return, Fort Keogh, November and December 1880, and January 1881.

28 Record of Events, Post Return, Fort Keogh, November and December 1880, and January 1881; Alfred H. Terry, Report, October 9, 1881, *Annual Report* 1881, 1:91–93, 101–6; Montana Lou Grill, "The Capture of Chief Gall and Crow, the Last except Sitting Bull to Surrender to the Military Authorities in the Early Part of 1881" (six-page typescript, n.d.), Archives and Special Collections, Mansfield Library, University of Montana; Ojibwa, "The Sioux Return," Native American Netroots, April 29, 2011, http://nativeamericannetroots.net/diary/939.

29 Record of Events, Post Return, Fort Keogh, March and April 1881. The situation would repeat itself in February 1881, when warmer temperatures quickly melted the

heavy winter snowpack within a three-day period and the ice in the Yellowstone River began to crack. "From the Flooded Districts," *New York Times*, February 27, 1884.

30 Hunter Liggett to Adjutant General, April 24, 1881, ACP. It is also possible that Harriet's father had business at Fort Keogh and brought the family along.

31 Post Return, Fort Keogh, June 1881; Alfred H. Terry, Report, October 9, 1881, *Annual Report* 1881, 1:96. General Terry's Report indicates that the guard consisted of five officers and one hundred enlisted men aboard five steamers (*Eclipse*, *Josephine*, *Helena*, *General Terry*, and *General Sherman*). The post return for the month of June 1881 states quite clearly that five full companies (A, C, E, F, and G) left the post on June 13 and that Liggett was on duty with his company. I consider the latter to be more accurate.

32 *Dictionary of American Biography, Supplement One*, 494–95 ("Harriet Lane"); Fox, *Reading and Berks County*, 2:169; Post Return, Fort Keogh, July (including "1st Endorsement dated September 3, 1881") and August 1881; Robert Lee Bullard, *Personalities and Reminiscences of the War* (Garden City, NY: Doubleday, 1925), 143 ("sing his praises").

33 Certificate of Death, April 29, 1939, Office of the County Clerk, City and County of San Francisco, CA, April 29, 1939; 1860 US Census, Texas, Fredericksburg, Gillespie County (Series M653, Roll 1295, Page 26); 1870 US Census, Texas, San Antonio, Bexar County (Series M593, Roll ___, Page 182); 1870 US Census, Wyoming Territory, Fort Sanders, Albany County (Series M593, Roll ___, Page 26); 1880 US Census, Wyoming Territory, Fort Sanders, Albany County (Series T9, Roll 1454, Page 53C).

34 Fox, *Reading and Berks County*, 2:169; Post Return, Fort Keogh, July (including "1st Endorsement dated September 3, 1881") and August 1881.

35 Post Return, Fort Keogh, August 1881; Baldwin, *Memoirs*, 13–15, 31.

36 Post Return, Fort Keogh, September through December 1881 ("usual company duties"); Report, Alfred H. Terry, October 9, 1881, *Annual Report* 1881, 1:99; Report, Alfred H. Terry, October 6, 1882, *Annual Report* 1882, 1:83, 85.

37 *The River Press* (Fort Benton), December 14, 1881, p. 8 ("great rejoicing").

38 Post Return, Fort Keogh, January through August 1882.

39 Post Return, Fort Keogh, September and October 1882; Report, Terry, October 6, 1882, *Annual Report* 1882, 1:92.

40 *Daily Yellowstone Journal*, February 8, 1883, p. 4; Post Return, Fort Keogh, December 1883, January through May 1883, and November 1883.

41 Post Return, Fort Keogh, May 1883 through June 1884; Efficiency Report, May 1, 1890, ACP ("surveying course").

42 Hunter Liggett to Adjutant General, July 16, 1884, ACP; and Oath of Office, July 16, 1884, ACP; Statement of the Military Service of Hunter Liggett; Post Return, Fort Keogh, June and July 1884; *Daily Enterprise*, July 5, 1884, p. 4.

43 *Daily Yellowstone Journal*, January 24, 1885, p. 3; Post Return, Fort Keogh, November 1884 and January 1885; Miki Pfeffer, "Memories of the 1884 Cotton Centennial Exposition," *New Orleans Historical*, http://www.neworleanshistorical.org/items/show/196, accessed August 6, 2018; "1884: World Cotton Exposition Opens in New Orleans," *Times-Picayune*, December 1, 2014.

44 Post Return, Fort Keogh, February 1885 through November 1885; Liggett, *Ten Years Ago*, 291 ("map making").

45 Record of Events, Post Return, Fort Keogh, November and December 1885; Report, Thomas H. Ruger, September 6, 1886, *Annual Report* 1886, 1:130–31; *Daily Yellowstone Journal*, November 24, 1885, p. 1; *Semi-Weekly Miner*, November 30, 1885.

46 *Daily Yellowstone Journal*, December 25, 1885, p. 1.

47 *Daily Yellowstone Journal*, January 12, 1886, p. 3 ("subdivision"); Post Return, Fort Keogh, January through June 1886.

48 "Pretty Hot at Fort Keogh," *New York Times*, July 16, 1886; Post Return, Fort Keogh, July 1886.

49 Report, Thomas H. Ruger to Assistant Adjutant General, August 30, 1887, *Annual Report* 1887, 1:137.

50 Ruger to Assistant Adjutant General, *Annual Report* 1887, 1:138–40, 148; Post Return, Fort Keogh, August 1886; *Daily Yellowstone Journal*, August 17, 1886, p. 1. The *Journal* reported that Company F left Keogh on Sunday (August 15) and that Liggett had left the following night. I have followed the official *Annual Report*.

51 Cullum, *Biographical Register*, 3:321; Post Return, Fort Totten, Dakota Territory, August, September, and October 1886 ("Harriet").

52 Post Return, Fort Totten, September 1886; *Devils Lake Inter-Ocean*, September 4, 1886, p. 1.

53 Harold W. Schunk, "History of Fort Totten," United States Department of the Interior (scanned and formatted by Kathryn Thomas at North Dakota State Libraries, February 26, 2004), available at http://www.library.ndsu.edu/exhibit/text/forttotten.html, accessed August 31, 2015.

54 Baldwin, *Memoirs*, 32–34. The American Indians called the lake "Minnewaukan," which means "Spirit Water." However, a later legend involving the drowning of two bands of Indians at the hands of the lake's spirit, resulted in the lake being called "Devils Lake." Schunk, "History of Fort Totten."

55 Post Return, Fort Totten, October 1886, July 1887, August 1887, December 1887, and January 1888; *Bismarck Weekly Tribune*, July 15, 1887, p. 1 ("post commissary").

56 Coffman, *The Old Army*, 355; Rickey, *Forty Miles a Day*, 86; Thomas R. Buecker, *Fort Robinson and the American West 1874–1899* (Norman: University of Oklahoma Press, 2003), 155; Alfred H. Terry, Report, October 8, 1883, *Annual Report* 1883, 1:117 (discussing marksmanship); *Daily Yellowstone Journal*, September 28, 1884, p. 1. Qualification for sharpshooter required a score of 88 percent at two hundred, three hundred, and six hundred yards, as well as 76 percent at eight hundred, nine hundred, and one thousand yards. The US Army also sponsored shooting competitions and encouraged all officers and enlisted men to compete on behalf of their company or regiment. In an ironic twist, since the US Army did not pay for travel expenses to these events, some soldiers purposely depressed their scores so as not to be pressured to compete. Alfred H. Terry, Report, September 16, 1885, *Annual Report* 1885, 1:121 ("depressing scores").

57 Post Return, Fort Totten, October 1886; *Devils Lake Inter-Ocean*, October 16, 1886.

58 Baldwin, *Memoirs*, 32–34; *Devils Lake Inter-Ocean*, December 4, 1886, p. 1 ("sleigh"); Post Return, Fort Totten, December 1886 and January 1887 ("cutting and putting up").

59 Post Return, Fort Totten, June and August 1887; Baldwin, *Memoirs*, 33; *Devils Lake Inter-Ocean*, June 18, 1887 ("aquatic picnic").

60 Post Return, Fort Totten, September and October 1887; Obituary, *Reading Eagle*, September 27, 1887; "Tombstone Inscriptions," St. Paul's Methodist Episcopal Church, Geigertown, PA, BHC. While I cannot be certain that Liggett went to

see his father, given the timing and the circumstances, I believe that it is reasonable to assume that he did so.

61 Baldwin, *Memoirs*, 34 ("salubrious"); Post Return, Fort Totten, May 1888, RG94 NARA ("march out").

62 *Jamestown (ND) Weekly Alert*, June 7, 1888; *Bismarck Weekly Tribune*, June 1, 1888.

63 Record of Events, Post Return, Fort McIntosh, Texas, June 1888; *Omaha Daily Bee*, June 11, 1888, p. 8.

64 *Omaha Daily Bee*, June 12, 1888, p. 5; *Jamestown Weekly Alert*, June 14, 1888, p. 8.

65 Record of Events, Post Return, Fort McIntosh, June 1888; *Omaha Daily Bee*, June 13, 1888, p. 5.

66 *Omaha Daily Bee*, June 24, 1888, p. 8.

CHAPTER THREE

1 Garna L. Christian, "Fort McIntosh," *Handbook of Texas Online* (Denton: Texas State Historical Association, 2010), available at http://www.tshaonline.org/handbook/online/articles/qbf35, accessed August 31, 2015; Robert G. Carter, *On the Border with Mackenzie, or Winning West Texas from the Comanches* (Austin: Texas State Historical Association, 2007), 35, 56–57.

2 Post Return, Fort McIntosh, June through August 1888.

3 Post Return, Fort McIntosh, October 1888 through January 1889.

4 Post Return, Fort McIntosh, March 1889 through March 1890.

5 Coffman, *The Old Army*, 281.

6 Efficiency Report, May 1, 1890, ACP.

7 Post Return, Fort McIntosh, March through August 1890; Special Return, Fort McIntosh, Texas, August 1890, RG94 NARA.

8 Robert Wooster, *Frontier Crossroads: Fort Davis and the West* (College Station: Texas A&M University Press, 2006), 15, 30–32, 76–78, 101–7 ("Victorio Campaign").

9 Post Return, Fort Davis, Texas, October and November 1890; Statement of the Military Service of Hunter Liggett; Thomas A. Britten, *A Brief History of the Seminole-Negro Indian Scouts* (Lewiston, NY: Edwin Mellen Press, 1999), 93–98. Dr. Britten's account of these soldiers presents an excellent picture of their history and exploits.

The Seminole-Negro Indian Scouts were not American Indians at all. Rather, they were African Americans, sometimes referred to as "maroons," mostly former slaves who had fled to Florida and were received by the Seminoles in a mainly servile capacity at first. As the close relationship between the two peoples evolved over time, they continued to maintain a separate identity, and were often referred to as "Black Seminoles." They followed the Seminoles from Florida to Oklahoma and even into Mexico, where they earned a solid reputation as reliable scouts and excellent fighters. With the continuing border troubles with Mexico following the Civil War, the US Army enticed some Black Seminoles to return, and in August 1870, Maj. Zenas Bliss enlisted the first Seminole-Negro Indian Scouts at Fort Duncan, Texas. Even he was surprised to learn that they were in fact not Native American when he saw them for the first time. They and their families settled near Fort Duncan at first, but later at Fort Clark in Brackettville, Texas, which became their base. For the next forty-plus years until they were finally disbanded in 1914, these loyal scouts, led by white officers, patrolled the border area for raiders and cattle thieves, in addition to pursuing hostile Apache and Comanche. Sadly, despite their long, loyal service, the US government failed to honor its initial commitment to provide land based on a number of specious excuses. David S. Heidler and Jeanne T. Heidler, *Old Hickory's War: Andrew Jackson and the Quest for Empire* (Mechanicsburg, PA: Stackpole, 1996), 36 ("maroons").

10 N. W. Osborne to Adjutant General, October 18, 1890, ACP; H. Liggett to Regimental Adjutant, October 31, 1890, ACP. The Fort at Willets Point (now Fort Totten) was home to the Army Engineer School of Application. The brightest graduates West Point were appointed to the corps of engineers, so for Liggett, this would definitely have been a choice assignment and made in recognition of his drive to educate himself as a US Army officer, especially this early in his career. In addition to standard engineering training, the Torpedo School there was a laboratory for the design of improved weaponry. The course length was two and a half years, which is why Liggett may have balked at the assignment. Marjorie Pearson, "Fort Totten Historic District, Borough of Queens, a Designation Report," New York City Landmarks Preservation Commission (New York: City of New York, 1999), 13–17; McGovern, "The School of Experience," 403–4 ("Point").

11 Post Return, Fort Davis, November and December 1890; Shay, *Revered Commander*, 29–30.

12 Post Return, Fort Davis, January through May 1891.

13 Post Return, Fort Davis, June 1891; Wooster, *Frontier Crossroads*, 137–39.

14 John Manguso, "Fort Sam Houston," *Handbook of Texas Online* (Denton: Texas State Historical Association, 2010), available at http://www.tshaonline.org/handbook/online/articles/qbf43, accessed August 31, 2015; Post Return, Fort Sam Houston, Texas, July 1891.

15 Buecker, *Fort Robinson*, 154–55 ("camps of instruction"); Post Return, Fort Sam Houston, August 1891.

16 Post Return, Fort Sam Houston, September 1891 through January 1892.

17 Efficiency Report, January 1, 1892, ACP.

18 Efficiency Report, December 15, 1891, ACP; Officer's Individual Report, February 5, 1894, and Efficiency Report, February 5, 1894, ACP.

19 Special Orders No. 38, Headquarters 5th US Infantry, April 25, 1892, ACP; Special Orders No. 103, par. 17, Headquarters of the Army, Adjutant General's Office, May 2, 1892, ACP ("appointment as Regimental Adjutant"); Post Return, Fort Sam Houston, January through May 1892.

20 Post Return, St. Francis Barracks, Florida, May 1892.

21 Robert Hawk, "St. Francis Barracks: From Monastery to State Arsenal" (St. Augustine: Florida Department of Military Affairs, 2011), available at http://www.dma.myflorida.com, accessed August 31, 2015.

22 Post Return, St. Francis Barracks, May, July, and September 1892; King, "General Hunter Liggett," 8.

23 Post Return, St. Francis Barracks, October ("leave") and December 1892 ("examination board"); Special Orders No. 292, par. 12, Headquarters of the Army, Adjutant General's Office, December 14, 1892, ACP; Report of Examination, December 27, 1892, ACP; Notice, Adjutant General's Office, January 18, 1893, ACP.

24 Officer's Individual Report, February 5, 1894, and Efficiency Report, February 5, 1894, ACP.

25 Post Return, St. Francis Barracks, January through March, September and October 1893; *New York Times*, September 22, 1893.

26 Post Return, St. Francis Barracks, January through April 1894, RG94 NARA.
27 Efficiency Report, February 28, 1894, ACP; and Officer's Individual Report, February 5, 1894, ACP.
28 H. Liggett to Adjutant General, Telegram, September 5, 1894, ACP; Post Return, St. Francis Barracks, January, and August and September 1894.
29 Record of Events, Post Return, St. Francis Barracks, October 1894.
30 Elizabeth J. Whaley, *Forgotten Hero: General James B. McPherson* (Fremont, OH: Lesher Printers, 1976), 159–60; Statement of the Military Service of Hunter Liggett; George W. Cullum, *Biographical Register of the Officers and Graduates of the U.S. Military Academy at West Point, New York, since Its Establishment in 1802, Supplement*, vol. 4, *1890–1900* (Cambridge, MA: Riverside Press, 1901), 315.
31 Record of Events, Post Return, Fort McPherson, Georgia, October through December 1894; Special Field Return, Fort McPherson, Georgia, October 19, 1894, RG94 NARA.
32 Post Return, Fort McPherson, October 1894; Jack McCallum, *Leonard Wood: Rough Rider, Surgeon, Architect of American Imperialism* (New York: New York University Press, 2006), 49–52; Post Return, Fort McPherson, September 1895.
33 Post Return, Fort McPherson, May 1895.
34 Efficiency Report, June 30, 1895, ACP; Officer's Individual Report, June 30, 1895, ACP.
35 Post Return, Fort McPherson, July 1895.
36 Record of Events, Post Return, Fort McPherson, September through December 1895; "The Atlanta Exposition," *New York Times*, September 19, 1895; "The Atlanta Exposition," *New York Times*, October 22, 1895.
37 Joseph C. Breckinridge to Secretary of War, May 28, 1896, ACP.
38 Record of Events, Post Return, Fort McPherson, March and April 1896.
39 Efficiency Report, June 30, 1896, ACP; Officer's Individual Report, June 22, 1896, ACP.
40 Record of Events, Post Return, Fort McPherson, July through September 1896.
41 Post Return, Fort McPherson, October and November 1896 and January 1897 ("court marshal").
42 Record of Events, Post Return, Fort McPherson, April 1897; Efficiency Report, June 30, 1897, ACP.
43 "Nashville's Exposition," *New York Times*, June 20, 1897. The actual centennial of the city's founding was a year earlier on May 1, 1896; however, given the difficult economic times, the organizers had exercised fiscal restraint during the planning process.
44 Special Orders No. 93, Adjutant General's Office, April 22, 1897, RG94 NARA; Record of Events, Post Return, Fort McPherson, May and June 1897, ACP; H. Liggett to Adjutant General, July 4, 1897 (Request to Correct Muster Roll and Post Return for May), ACP; and Correction to Muster Roll and Post Return, July 10, 1897, ACP.
45 Acknowledgement of Receipt of Commission, June 21, 1897, and Oath of Office, June 21, 1897, ACP; "Captain Romeyn Retired," *New York Times*, June 2, 1897; Post Return, Fort McPherson, June 1897; Statement of the Military Service of Hunter Liggett; Cullum, *Biographical Register, Supplement*, vol. 4, *1890–1900*, 315; Coffman, *The Old Army*, 31, 233 ("promotion policy"). Henry Romeyn was a valiant officer, who saw extensive service as a volunteer during the Civil War, where he was brevetted as

a brigadier general, and he remained in the US Army thereafter. He was awarded the Medal of Honor and brevetted captain for his courage and gallantry during the fight at Bear Paw Mountain, Montana Territory, on September 30, 1877, at which time he was wounded. As a result of that engagement, Chief Joseph of the Nez Percé surrendered to General Miles. "Henry Romeyn, Major, United States Army," Arlington National Cemetery Website, last updated August 17, 2003, http://arlingtoncemetery.net/henryrom.htm, accessed June 2, 2016.

46 Efficiency Record, June 30, 1897, ACP; Officer's Individual Report, June 30, 1897, ACP.

47 Post Return, Fort McPherson, September and October 1897.

48 Robert J. Lowry to Mark A. Hanna, July 3, 1897, ACP; and Robert J. Lowry to William McKinley, January 7, 1898, ACP.

49 W. Y. Atkinson to the President of the United States, February 3, 1898 ("Georgia"), ACP; William T. Newman to the President of the United States, February 1, 1898, ACP; W. L. Strong to the President of the United States, October 5, 1897, ACP; Memorandum for the Secretary of War, February 28, 1898, ACP.

50 Record of Events, Post Return, Fort McPherson, October 1898.

51 George T. Fry, "Gen. Liggett's Rise Due to Sheer Industry," *Sun*, March 17, 1918.

52 Record of Events, Post Return, Fort McPherson, October and November 1898.

53 Post Return, Fort McPherson, December 1897 and February 1898.

54 Record of Events, Post Return, Fort McPherson, April 1898.

CHAPTER FOUR

1 Brian McAllister Linn, *The Philippine War 1899–1902* (Lawrence: University Press of Kansas, 2000), 16–19 (rise of Philippine nationalism); Stuart Creighton Miller, *"Benevolent Assimilation": The American Conquest of the Philippines, 1899–1903* (New Haven, CT: Yale University Press, 1982), 34–36 ("Philippine nationalists"); David Traxel, *1898: The Birth of the American Century* (New York: Knopf, 1998), 78–80 ("Cuban insurgency"); Gregg Jones, *Honor in the Dust: Theodore Roosevelt, War in the Philippines, and the Rise and Fall of America's Imperial Dream* (New York: New American Library, 2012), 93–95; David Trask, *The War with Spain in 1898* (Lincoln: University of Nebraska Press, 1996), 8, 30–37; Ivan Musicant, *Empire by Default: The Spanish-American War and the Dawn of the American Century* (New York: Henry Holt, 1998), 96; Frederick Funston, *Memories of Two Wars: Cuban and Philippine Experiences* (Lincoln: University of Nebraska Press, 2009), 3–28.

2 Trask, *War with Spain*, 145–46; Musicant, *Empire by Default*, 239–45; Millett, *The General*, 82–83 ("Quartermaster").

3 Trask, *War with Spain*, 183; Musicant, *Empire by Default*, 243.

4 H. Liggett to Adjutant General, Personal Report, July 6, 1898, ACP ("Ft. St. Philip"); Post Return, Fort St. Philip, Louisiana, May and June 1898; Return of Captain Hunter Liggett, Company D of the 5th Regiment Infantry, Army of the United States, Santiago de Cuba, August 1898, RG94 NARA.

5 Shay, *Revered Commander*, 29–30.

6 "Many Officers Mustered Out," *New York Times*, March 14, 1899; Cullum, *Biographical Register, Supplement*, vol. 4, *1890–1900*, 315.

7 Notation for File, Adjutant General's Office, ACP.

8 Liggett to Adjutant General, April 12, 1899, ACP ("brief respite"); Liggett to Adjutant General, April 30, 1899, ACP ("left post"); Post Return, Santiago de Cuba

Barracks, Cuba, May and June 1899; Post Return, El Caney, Cuba, July 1899; Return of Captain Hunter Liggett, Company D of the 5th Infantry, Army of the United States, El Caney, Cuba, July 1899, RG94 NARA; Efficiency Report, June 30, 1899, ACP; Statement of the Military Service of Hunter Liggett. One source indicates that Liggett was invalided home from Cuba with typhoid fever; this was not the case. *Birdsboro Dispatch*, January 3, 1936.

9 "Succinct Account of Services," Efficiency Report, Part A, July 1, 1900, ACP. At some point during the initial sorting process at Fort Thomas, Liggett was assigned to the 2nd Battalion, but when all was said and done his final assignment was the 3rd Battalion. Statement of the Military Service of Hunter Liggett; Cullum, *Biographical Register, Supplement*, vol. 4, *1890–1900*, 315; General Orders No. 20, August 13, 1899, 31st US Volunteer Infantry Order Book, p. 4, RG94 NARA ("Summary Court Officer"); General Orders No. 2, par. 2, August 23, 1899, 31st US Volunteer Infantry Order Book, p. 5, RG94 NARA ("thievery"); General Orders No. 14, August 4, 1899, 31st US Volunteer Infantry Order Book, p. 2, RG94 NARA ("bathing naked").

Webb Cook Hayes (1856–1934) was the second son of Rutherford and Lucy Hayes. He served at various times as his father's secretary and was a cofounder of the National Carbon Company, the predecessor of Union Carbide. Hayes served with distinction during the Spanish-American War and in the Philippines. Later, during World War I, he received a commission as a colonel, and he served in both France and Italy in special assignments. "Webb Cook Hayes [1856–1934]," Rutherford B. Hayes Presidential Library & Museums, https://www.rbhayes.org/hayes/webb-cook-hayes/, accessed July 11, 2016.

10 "Succinct Account of Services"; Trask, *War with Spain*, 158 ("Presidio").

11 Webb C. Hayes, diary, October 26 through November 3, 1899, RBHL.

12 Hayes, diary, November 3 and November 4, 1899.

13 Hayes, diary, November 3 and November 4, 1899.

14 Hayes, diary, November 4 and November 5, 1899.

15 Hayes, diary, November 6 through November 16, 1899.

16 Hayes, diary, November 17 through November 19, 1899. Hayes refers to the island as "Assumption Island" and refers to it as "essentially a volcano." Since the actual Assumption Island is in the Seychelles near Madagascar, he is mistaken in the name, but not the fact that the ship stopped at an island with a volcanic cone that was "belching out smoke and probably lava." No doubt he was referring to Asuncion Island (Spanish for Assumption, hence the confusion) in the Northern Marianas, with a 2,800-foot volcanic cone, which last erupted in 1906. https://www.volcanodiscovery.com/asuncion.html, accessed August 6, 2018.

17 Fry, "Gen. Liggett's Rise." This anecdote was written nearly twenty years after the fact, no doubt to demonstrate Liggett's sense of humor and his fierce determination to succeed. Hayes makes no specific mention of it in his diary, but it would be consistent with Liggett's character and leadership style, and as it was his battalion, he would not have taken a "hands-off" approach under those extraordinary circumstances. The *Sun* article was written by George T. Fry, who had met Liggett during the run up to the war with Spain and who, more important, was then a passenger on the *City of Peking* en route to the Philippines and in a position to write about the voyage. The two men remained friends for decades. While Fry could well have "made a good story better," I believe that at the core, the story rings true. The

story is retold in other newspaper accounts. *Chattanooga News*, August 8, 1918, p. 10; "General Liggett in Work and War," *New York Times*, September 29, 1918 ("lick anything").

18 Hayes, diary, November 20 through November 22, 1899.

19 Fry, "Gen. Liggett's Rise"; *Chattanooga News*, August 8, 1918, p. 10; Hayes, diary, November 22 through November 25, 1899.

20 Gene Smith, *Until the Last Trumpet Sounds: The Life of General of the Armies John J. Pershing* (New York: Wiley, 1998), 57. The command had recently passed to Kobbé from Brig. Gen. John Bates, who was recalled to Manila after the sudden death of Maj. Gen. Henry Ware Lawton in battle at San Mateo in Luzon, on December 19, 1899. Hayes, diary, December 29, 1899.

21 "Succinct Account of Services"; Hayes, diary, November 28 and November 29, 1899. In his diary, Hayes called his steamship the *Jupiter*, when in fact it was the SS *Brutus*. No doubt, though, it fit the description of the old tub *Immanuense*. Record of Events, Post Return, Post of Zamboanga, Mindanao, Philippines, December 1899. Built in Great Britain in 1894, the SS *Brutus* (originally the SS *Peter Jebsen*) was acquired by the US Navy in San Francisco, California, on April 21, 1898. She was commissioned as a collier (Fuel Ship #15) on May 27 of that same year and served off and on until she was finally decommissioned in 1921. Gary P. Priolo, "USS *Brutus* (AC-15)" NavSource Naval History, last updated February 2, 2018, http://www.navsource.org/archives/09/02/0215.htm.

22 Record of Events, Post Return, Post of Zamboanga, Mindanao, Philippines, December 1899; "Succinct Account of Services"; Post Return, Davao, Mindanao, Philippines, February and May 1900; William A. Kobbé, diary, May 13 and 14, 1900, MHI ("transfer of Company K"); Statement of the Military Service of Hunter Liggett.

23 Linn, *The Philippine War*, 225–26; McCallum, *Leonard Wood*, 205–6.

24 John M. Gates, *Schoolbooks and Krags: The United States Army in the Philippines, 1898–1902* (Westport, CT: Greenwood, 1973), vii ("Civilize 'em"), 88–92, 199–200 ("Kobbé's plan for self-government"); McCallum, *Leonard Wood*, 205–6.

25 Brian McAllister Linn, *Guardians of Empire: The U.S. Army and the Pacific, 1902–1940* (Chapel Hill: University of North Carolina Press, 1997), 47–48 ("four-fifths"); Kobbé, diary, May 2, 1900 ("singularly unfortunate"); Linn, *The Philippine War*, 227–28 ("needless antagonism").

26 Kobbé, diary, October 31, 1900 ("quarterly returns").

27 Special Orders No. 1, Post Davao, December 26, 1899, Company Orders, 31st US Volunteer Infantry Order Book, RG94 NARA; General Orders No. 1, Post Davao, December 26, 1899, Company Orders, 31st US Volunteer Infantry Order Book, RG94 NARA.

28 Memorandum, Post Davao, February 14, 1900, Company I, Company Orders, 31st US Volunteer Infantry Order Book, p. 13, RG94 NARA.

29 General Orders No. 13, Post Davao, May 19, 1900, Company Orders, 31st US Volunteer Infantry Order Book, RG94 NARA.

30 Memorandum, Post Davao, May 22, 1900, 31st US Volunteer Infantry Order Book, RG94 NARA.

31 General Orders No. 17, June 13, 1900, RG94 NARA; Memorandum, June 25, 1900 ("spoiled children"), Company Orders, 31st US Volunteer Infantry Order Book, RG94 NARA.

32 Kobbé, diary, May 14, 1900 ("$3,000.00"); Post Return, Davao, Mindanao, Philippines, May 1900.
33 Efficiency Report, July 1, 1900, ACP; Special Orders No. 38, Post Davao, July 26, 1900, Company Orders, 31st US Volunteer Infantry Order Book, RG94 NARA.
34 Kobbé, diary, August 25, 1900; Post Return, Davao, Mindanao, Philippines, August 1900.
35 Post Return, Davao, Mindanao, Philippines, November 1900 ("Pettit"); Kobbé, diary, November 29, 1900 ("murders").
36 Post Return, Davao, Mindanao, Philippines, December 1900.
37 Post Return, Davao, Mindanao, Philippines, January, February, and March 1901.
38 Memorandum, Post Davao, March 26, 1901, Company Orders, 31st US Volunteer Infantry Order Book, RG94 NARA.
39 Special Orders No. 80, Headquarters Department of Mindanao and Jolo, April 26, 1901, Company Orders, 31st US Volunteer Infantry Order Book, RG94 NARA ("relief"); Special Orders No. 41, Part I, Post Davao, May 1, 1901 ("turn in equipment").
40 Post Return, Davao, Mindanao, Philippines, May and June 1901.
41 Kobbé, diary, May 12, 13, and 14, 1901.
42 Shay, *Henry Ware Lawton*, 199 ("six weeks behind"); Harriet to Henry C. Corbin, June 10, 1901, ACP; Henry C. Corbin to Harriet Liggett, June 15, 1901, ACP.
43 Post Return, Davao, Mindanao, P. I., July, August, and September and October 1901; Special Field Return, Davao, Mindanao, P. I., September 1901, RG94 NARA.
44 Statement of the Military Service of Hunter Liggett; George W. Cullum, *Biographical Register of the Officers and Graduates of the U.S. Military Academy at West Point, New York, since Its Establishment in 1802, Supplement*, vol. 5, *1900–1910* (Saginaw, MI: Seemann & Peters, 1910), 295.
45 Special Orders No. 91, Headquarters Department of North Philippines, April 9, 1902, ACP; Adjutant General to Hunter Liggett, May 21, 1902, ACP; Summary of Examination, April 14, 1902, ACP; Acknowledgement of Receipt of Commission and Oath of Office, July 9, 1902, ACP.
46 Harriet Lane Liggett to Henry C. Corbin, June 5, 1902, ACP.
47 J.[Jefferson] R. Kean to Adjutant General, March 30, 1903, ACP ("disappointed"); General Orders No. 69, par. 4, Headquarters 31st Volunteer Infantry, Zamboanga, Philippines, December 12, 1899, 31st US Volunteer Infantry Order Book, p. 11, RG94 NARA ("insulting native women"). As a case in point, soon after arriving at Zamboanga, Liggett issued a memo to the men of the 3rd Battalion to the effect that when they were outside the "immediate vicinity of their tents" they were to be "properly dressed," wearing their blue shirts and khaki pants. For emphasis, he added, "The habit of going to meals or elsewhere in undershirts will be stopped at once." Memorandum, Zamboanga, Philippines, December 15, 1899, Company I, 31st US Volunteer Infantry Order Book, p. 13, RG94 NARA.

CHAPTER FIVE

1 Minnesota Historical Society, "Historic Fort Snelling," historicfortsnelling.org/history/timeline, accessed June 11, 2016.
2 Special Orders No. 155, Headquarters Department of Dakota, September 17, 1902, ACP; H. Liggett to Adjutant General, September 19, 1902, ACP; Special Orders No. 226, Headquarters of the Army, Adjutant General's Office, September 25, 1902,

ACP; Post Return, Fort Snelling, Minnesota, December 1902 and January through March 1903; *New York Times*, December 28, 1902 ("summary court"); *New York Times*, March 21, 1903 ("promotion board").

3 Record of Events, Post Return, Fort Snelling, April 1903.

4 *St. Paul Globe*, April 23, 1903, p. 1, available at http://sites.mnhs.org/historic-sites/alexander-ramsey-house/history, accessed June 9, 2016.

5 Record of Events, Post Return, Fort Snelling, April 1903; *St. Paul Globe*, April 26, 1903, p. 1.

6 Record of Events, Post Return, Fort Snelling, May 1903.

7 Record of Events, Post Return, Fort Snelling, July and August 1903.

8 Special Orders No. 17, pars. 8, 9, War Department, September 3, 1903, ACP; Statement of the Military Service of Hunter Liggett; Cullum, *Biographical Register, Supplement*, vol. 5, *1900–1910*, 295; Perret, *Eisenhower*, 90 ("rotating assignments").

9 "Bull Run Manoevers to Be like Real Warfare," *New York Times*, August 14, 1904.

10 Brig. Gen. Funston to Military Secretary, Telegram, January 4, 1905, ACP; Special Orders No. 4, War Department, January 6, 1905, ACP.

11 Sharon Shugart, *The Hot Springs of Arkansas through the Years: A Chronology of Events, Excerpts* (Hot Springs, AR: Department of the Interior, National Park Service, 2004); Richard T. Smith, "Rheumatic Diseases," chap. 18 in *History of the Office of Medical History* (Fort Sam Houston, TX: US Army Medical Department, Office of Medical History, n.d.), 477–82 ("mecca"), available at http://history.amedd.army.mil/history.html, accessed July 2, 2016.

12 Taylor to Military Secretary, Telegram, February 23, 1905, ACP; Special Orders No. 46, War Department, February 25, 1905, ACP.

13 Field Return, Fort Benjamin Harrison, Indiana, September 1906, RG94 NARA.

14 Statement of the Military Service of Hunter Liggett; Cullum, *Biographical Register, Supplement*, vol. 5, *1900–1910*, 295.

15 Merrill J. Mattes, *The Great Platte River Road: The Covered Wagon Mainline via Fort Kearny to Fort Laramie* (Lincoln: University of Nebraska Press, 1969), 110–12; Edward M. Coffman, *The Regulars: The American Army, 1898–1941* (Cambridge, MA: Harvard University Press, 2007), 179.

16 Coffman, *The Regulars*, 177; Liggett, *Ten Years Ago*, 286–87; Harry P. Ball, *Of Responsible Command: A History of the U.S. Army War College, the School That Shaped the Military Leaders of the Free World* (Carlisle Barracks, PA: Alumni Association of the US Army War College, 1994), 24–25, 29; Forrest C. Pogue, *George C. Marshall: Education of a General, 1880–1939* (New York: Viking, 1963), 62 ("resumed").

17 Ball, *Of Responsible Command*, 90–91; Coffman, *The Old Army*, 269–70, 281, 355–65 ("efficiency reports, etc."); Rickey, *Forty Miles a Day*, 86, 103–5 ("marksmanship"); Buecker, *Fort Robinson*, 154–55 ("camps of instruction"); Utley, *Frontier Regulars*, 44 ("professional journals"); Coffman, *The Regulars*, 177–82 ("Command and Staff School").

18 Post Return, Fort Leavenworth, Kansas, October 1907; Statement of the Military Service of Hunter Liggett; Cullum, *Biographical Register, Supplement*, vol. 5, *1900–1910*, 295.

19 Post Return, Fort Leavenworth, December 1907 through June 2008.

20 Report of Physical Examination and Riding or Walking Test, October 12, 1908, ACP.

21 Ball, *Of Responsible Command*, 37 ("catalyst"), 57 ("to prepare for war"), 61–67 ("Ludlow Board"); Pogue, *Education of a General*, 58–63; McGovern, "The School of Experience," 397, 417–18 ("Root Reforms"). Nelson Miles was the last commanding general of the US Army, and, quite understandably, he felt that the position should have stronger powers. On the other hand, he did support the consolidation of some bureaus and the merit selection of officers. Wooster, *Nelson Miles*, 73–74, 242–44.

22 Liggett, *Ten Years Ago*, 285; Bullard, *Personalities and Reminiscences of the War*, 143 ("military highbrow"); Coffman, *The Regulars*, 95 ("one of the finest minds").

23 Larry I. Bland, ed., *The Papers of George Catlett Marshall*, vol. 1, *"The Soldierly Spirit," December 1880–June* 1939 (Baltimore: Johns Hopkins University Press, 1981), 93; Liggett, *Ten Years Ago*, 288.

24 Post Return, Fort Leavenworth, August and November 1908, and April and May 1909.

25 H. Liggett to Adjutant General, November 1, 1908, ACP; and Adjutant General to Quartermaster General of the Army, December 4, 1908, ACP; Statement of the Military Service of Hunter Liggett; George W. Cullum, *Biographical Register, Supplement of the Officers and Graduates of the U.S. Military Academy at West Point, New York, since Its Establishment in 1802*, vol. 6A, *1910–1920* (Saginaw, MI: Seemann & Peters, 1920), 295; Hunter Liggett to Adjutant General, June 30, 1909, ACP; Acknowledgement of Promotion and Oath of Office, ACP.

26 Ball, *Of Responsible Command*, 83; Pogue, *Education of a General*, 61; Perret, *Eisenhower*, 99 ("role of Army War College"). Not all senior officers were entirely satisfied with the procedures followed at the Command and General Staff School at Fort Leavenworth. A former chief of staff, General Charles P. Summerall wrote that the grading system was too rigid and kept many officers from being selected to advance to the Army War College. During his tenure as chief of staff, Summerall eliminated all grades, stating simply whether a student officer's performance was "satisfactory" or not. Summerall, *The Way of Duty*, 213.

27 Ball, *Of Responsible Command*, 81–83, 86, 100–102, 105–6; George P. Ahern, ed., *A Chronicle of the Army War College* (Carlisle, PA: US Army War College, 1919), 1:61, 75, 123 ("Swift").

28 Ahern, *A Chronicle of the Army War College*, 1:125–28.

29 Special Orders No. 111, War Department, par. 26, May 14, 1909, ACP ("leave"); Post Return, Officers Present, Army War College, Washington, DC, August 1909 through July 1910; Statement of the Military Service of Hunter Liggett; 1910 US Census, District of Columbia, Washington City (Series T624, Roll 151, Page 7B); Ahern, *A Chronicle of the Army War College*, 1:124, 142.

30 Ahern, *A Chronicle of the Army War College*, 1:123–24, 132–33.

31 Report of Physical Examination and Riding or Walking Test, October 23, 1909, ACP. The report listed his height as "74 inches" which is clearly an error, since all other examinations found him to be about six feet tall.

32 Ahern, *A Chronicle of the Army War College*, 1:133–36.

33 Ahern, *A Chronicle of the Army War College*, 1:136–37.

34 Ahern, *A Chronicle of the Army War College*, 1:137–38, 149 ("supervise Preliminary Course").

35 H. Liggett to Secretary Army War College, August 4, 1910, ACP; Special Orders No. 185, par. 19, War Department, August 9, 1910, ACP; Millett, *The General*, 230–32

("reshape curriculum"); Post Return, Officers Present, Army War College, August 1910 ("Conferring with authorities"); "Serving America's Armed Forces Since 1909," *The Real McCoy*, Spring 1916 (Fort McCoy, WI: Fort McCoy Public Affairs Office, 2016), available at http://www.mccoy.army.mil/vnewspaper/newspaper/areaguide/history.html, accessed July 2, 2016; Ahern, *A Chronicle of the Army War College*, 1:142, 147 ("Director"); Perret, *Eisenhower*, 97 ("retention of outstanding graduates").

36 Ball, *Of Responsible Command*, 105–6, 118 ("preparatory course in military art"). *Military art* included military history, tactics, map reading, and tactical rides, among other things.

37 Report of Physical Examination and Riding or Walking Test, October 20, 1910, ACP.

38 Ahern, *A Chronicle of the Army War College*, 1:153–55.

39 Report of Physical Examination and Riding or Walking Test, October 9, 1911, ACP. The standard report of physical examination form does not call for a waist measurement, which would be a better indicator. However, the surgeon's characterization was no doubt based on a visual observation, and appearances were becoming increasingly important. The same surgeon appears to have signed off on the exam for both 1910 and 1911.

40 Memorandum for Adjutant General, Office of Chief of Staff, July 3, 1911, ACP; Special Orders No. 157, par. 27, War Department, July 7, 1911, ACP.

41 Ahern, *A Chronicle of the Army War College*, 1:168–73.

42 Ahern, *A Chronicle of the Army War College*, 1:173–74; Post Return, Officers Present, Army War College, July 1913, RG94 NARA; Ball, *Of Responsible Command*, 115 ("appointed President"); Millett, *The General*, 230–32 ("exhilarating"). While in France, Liggett had a fall with his horse on rough terrain, and witnesses told of how quickly he got back up without apparent injury to himself. King, "General Hunter Liggett," 26.

43 Acknowledgement of Promotion and Oath of Office, April 10, 1912, ACP; H. Liggett to Adjutant General, April 10, 1912, ACP ("application for rank of brigadier general"); Nelson A. Miles to President [Taft], April 10, 1912, ACP.

44 Statement of the Military Service of Hunter Liggett; Ahern, *A Chronicle of the Army War College*, 1:180; "Army Officers Coming," *New York Times*, July 28, 1912 ("Connecticut Manoeuvers"); John Q. Tilson to Henry L. Stimson, September 18, 1912, ACP; "Tilson, John Quillin (1866–1958)," Biographical Directory of the United States Congress, http://bioguide.congress.gov/scripts/biodisplay.pl?index=T000279, accessed August 6, 2018.

45 Ahern, *A Chronicle of the Army War College*, 1:186–87; Post Return, Officers Present, Army War College, May 1913.

46 Report of Physical Examination and Riding Test, October 20, 1912, ACP. Since the surgeon who conducted the examination was different from the one for the previous two years, his subjective judgment as to Liggett's appearance was his own.

47 Memorandum, November 9, 1912, ACP; S. B. M. Young to President [Taft], November 9, 1912, ACP.

48 Ahern, *A Chronicle of the Army War College*, 1:189; Post Return, Officers Present, Army War College, May 1913, RG94 NARA. The permanent party, or detachment, at the Army War College was composed of one officer and thirty-six to forty enlisted men. It was quartered at Fort Myer, Virginia. In addition to their normal garrison duties, it provided mounts for the student officers for the staff rides, but it would appear that the detachment followed the route of the staff rides in order to

pitch and break camp for the student officers at the various stops. Record of Events, Return of the War College Detachment, May 1913, RG94 NARA.

49 Ahern, *A Chronicle of the Army War College*, 1:190.

50 Ahern, *A Chronicle of the Army War College*, 1:198–99.

51 Post Return, Officers Present, Army War College, January and February 1913; "Popular Officers Are Nominated," *San Francisco Call*, February 21, 1913, p. 7 ("nomination"); Acknowledgement of Promotion, March 6, 1913, and Oath of Office, March 7, 1913, ACP; Statement of the Military Service of Hunter Liggett; Cullum, *Biographical Register, Supplement*, vol. 6A, *1910–1920*, 295; Ahern, *A Chronicle of the Army War College*, 1:186, 199.

A biographical article in the *New York Times* written in September 1918, states that Liggett was "invalided home" from Cuba in 1899 after contracting typhoid fever. This is clearly an error, since he had received orders to report to the 31st Volunteer Infantry with no mention of illness. No doubt, the *Times* confused his more recent visit to Cuba in January 1913 while on duty at the Army War College with his earlier service there in 1899. The Post Return for January 1913 shows that he was sick in quarters with an "unspecified illness" from January 20 through February 3. "General Liggett in Work and War," *New York Times*, September 29, 1918; *New York Times*, March 4, 1913 ("promotion").

52 Hunter Liggett to George C. Marshall, April 23, 1913, GCML; Post Return, Officers Present, Army War College, April 1913.

53 Efficiency Report, February 21, 1913, ACP.

54 "Carlisle Indian School Holds Its Annual Commencement Exercises This Week—Fifteen Students to Be Graduated," *New York Times*, March 30, 1913 ("Carlisle Indian School"); Special Orders No. 81, par. 10, War Department, April 8, 1913, ACP ("Fort Sill"); Post Return, Officers Present, Army War College, June and July 1913; Record of Events, Return of the War College Detachment, June 1913.

55 King, "General Hunter Liggett," 13.

56 "Reference List, 50th Anniversary of the Battle of Gettysburg and Grand Reunion, 1913," Park Library & Research Center, Gettysburg Park Library & Research Center, Gettysburg, PA.

57 *Fiftieth Anniversary of the Battle of Gettysburg: Report of the Pennsylvania Commission, December 31, 1913* (Harrisburg, PA: W. Stanley Ray Printing, 1915), 40–42.

58 *Fiftieth Anniversary*, 26; "Wilson to Gettysburg," *New York Times*, June 29, 1913; "Pickett's Charge Fifty Years After," *New York Times*, July 4, 1913 ("one hour"). Irish-born John Kinley Tener (1863–1946) played baseball for the Chicago White Sox, worked as a Pittsburgh businessman, and served in Congress and as governor of Pennsylvania, and later as president of the National League. Daniel Ginsburg, "John Tener," Society for American Baseball Research, https://sabr.org/bioproj/person/c90d4ea9, accessed August 6, 2018.

59 "Pickett's Charge Fifty Years After," *New York Times*, July 4, 1913 ("walks to tent").

60 "Gettysburg Camp All But Deserted," *New York Times*, July 6, 1913 ("nine deaths"); *The Forest Republican*, July 2, 1913, p. 1 ("two deaths"); "Pickett's Charge Fifty Years After," *New York Times*, July 4, 1913 ("eight deaths" and "two tents"); "Blue Arms Link with Gray," *The Missoulian*, July 1, 1913, p. 9 ("Longstreet's widow"); *Fiftieth Anniversary*, 25 ("veterans only").

61 *Fiftieth Anniversary*, 233 ("congratulations"); "Gettysburg Camp All But Deserted," *New York Times*, July 6, 1913.

62 H. Liggett to Webb C. Hayes, July 23, 1913, RBHL.
63 Millett, *The General*, 260–62.
64 Mitchell A. Yockelson, *Borrowed Soldiers: Americans under British Command, 1918* (Norman: University of Oklahoma Press, 2008), 221–22; Ahern, *A Chronicle of the Army War College*, 1:200, 206.
65 Ahern, *A Chronicle of the Army War College*, 1:210–11.

CHAPTER SIX

1 In August 1912, Congress passed the so-called Manchu Law that required company grade officers to serve at least two of their last six years with troops. The policy was extended to field grade officers in 1915. Ball, *Of Responsible Command*, 130; Pogue, *Education of a General*, 61.
2 Hunter Liggett, Statement of Preferences, May 24, 1913, ACP; Liggett, *Ten Years Ago*, 288 ("requested relief"); Hunter Liggett to George C. Marshall, April 23, 1913, GCML. Robert L. Bullard observed that the Manchu Law has "struck a fatal blow at the regimental staff." He added, "From an honor to be sought [staff duty] it has come to be a pest to be shunned." Robert L. Bullard, "Impressions of Service with the 2d Division in Texas," *Infantry Journal*, no. 11 (November–December 1914): 356; "Garrison Shifts a Dozen Generals," *New York Times*, December 19, 1913.
3 John S. D. Eisenhower, *Intervention: The United States and the Mexican Revolution, 1913–1917* (New York: Norton, 1993), 10–29, 330–31; Eileen Welsome, *The General and the Jaguar: Pershing's Hunt for Pancho Villa: A True Story of Revolution and Revenge* (New York: Little, Brown, 2006), 28–30 ("Huerta"); Millett, *The General*, 251–52.
4 Millett, *The General*, 253–54; Shay, *Revered Commander*, 102–3 ("gray wolves of the air"); James Parker, *The Old Army, Memories, 1872–1918* (Mechanicsburg, PA: Stackpole, 2003), 419 ("heat, dust"); Bullard, "Impressions of Service," 354.
5 Ball, *Of Responsible Command*, 132; Ahern, *A Chronicle of the Army War College*, 1:201, 206, 210; Statement of the Military Service of Hunter Liggett.
6 Eisenhower, *Intervention*, 82–83, 108, 123–27, 166; Welsome, *The General and the Jaguar*, 44–47; Millett, *The General*, 262–65.
7 War Department, Memorandum for the Adjutant General, April 17, 1914, ACP; Special Orders No. 94, par. 15, April 22, 1914, ACP; H. Liggett to Adjutant General, Telegram, April 29, 1914, ACP; Special Orders No. 100, par. 13, War Department, April 29, 1914, ACP; Statement of the Military Service of Hunter Liggett; Cullum, *Biographical Register, Supplement*, vol. 6A, *1910–1920*, 295.
8 Liggett, *Commanding an American Army*, 6 ("first time"); Millett, *The General*, 253.
9 Liggett, *Commanding an American Army*, 1–3 ("made to understand"); Millett, *The General*, 257, 266 ("realistic and useful"). Bullard was not the only one frustrated by Carter's micromanagement. Clarence Edwards had tried to implement a gradual conditioning regimen for his men which he referred to as "progressive training," that involved gradually longer marches with and without packs. Carter told him to stop. Shay, *Revered Commander*, 103; Bullard, "Impressions of Service," 358 ("low morale").
10 Post Return, Army-Navy Hospital, Hot Springs, Arkansas, August and September 1914; H. Liggett to Adjutant General, Telegram, August 17, 1914, ACP; H. Liggett

to Adjutant General, October 1, 1914, ACP; Special Orders No. 238, par. 23, War Department, October 5, 1914, ACP.

11 Liggett, *Commanding an American Army*, 7 ("Provisional Infantry Brigade"). There is an obvious typographical error in Liggett's account as the text refers to the "Provincial" brigade. Post Return, Fort William McKinley, Philippines, January 1915; Statement of the Military Service of Hunter Liggett; Cullum, *Biographical Register, Supplement*, vol. 6A, *1910–1920*, 295.

12 Efficiency Report, October 1, 1915, ACP.

13 George C. Marshall to Captain Booth, January 2, [1915], in *Guardians of Empire*, 70 ("Fort McKinley"). (Marshall obviously dated the letter "1914" by mistake, since Liggett's new command commenced in January 1915.) George C. Marshall, interview, April 4, 1957, in Bland, *Papers of George Catlett Marshall*, 1:93 ("Batangas").

14 Liggett, *Commanding an American Army*, 6 ("a question of time").

15 Warren Zimmermann, *First Great Triumph: How Five Americans Made Their Country a World Power* (New York: Farrar, Strauss & Giroux, 2002), 300–301; Stanley Karnow, *In Our Image: America's Empire in the Philippines* (New York: Ballantine, 1989), 103–10; Trask, *War with Spain*, 450–56.

16 Linn, *Guardians of Empire*, 82–90; Ball, *Of Responsible Command*, 84–85; Edward S. Miller, *War Plan Orange: The U.S. Strategy to Defeat Japan, 1897–1945* (Annapolis, MD: Naval Institute Press, 1991), 13.

17 Robert Smith Thompson, *Empires on the Pacific: World War II and the Struggle for the Mastery of Asia* (New York: Basic Books, 2001), 115 ("Port Arthur"); Linn, *Guardians of Empire*, 84–88; Miller, *War Plan Orange*, 10, 19–23 ("anti-Japanese sentiment"), 89–90 ("Great White Fleet"); Morris, *Theodore Rex*, 482–85, 490 ("anti-Japanese"), 502–3 ("Great White Fleet").

18 Ball, *Of Responsible Command*, 109–11.

19 Linn, *Guardians of Empire*, 82–91; H. W. Brands, *Bound to Empire: The United States and the Philippines* (New York: Oxford University Press, 1992), 117–18 ("Panama Canal"); Miller, *War Plan Orange*, 24, 68, 122–23.

20 Post Return, Fort William McKinley, April 1915, RG94 NARA ("Board of Officers"); Linn, *Guardians of Empire*, 97–100, 113; Liggett, *Commanding an American Army*, 78 ("Board of Officers").

21 Linn, *Guardians of Empire*, 100–102.

22 Post Return, Fort William McKinley, May, June, and December 1915 through January 1916; Report of Physical Examination and Riding Test, December 17, 1915. ACP.

23 Efficiency Report, December 31, 1915, ACP.

24 Efficiency Report, April 15, 1916, ACP.

25 Post Return, Fort William McKinley, January 1916; Bland, *Papers of George Catlett Marshall*, 1:96; Linn, *Guardians of Empire*, 101 ("staff rides"); Brands, *Bound to Empire*, 190; Thompson, *Empires on the Pacific*, 115 ("Japanese invasion"). The date for the invasion would be recorded as December 21, 1941, in Washington, DC, as it is east of the International Dateline.

26 Liggett, *Commanding an American Army*, 8 ("effective defense")

27 Liggett, *Commanding an American Army*, 8–9; Post Return, Fort William McKinley, April 1916 ("assumed command"); Hunter Liggett to Webb C. Hayes, March 21, 1917, RBHL; Statement of the Military Service of Hunter Liggett; Cullum, *Biographical Register, Supplement*, vol. 6A, *1910–1920*, 295.

28 Liggett to Adjutant General, Cablegram, October 14, 1916, ACP; H. Liggett to Adjutant General, November 13, 1916, ACP; Liggett to Adjutant General, Cablegram, November 15, 1916, ACP.

29 [Hugh] Scott to Liggett, Telegram, March 6, 1917, ACP; Frank M. McIntyre to Adjutant General, Memorandum (enclosing letter from Burton Harrison), February 23, 1917, ACP; Liggett to Adjutant General, March 22, 1917, ACP; Statement of the Military Service of Hunter Liggett; Thomas Bruscino, introduction to Funston, *Memories of Two Wars*, x; "Nominates Grayson Again," *New York Times*, March 7, 1917 ("Wilson nominates Liggett"); Cullum, *Biographical Register, Supplement*, vol. 6A, *1910–1920*, 295.

30 Hunter Liggett to Clarence R. Edwards, March 12, 1917, CRE 12.5.

31 Hunter Liggett to Webb C. Hayes, March 21, 1917, RBHL.

32 Liggett to Adjutant General, Telegram, May 15, 1917, ACP; Oath of Office, San Francisco, California, May 15, 1917, ACP; Statement of the Military Service of Hunter Liggett; Cullum, *Biographical Register, Supplement*, vol. 6A, *1910–1920*, 295.

CHAPTER SEVEN

1 Winston S. Churchill, *The World Crisis 1911–1918* (New York: Free Press, 2005), 96 ("some damned foolish thing"), 684–97; Coffman, *War to End All Wars*, 6–8.

2 Liggett, *Commanding an American Army*, 11–13; Frederick Palmer, *Newton D. Baker: America at War*, vols. 1–2 (New York: Dodd, Mead, 1931), 1:238–43 ("choice cantonments").

3 Cullum, *Biographical Register*, vol. 6A, *1910–1920*, 275; Statement of the Military Service of Hunter Liggett; Liggett, *Ten Years Ago*, 14; Laurence Stallings, *The Doughboys: The Story of the AEF, 1917–1918* (New York: Harper, 1963), 375.

4 Liggett, *Ten Years Ago*, 14; Millett, *The General*, 335 ("quick to censure"); Summerall, *The Way of Duty*, 120; Shay, *Revered Commander*, 161, 198. Historian Terrence Finnegan offers another assessment of Craig, who received a Jesuit education at Georgetown University prior to West Point, as "aggressively resolute in his loyalty to higher authority such as Pershing and Liggett," posing as a "grand inquisitor to the heretics." Terrence J. Finnegan, *A Delicate Affair on the Western Front: America Learns How to Fight a Modern War in the Woëvre Trenches* (Stroud, UK: Spellmount, 2015), 136–37.

5 Edward T. James, ed., *Dictionary of American Biography, Supplement Three, 1941–45* (New York: Scribner, 1973), 193–94.

6 Stallings, *The Doughboys*, 153–54 ("Greek cook"); Mitchell Yockelson, *Forty-Seven Days: How Pershing's Warriors Came of Age to Defeat the German Army in World War I* (New York: New American Library, 2016), 51; Byron Farwell, *Over There: The United States in the Great War, 1917–1918* (New York: Norton, 1999), 187; Ferrell, *In the Company of Generals*, 4 ("special mess"); King, "General Hunter Liggett," 46.

7 Liggett, *Ten Years Ago*, 14 ("SS *Finland*"); History of the One Hundred Second Field Artillery, July 1917–April 1919 (Boston: n.p., 1927), 4–7; Millett, *The General*, 315–17 ("audition").

8 Liggett, *Ten Years Ago*, 14–18; Liggett, *Commanding an American Army*, 14–15; John Keegan, *The First World War* (New York: Knopf, 1999), 367–69.

9 Liggett, *Ten Years Ago*, 23; Liggett, *Commanding an American Army*, 16. Liggett was not the only one to notice this attitude. Chaplain Malcolm E. Peabody served in Flanders as a chaplain with the Harvard Unit, a hospital/surgical team. He, too, was

impressed with the attitude of the British soldier, particularly the ones he visited in the hospital. "The Tommies are too marvelously wonderful and brace me up no end," he would write. Shay, *Sky Pilots*, 25.

10 Liggett, *Ten Years Ago*, 24–26; Liggett, *Commanding an American Army*, 16–17.

11 Liggett, *Ten Years Ago*, 24–26; Liggett, *Commanding an American Army*, 16–17; John J. Pershing, *My Experiences in the First World War* (New York: Da Capo, 1995), 1:193–94, 213 ("Paris"); Coffman, *War to End All Wars*, 250 ("too old").

12 Ahern, *A Chronicle of the Army War College*, 1:126; Liggett, *Ten Years Ago*, 21.

13 Palmer, *Newton D. Baker*, 2:228 ("cable"); Donald Smythe, *Pershing: General of the Armies* (Bloomington: University of Indiana Press, 2007), 54 ("good soldier"). Aside from the praise of Baldwin and Bullard, Pershing even recommended Liggett for the American position on the Supreme War Council, one that ultimately went to Tasker Bliss. Coffman, *War to End All Wars*, 248–50 ("praise from Baldwin and Bullard").

14 Hunter Liggett, Physical Examination, December 17, 1917, ACP.

15 Liggett, *Commanding an American Army*, 19.

16 Hunter Liggett to Colonel Hayes, November 15, 1917, Webb Hayes Papers, RBHL.

17 Hunter Liggett to Colonel Hayes, December 18, 1917, Webb Hayes Papers, RBHL; Liggett, *Commanding an American Army*, 19. Liggett refers to the town as "La Courtaine."

18 Stallings, *The Doughboys*, 375–77 ("41st Division").

19 James G. Harbord, "Personalities and Personal Relationships in the American Expeditionary Forces," 12, USMC ("hung by a thread"); James G. Harbord, *Leaves from a War Diary* (New York: Dodd, Mead, 1925), 201. According to one source, anticipating his likely relief, Liggett is said to have told Pershing to "withhold action until he saw him in command." If so, the tactic obviously worked. James J. Cooke, *The All-Americans at War: The 82nd Division in the Great War, 1917–1918* (Westport, CT: Praeger, 1999), 57; Yockelson, *Forty-Seven Days*, 50–51.

20 Pershing, *My Experiences*, 1:290; Harbord, *Leaves from a War Diary*, 202 ("unsought"); Cullum, *Biographical Register*, vol. 6A, *1910–1920*, 275–76; Statement of the Military Service of Hunter Liggett.

21 Harbord, *Leaves from a War Diary*, 202 ("Blatchford sent home instead of Liggett"); Harbord, "Personalities and Personal Relationships in the American Expeditionary Forces," 12 ("unsent cablegram"); Liggett, *Ten Years Ago*, 255 ("hearsay"). According to Harbord, the officer in charge of the code room was court-martialed.

22 Palmer, *Newton D. Baker*, 2:135–36 ("Pioneer"); John S. D. Eisenhower and Joanne T. Eisenhower, *Yanks: The Epic Story of the American Army in World War I* (New York: Free Press, 2001), 84 ("Old Reliables"); Mark Ethan Grotelueschen, *Doctrine under Trial: American Artillery Employment in World War I* (Westport, CT: Greenwood, 2001), 150 ("30%"); Coffman, *War to End All Wars*, 135–37 ("training").

23 Stackpole, diary, January 26 through February 26, 1918. During the war, at least ten American divisions (4th, 27th, 28th, 30th, 33rd, 35th, 77th, 78th, 80th, and 82nd) would train with the British Army. Of them, at least three (27th, 30th, and 37th) would actually serve under British command in the British Sector. Yockelson, *Borrowed Soldiers*, xiv.

24 Ferrell, *In the Company of Generals*, 15–18 ("complaints"); Michael E. Shay, *The Yankee Division in the First World War: In the Highest Tradition* (College Station: Texas A&M University Press, 2008), 26–27 ("worst winter").

25 Shay, *The Yankee Division*, 45–46; Coffman, *War to End All Wars*, 135–37 ("training"); Pershing, *My Experiences*, 1:369 ("four available divisions"); Liggett, *Commanding an American Army*, 22–24 ("training").

26 Millett, *The General*, 320 ("favors 1st Division"); Palmer, *Newton D. Baker*, 2:213 ("choice officers"); James J. Cooke, *The Rainbow Division in the Great War, 1917–1919* (Westport, CT: Praeger, 1994), 240; Bullard, *Personalities and Reminiscences of the War*, 144–45 ("private wire"). As a case in point, Liggett had sent a letter to Bullard with some critical comments about how Bullard's division was handling its animals, with some suggestions as to how to improve the situation. Bullard took it personally, and Liggett and his aide went to 1st Division Headquarters for the "purpose of smoothing out Bullard, who had called up night before and showed feeling about language of letter." Stackpole, diary, March 15, 1918.

27 H. Liggett, Endorsement to Application for Commission, February 2, 1918, Webb Hayes Papers, RBHL; Stackpole, diary, February 1, 1918.

28 Stackpole, diary, March 2, 1918.

29 Hunter Liggett to Colonel Hayes, March 16, 1918, Webb Hayes Papers, RBHL.

30 Robert H. Ferrell, *Collapse at Meuse-Argonne: The Failure of the Missouri-Kansas Division* (Columbia: University of Missouri Press, 2004), 7 ("micromanager"); Smythe, *Pershing*, 25 ("too many hats"); James J. Cooke, *Pershing and His Generals: Command and Staff in the AEF* (Westport, CT: Praeger, 1997), 26–27 ("fear and loyalty"); Thomas Fleming, *The Illusion of Victory: America in World War I* (New York: Basic, 2003), 185–86 ("not loved"); Yockelson, *Forty-Seven Days*, 35 ("micromanager"); Robert H. Ferrell, *Five Days in October: The Lost Battalion of World War I* (Columbia: University of Missouri Press, 2005), 1–6 ("Pershing's shortcomings"); David F. Trask, *The AEF and Coalition Warfare, 1917–1918* (Lawrence: University Press of Kansas, 1993), 175–76 ("full support").

31 Bullard, *Personalities and Reminiscences of the War*, 144 ("valuable faculty"); Stackpole, diary, February 6 ("prejudice") and July 26, 1918 ("prejudice against 26th Division").

32 Shay, *Revered Commander*, 212 ("Harbord").

33 Hugh A. Drum to John J. Pershing, undated draft of letter [circa 1939], Drum Papers, MHI; Stackpole, diary, March 7 ("spirit and discipline") and March 9, 1918 ("chided").

34 Clarence R. Edwards, "Memorandum of the News," January 29, 1918, CRE 14.7; Millett, *The General*, 335 ("Craig as driving force"). This enmity could well have begun at Neufchâteau during the evening of January 25, 1918, during a conference with General Liggett and some of his staff, including Craig. General Edwards was present, along with some of his division officers. According to Craig, Edwards, in his inimitable manner, monopolized the entire evening and in the process ridiculed colonels Harold B. Fiske, Paul B. Malone, and Leroy S. Upton about "training matters" relating to machine guns and ammunition. From that point on, it is likely that the damage had been done, and Craig had become a mortal enemy. Malin Craig to Hugh A. Drum, Confidential Memorandum, December 8, 1920, Drum Papers, MHI; Ferrell, *In the Company of Generals*, 10–11 ("conference").

35 Liggett, *Commanding an American Army*, 23–24 ("no open warfare training"); Liggett, *Ten Years Ago*, 67–70 ("Cantigny"); Robert H. Ferrell, *America's Deadliest Battle: Meuse-Argonne, 1918* (Lawrence: University Press of Kansas, 2007), 27–28 ("small raids"), 28–29 ("Cantigny"); Yockelson, *Forty-Seven Days*, 48 ("Cantigny").

36 Shay, *The Yankee Division*, 74–78 ("Apremont"), 78–89 ("Seicheprey"); Finnegan, *Delicate Affair*, 254–55 ("prisoners"); Liggett, *Ten Years Ago*, 67 ("check"); Stackpole, diary, April 23, 1918 ("Passaga"); Pershing, *My Experiences*, 2:16 ("softened").

37 Martin Gilbert, *The First World War: A Complete History* (New York: Henry Holt, 1994), 406–19, 425–27, 434–35 ("German Offensive"); Pershing, *My Experiences*, 1:353 ("German Offensive"), 2:129 ("Vaux"); Coffman, *War to End All Wars*, 212–22 ("Belleau Wood and Vaux").

38 Stackpole, diary, July 17, 1918, and August 19, 1918 ("first time since Revolution").

39 Stackpole, diary, July 4 and 13, 1918.

40 Trask, *AEF and Coalition Warfare*, 92; Stackpole, diary, October 3, 1918; Liggett, *Ten Years Ago*, 175.

41 Coffman, *War to End All Wars*, 251–61 ("Aisne-Marne Offensive"); Stallings, *The Doughboys*, 125–35 ("Rock of the Marne"); Rod Paschall, *The Defeat of Imperial Germany, 1917–1918* (Chapel Hill, NC: Algonquin, 1989), 161 ("lost initiative").

42 Shay, *Revered Commander*, 157; Stackpole, diary, April 12 ("Pershing's chestnuts") and July 21, 1918 ("Brewster").

43 Stackpole, diary, July 20 and 21 ("by-pass") and July 23, 1918 ("artillery preparation").

44 Mark Ethan Grotelueschen, *The AEF Way of War: The American Army and Combat in World War I* (New York: Cambridge University Press, 2007), 236–37 ("coordination").

45 Stackpole, diary, July 18, 1918 ("guide left"), through July 22, 1918; Liggett, *Commanding an American Army*, 37–38.

46 Liggett, *Ten Years Ago*, 124–26 ("pinching out"); Stackpole, diary, July 23, 1918; Liggett, *Commanding an American Army*, 39–40 ("bound to go astray"); Stackpole, diary, July 24, 1918 ("never obey"); Coffman, *War to End All Wars*, 252 ("Liggett and staff in part to blame"); Stackpole, diary, July 27 ("reconstitute") and August 7, 1918 ("break up division").

47 Shay, *The Yankee Division*, 133–39; Stackpole, diary, July 30, 1918 ("careless and prodigal"), and August 1 and 3, 1918 ("too many in front line").

48 Stackpole, diary, August 3 ("don't bunch"), and August 7, 1918 ("poor liaison"); Coffman, *War to End All Wars*, 253–58; Liggett, *Commanding an American Army*, 53–54.

49 Stackpole, diary, August 30, 1918 ("dysentery"); Shay, *The Yankee Division*, 137–38 ("Sgt. Forbush"); Michael E. Shay, *A Grateful Heart: The History of a World War I Field Hospital* (Westport, CT: Greenwood, 2001), 79 ("promiscuous defecation").

50 Stackpole, diary, August 10, 1918. Benjamin Andrew Poore retired in 1927 as a major general following a long career, which began as a cadet at the United States Military Academy (class of 1886). In addition to his line assignments, Poore served as a director of the Army War College from 1912 to 1916, where he overlapped with Liggett. He won the Distinguished Service Cross for twice personally leading elements of his brigade against enemy fire, on September 27 and October 11, 1918. Michael Stein, "Benjamin Andrew Poore, Major General, United States Army," Arlington National Cemetery Website, last updated October 14, 2007, http://www.arlingtoncemetery.net/bapoore.htm.

51 Stackpole, diary, August 14 ("rheumatism") and August 20, 1918 ("Saizerais"); Coffman, *War to End All Wars*, 273; Millett, *The General*, 313 ("importance of Metz"); Trask, *AEF and Coalition Warfare*, 102 ("communications center"); Liggett, *Commanding an American Army*, 64 ("make-up of I Corps"), 133–34 ("Franco-Prussian War").

52 Pershing, *My Experiences*, 2:241–55; George C. Marshall, *Memoirs of My Services in the World War, 1917–1918* (Boston: Houghton Mifflin, 1976), 132–33; Paschall, *The*

Defeat of Imperial Germany, 171–72; Coffman, *War to End All Wars*, 270–72; Trask, *AEF and Coalition Warfare*, 102–5.

53 Stackpole, diary, August 30 ("Ligny-en-Barrois") and September 1 ("dominating artillery"), 1918; Liggett, *Commanding an American Army*, 59–60; Liggett, *Ten Years Ago*, 150.

54 Stackpole, diary, August 24 ("Burnham") and September 7 ("undisciplined"), 1918.

55 Stackpole, diary, August 27, 30, and 31 ("front line") and September 11, 1918 ("boots"); Coffman, *War to End All Wars*, 275 ("dandy").

56 Stackpole, diary, September 9, 1918 ("McMahon").

57 Coffman, *War to End All Wars*, 268, 273; Pershing, *My Experiences*, 2:261–63. During the battle, fewer than one-half of the assembled American force actually took part in the fighting. Ferrell, *America's Deadliest Battle*, 33 ("230,000").

58 Coffman, *War to End All Wars*, 279–83; Paschall, *The Defeat of Imperial Germany*, 173–81; Digest of Operations, First Army, AEF, September 12, 1918, *United States Army in the World War, 1917–1919* (Washington, DC: GPO, 1968), 8:255 ("5:00 a.m.").

59 Liggett, *Commanding an American Army*, 68–69 ("positive results"); Coffman, *War to End All Wars*, 283 ("MacArthur"); Liggett, *Ten Years Ago*, 159 ("Metz"); Ferrell, *America's Deadliest Battle*, 35; Smythe, *Pershing*, 188–89 ("serious deficiencies").

60 Stackpole, diary, August 12 and 13 ("liaison"), and September 14 ("somewhat shaky"), 1918; Ferrell, *In the Company of Generals*, 128, 169–70 ("McMahon relieved").

CHAPTER EIGHT

1 Stackpole, diary, October 5, 1918 ("Argonne country").

2 Coffman, *War to End All Wars*, 301–6; Paschall, *The Defeat of Imperial Germany*, 183–84; Ferrell, *America's Deadliest Battle*, 38.

3 Liggett, *Commanding an American Army*, 75; Ferrell, *America's Deadliest Battle*, 40–41.

4 Stackpole, diary, September 25, 1918.

5 Stackpole, diary, October 3, 1918 ("Liggett tells Pershing"); Yockelson, *Forty-Seven Days*, 123–24.

6 Liggett, *Ten Years Ago*, 174–75 ("anodyne"); Edward G. Lengel, *To Conquer Hell: The Meuse-Argonne, 1918* (New York: Henry Holt, 2008), 107 ("solitaire"); Liggett, *Commanding an American Army*, 75 ("Rarécourt").

7 Ferrell, *America's Deadliest Battle*, 45–46 ("mixed results"); Ferrell, *In the Company of Generals*, 143–44 ("lack of control").

8 Stackpole, diary, September 26, 1918 ("poor liaison").

9 Stackpole, diary, September 26 to 29, 1918 ("poor liaison").

10 Coffman, *War to End All Wars*, 311–12 ("lost cohesion"); Stackpole, diary, September 26 through October 3, 1918.

11 Stackpole, diary, September 28, 1918 ("Kamerad").

12 Shay, *The Yankee Division*, 124 ("We never take a machine gunner").

13 Lengel, *To Conquer Hell*, 190–91; Ferrell, *America's Deadliest Battle*, 73–74 ("1st replaced 35th"); Liggett, *Commanding an American Army*, 84 ("1st replaced 35th").

14 Stackpole, diary, October 3, 1918; Liggett, *Ten Years Ago*, 175 ("own initiative").

15 Stackpole, diary, October 3, 1918.

16 Yockelson, *Forty-Seven Days*, 134; Coffman, *War to End All Wars*, 322 ("Cunel") and 325–27 ("east of Meuse"); Pershing, *My Experiences*, 2:323–24 ("resumed attack"); Grotelueschen, *The AEF Way of War*, 252–66 ("Blanc Mont").

17 Stackpole, diary, October 7, 1918 ("imperious and bull-headed"); Coffman, *War to End All Wars*, 323–25 ("Lost Battalion"); Ferrell, *Five Days in October*, 54.

18 Stackpole, diary, October 6 and 7, 1918 ("flanking maneuver"); Liggett, *Commanding an American Army*, 86–89 ("flanking maneuver"). In his account of the maneuver, Liggett noted that only a portion of the brigade from the 82nd Division ("six companies of one regiment") actually was able to participate in the fight, and he speculated just what the result would have been if undertaken by the entire brigade. Cooke, *The All-Americans at War*, 88–94; Coffman, *War to End All Wars*, 323–25 ("flare for tactics"); Ferrell, *America's Deadliest Battle*, 74 ("82nd Division").

19 Statement of the Military Service of Hunter Liggett; Liggett, *Commanding an American Army*, 95 ("Souilly"); Cullum, *Biographical Register*, vol. 6A, *1910–1920*, 275–76.

20 Stackpole, diary, October 12 through 18, 1918 ("butting into details"); Ferrell, *In the Company of Generals*, 169–73; Yockelson, *Forty-Seven Days*, 267–68. Most accounts list the official transfer of command as October 16, but as is obvious from Stackpole's account that things were actually somewhat more complicated. On October 18, Pershing's aide, Maj. Edward Bowditch Jr., was sent to First Army, and without consulting Liggett, General Drum, who remained as chief of staff, assigned him to the headquarters mess. Liggett, sensing what was up, immediately had him assigned to a different mess. That did not stop Bowditch from asking Stackpole about "everything General Liggett [did]." Obviously, Bowditch was placed there by Pershing to keep tabs on Liggett.

21 Marshall, *Memoirs of My Services*, 187.

22 Stephen L. Harris, *Duffy's War: Fr. Francis Duffy, Wild Bill Donovan, and the Irish Fighting 69th in World War I* (Washington, DC: Potomac, 2006), 92–93 ("well-liked"); Cooke, *The Rainbow Division*, 178 ("strongly recommended"); Ferrell, *America's Deadliest Battle*, 103–7 ("indecisive").

23 Harris, *Duffy's War*, 332–57; Cooke, *The Rainbow Division*, 168–78; William M. Wright and Robert H. Ferrell, ed., *Meuse-Argonne Diary: A Division Commander in World War I* (Columbia: University of Missouri Press, 2004), 110; Yockelson, *Forty-Seven Days*, 260–64; Lengel, *To Conquer Hell*, 352–55; Ferrell, *America's Deadliest Battle*, 103–7.

24 Harris, *Duffy's War*, 358–59; Cooke, *The Rainbow Division*, 178; Ferrell, *America's Deadliest Battle*, 103–7; Wright and Ferrell, *Meuse-Argonne Diary*, 110 ("unjustified"). For the opposing point of view see Stackpole, diary, October 17, 1918; Summerall, *The Way of Duty*, 144–45 ("confused and unstrung").

25 Cooke, *The Rainbow Division*, 178; Ferrell, *America's Deadliest Battle*, 106; Wright and Ferrell, *Meuse-Argonne Diary*, 110.

26 Stackpole, diary, October 20 ("local operations") and October 25 through 26 ("French cooperation"), 1918; Liggett, *Ten Years Ago*, 214–20 ("two week pause"); Yockelson, *Forty-Seven Days*, 292 ("pause"); Paschall, *The Defeat of Imperial Germany*, 191 ("casualties and influenza"); Wright and Ferrell, *Meuse-Argonne Diary*, 119 ("pause").

27 Stackpole, diary, October 25 through 28, 1918.

28 Stackpole, diary, November 1, 1918 ("promotion"); Statement of the Military Service of Hunter Liggett; Grotelueschen, *The AEF Way of War*, 267–68 ("artillery support")

29 Liggett, *Ten Years Ago*, 218–25; Liggett, *Commanding an American Army*, 113–15.

30 Shay, *Revered Commander*, 169; Hugh A. Drum to John J. Pershing, undated handwritten draft of letter [1939], Hugh A. Drum Papers, MHI ("vindictiveness"); Summerall, *The Way of Duty*, 120 ("blighted career").

31 Stackpole, diary, March 16, 1919. On January 31, 1919, when a similar issue arose regarding the possible relief of Maj. Gen. Robert Alexander (77th Infantry Division), Liggett told Stackpole that it had been "a mistake to relieve Edwards at the time selected." Stackpole, diary, January 31, 1919; Stackpole, diary, June 3, 1919 ("best he knew how").

It was not the first time that Pershing went around Liggett to relieve a senior commander. On October 16, 1918, Maj. Gen. John McMahon (5th Division) and Maj. Gen. Beaumont Buck (3rd Division) were both relieved upon direct orders from Pershing without apparent consultation with Liggett. Sometime earlier, Liggett had recommended McMahon's relief, which distinguishes this from the case of General Edwards. Stackpole, diary, October 16, 1918.

32 Hunter Liggett to Clarence Edwards, October 25, 1918, CRE 14.24.

33 Grotelueschen, *The AEF Way of War*, 199 ("combat effectiveness").

34 Stackpole, diary, October 29, 1918; Cooke, *The Rainbow Division*, 192; Coffman, *War to End All Wars*, 348; Liggett, *Ten Years Ago*, 226–27.

35 Ferrell, *America's Deadliest Battle*, 139–40 ("November 3 meeting"); Pershing, *My Experiences*, 2:370, 381 ("warmly approved"); Ferrell, *In the Company of Generals*, 188 ("Liggett supports French claim to priority").

36 H. A. Drum, Memorandum For: Commanding Generals I Corps and V Corps, November 5, 1918, Drum Papers, MHI; Marshall, *Memoirs of My Services*, 187–91; Ferrell, *In the Company of Generals*, 189 ("Drum added"); Stackpole, diary, November 8, 1918 ("Pershing visited").

37 Commanding General, Third Army to Adjutant General, GHQ, Memorandum, December 24, 1919, Drum Papers, MHI; Liggett, *Ten Years Ago*, 228–29. In his memoir written years after the war, Summerall laid the blame on Parker for misinterpreting the order by moving laterally into the zone of the First Army Corps instead of continuing forward toward the Meuse. He said that when he found out, he ordered Parker to return to the Fifth Army Corps zone. This seems disingenuous, as the order to disentangle came directly from Liggett to him. Later that day when he received "violent criticism" from Liggett, he blamed Dickman for unleashing the problem with his "unjustified" criticism. Summerall, *The Way of Duty*, 152–54.

38 Cooke, *The Rainbow Division*, 193–94; Liggett, *Ten Years Ago*, 229–30; Ferrell, *America's Deadliest Battle*, 141.

39 Stackpole, diary, November 7, 1918.

40 Stackpole, diary, November 8, 1918; Drum to Commanding General, I Corps, Telegram, November 7, 1918, and Drum to Commanding General, V Corps, Telegram, November 7, 1918, Drum Papers, MHI; Liggett, *Ten Years Ago*, 229–30; Summerall, *The Way of Duty*, 154 ("violent criticism"). Years later, in the same memoir, Summerall put his own twist on things, not only blaming Frank Parker for the movement but also denying any confusion with units of the 42nd Division and criticizing General Dickman for overreacting, referring to him as "abusive and foul-mouthed." He chose to totally ignore the reaction of the French. Summerall, *The Way of Duty*, 136, 153–54.

41 Liggett spoke of the "craziness" of Parker and of Summerall's "ambition," whose explanation was a "lame affair." Months later, he told Stackpole that even though

he liked Summerall, he "would never trust him again in any affair where sentiment might be involved." He went on to rate Parker as capable of no more than the command of a regiment, and that Summerall should be limited to division command. For his part, Hugh Drum was not quite convinced that he himself was in any way to blame, and on November 8, he suggested the relief and a possible court-martial for both Parker and Summerall. Liggett, in no uncertain terms, made his point that it was Drum's wording that was to blame for the confusion, and Drum "reluctantly agreed." Stackpole, diary, November 8 and 10, 1918, and May 6, 1919.

42 Stackpole, diary, November 9, 1918 ("much amused"). Years later in his memoir, Pershing continued to ignore his role in the affair. He wrote, "Under normal conditions, the action of the officer or officers responsible for this movement of the 1st Division directly across the zones of action of two other divisions could not have been overlooked, but the splendid record of that unit and the approach of the end of hostilities suggested leniency." Pershing, *My Experiences*, 2:381. Liggett remained convinced that GHQ was at fault and had "encouraged the faulty maneuver by their meddling." Stackpole, diary, June 29, 1919. Historian Robert H. Ferrell called Liggett's restraint and focus on the offensive a "singular tribute to [his] judgment." Ferrell, *America's Deadliest Battle*, 142.

43 Yockelson, *Forty-Seven Days*, 267–68 ("meddling") and 304 ("road congestion"); Coffman, *War to End All Wars*, 355–56; Shay, *The Yankee Division*, 202–5; Liggett, *Ten Years Ago*, 237 ("Fourth of July"); Liggett, *Commanding an American Army*, 125 ("stunning silence"); Stanley Weintraub, *A Stillness Heard Round the World: The End of the Great War, November 1918* (New York: Oxford University Press, 1987), 193–208; Ann Hagedorn, *Savage Peace: Hope and Fear in America, 1919* (New York: Simon & Schuster, 2003), 3.

44 Margaret Macmillan, *Paris 1919: Six Months That Changed the World* (New York: Random House, 2003), 15–16, 33; John Milton Cooper, *Woodrow Wilson: A Biography* (New York: Knopf, 2009), 462–63.

45 Emerson Gifford Taylor, *New England in France 1917–1919: A History of the Twenty-Sixth Division USA* (Boston: Houghton Mifflin, 1920), 284–86 ("longest period of service in France"); James T. Duane, *Dear Old "K"* (Boston: Thomas Todd, 1922), 159. Taylor quotes in full the memorandum from H. A. Drum, chief of staff, First Army, to commanding general, 26th Division, on December 20, 1918, outlining the terms of the presidential visit, including Wilson's "desire [to] visit at dinner time and eat the soldier's dinner with the men." The American flag that was hung in the dining area during Wilson's visit is on display in a case in the vestibule of St. Bridget's Church in Framingham Center, Massachusetts, along with the original battle flag of the 101st Infantry Regiment.

46 Stackpole, diary, December 27, 1918; Shay, *The Yankee Division*, 212.

47 Shay, *The Yankee Division*, 210; Stackpole, diary, December 25, 1918; Summerall, *The Way of Duty*, 156–57 ("bad grace"); Taylor, *New England*, 284–86; Duane, *Dear Old "K,"* 160 ("circular"). To add insult to injury, during the second week of January 1919, a circular from division HQ to all of the units of the division, "suggested" that each company contribute fifteen French francs, and each company commander ten. This was to cover the cost of the Christmas dinner with the president and the replacement of tableware that had been broken or taken as souvenirs.

48 Shay, *The Yankee Division*, 219–20.

49 Shay, *The Yankee Division*, 208.
50 Stackpole, diary, December 16, 1918, and January 3 through 14, 1919.
51 Stackpole, diary, January 20 through 29, 1919.
52 Edmund Morris, *Colonel Roosevelt* (New York: Random House, 2011), 553; Shay, *Sky Pilots*, 116–17; Stackpole, diary, February 9, 10, 12, and 26, 1919.
53 Stackpole, diary, February 26, 1919; Julius Caesar, *The Conquest of Gaul* (New York: Penguin, 1976), 220–33.
54 H. Liggett to Mrs. Drum, undated copy of letter [1919], Hugh A. Drum Papers, MHI.
55 Stackpole, diary, February 25 and March 1, 1919 ("*La Pipiere*"), and January 1 and February 5, 1919 ("lumber shortage").
56 Stackpole, diary, December 4, 1918, and March 23, 1919 ("Distinguished Service Medal"); Cullum, *Biographical Register*, vol. 6A, *1910–1920*, 275–76.
57 Stackpole, diary, March 20 and April 9, 1919. Stackpole wrote that two journalists "commented . . . on the pro-German and anti-French sentiments and policy" of Dickman. Stackpole, diary, May 3 ("pro-Boche tendencies") and May 27, 1919.
58 Stackpole, diary, April 28, 1919 ("¶VII, General Orders 68"), and April 26, 1919 ("Secretary Baker").
59 Stackpole, diary, April 30 through May 3, and May 8, 1919.
60 Stackpole, diary, May 14 through 15, and June 17, 1919.
61 Stackpole, diary, June 19, 1919. Stackpole referred to it as "the very casual attitude of G. H. Q., which is to regard martial preparation as a joke." He goes on to refer to the "extraordinarily unmilitary and casual attitude" there.
62 Stackpole, diary, May 3 ("badly demoralized"), June 5 ("restlessness"), and June 6 ("rowdyism"), 1919.
63 Stackpole, diary, May 18 ("clear the field") and June 2 ("harassment"), 1919.
64 "Foch Inspects Coblenz," *New York Times*, May 16, 1919; Stackpole, diary, May 16 and 16, 1919.
65 "British Commander Confers with Liggett," *New York Times*, May 25, 1919; Stackpole, diary, May 23, 1919.
66 Stackpole, diary, May 26 and 30, 1919.
67 Macmillan, *Paris 1919*, 474–78; Hagedorn, *Savage Peace*, 265–66; Stackpole, diary, June 27, 1919 ("last minute").
68 Stackpole, diary, June 10, 1919. Liggett held the belief that the final push should have begun several days earlier and continued for a week or two after November 11 and that the US Army alone was in the best position to push the enemy. That being the case, in his opinion, the German Army would have soon disintegrated into a "rout." Liggett, *Ten Years Ago*, 238–39.
69 Stackpole, diary, July 1 through 13, 1919; Wright and Ferrell, *Meuse-Argonne Diary*, 58*n*9 ("Allen").
70 Stackpole, diary, May 11, 1919 ("self-interest"), and July 16, 1919.
71 "Ella Wheeler Wilcox Sails, Very Ill," *New York Times*, July 13, 1919 ("stretcher"); Stackpole, diary, July 14, 1919. Ella Wheeler Wilcox was the author of the poem "Solitude," in which she wrote the oft-quoted stanza "Laugh and the world laughs with you; weep and you weep alone." Wilcox died on October 30, 1919, at the age of sixty-four, shortly after returning to her Branford, Connecticut home called "The Bungalow." "Ella W. Wilcox, Poetess, Dies at 64," *New York Times*, October 31, 1919.
72 Liggett, *Commanding an American Army*, 75; Stackpole, diary, July 20, 1919.

CHAPTER NINE

1 Stackpole, diary, July 20 through 22, 1919.
2 Stackpole, diary, July 23 through 27, 1919.
3 *Reading News-Times*, July 24, 1919, pp. 1, 3; *Reading News-Times*, July 25, 1919, pp. 1–2.
4 Stackpole, diary, July 28, 1919; *Reading Eagle*, July 6, 1975.
5 *Reading Eagle*, July 6, 1975; *Reading News-Times*, July 24, 1919, pp. 1, 3; *Reading News-Times*, July 25, 1919, pp. 1–2; *Reading News-Times*, July 29, 1919, p. 1; Stackpole, diary, July 28, 1919.
6 *Reading News-Times*, July 29, 1919, p. 1; *Reading Eagle*, July 6, 1975; Stackpole, diary, July 28, 1919.
7 *Reading News-Times*, July 29, 1919, pp. 1–2; *Reading Eagle*, July 6, 1975; Stackpole, diary, July 28, 1919.
8 *Reading News-Times*, July 29, 1919, pp. 1, 3; *Reading Eagle*, July 6, 1975; Stackpole, diary, July 28, 1919.
9 "Liggett Lost Is Rescued by Police," *Reading News-Times*, July 29, 1919; Stackpole, diary, July 28, 1919.
10 *Reading News-Times*, July 29, 1919, p. 1 ("gracious welcome"); *Los Angeles Herald-Express*, December 30, 1935 ("greatest fighting unit").
11 Excerpt of letter from Hunter Liggett to Albert N. Burkholder, [July] 1919, *Reading Eagle*, January 26, 1936.
12 George C. Marshall to Hunter Liggett, August 11, 1919, in Bland, *The Papers of George Catlett Marshall*, 1:192.
13 G. C. Marshall to Hunter Liggett, September 16, 1919, GCML; Yockelson, *Forty-Seven Days*, 322 ("rewrite"). At least one original "Report of the Commanding General First Army: Organization and Operations First Army A. E. F." signed by Liggett is in existence and can be found in the Hugh A. Drum Papers, Box 12, folder "FAAEF," at the Military History Institute, Carlisle, PA. Shortly after the armistice, word began to circulate that the reason for the halt in the initial attacks on September 26 was due to the failure of the services of supply. A concerned Gen. Johnson Hagood relayed this to Liggett, who said that he had not heard that at the time. Stackpole surmised that the story was circulated by Pershing to "neutralize any criticism of his performance in command." Stackpole, diary, November 18, 1918; Pershing, *My Experiences*, 2:301.
14 George W. Cullum, *Biographical Register of the Officers and Graduates of the U.S. Military Academy at West Point, New York, since Its Establishment in 1802, Supplement*, vol. 7, *1920–1930* (Chicago: Lakeside Press, 1930), 161; 1920 US Census, California, San Francisco (Series T625, Roll 136, Page 1A); Statement of the Military Service of Hunter Liggett; *Los Angeles Herald*, January 25 and December 23, 1919 ("Beecher Ray"). Maj. Beecher Ray was commissioned as a US Army paymaster in 1898 and served in the Philippines. Prior to that time, he had risen from railroad switchman to secretary of the Illinois Railroad and Warehouse Commission. While in the Philippines, Ray and several other paymasters were cited for irregularities in carrying out their duties. During the course of congressional investigations in 1911–12, it came out that Ray had been granted a leave of absence in 1907, at the request of William Howard Taft, to return home in order to help with the campaign. Efforts to locate certain incriminating documents related to that incident were met with foot-dragging—and

even stonewalling—by many prominent officers concerned for the reputation of both President Taft and the US Army. Ray was later passed over for promotion and retired to Los Angeles, where he died on August 24, 1920, at the age of sixty-one. Liggett had known Ray from his time as adjutant general of the Department of the Lakes, where Ray was chief paymaster. Shay, *Revered Commander*, 91–94.

15 *Sausalito News*, September 20, 1919; "The Great Fire of September, 1919, Marin County Fire History," http://www.marinfirehistory.org/1919-sausalito-hills.html, accessed June 3, 2017.

16 *Worcester Evening Post*, April 18, 1919, p. 1 ("telephone workers"); Francis Russell, *A City in Terror: Calvin Coolidge and the 1919 Boston Police Strike* (Boston: Beacon Press, 2005), 112–16, 222–23; Robert Sobel, *Coolidge: An American Enigma* (Washington, DC: Regnery, 1998), 133–58; Beverly Gage, *The Day Wall Street Exploded: A Story of America in Its First Age of Terror* (New York: Oxford University Press, 2009), 26–27; Glen Jeansonne, *Herbert Hoover: A Life* (New York: New American Library, 2016), 134 ("3,000 strikes"); Eliot Asinof, *1919: America's Loss of Innocence* (New York: Donald I. Fine, 1990), 130–38 ("Seattle"); "The I. W. W. in Washington," Centralia Massacre Collection, University of Washington Libraries, https://content.lib.washington.edu/iwwweb/readIWW.html, accessed August 6, 2018.

17 Gage, *The Day Wall Street Exploded*, 1, 27; David M. Kennedy, *Over Here: The First World War and American Society* (New York: Oxford University Press, 1982), 23–29 ("censorship and repression"), 291 ("Red Scare"); Edward Robb Ellis, *Echoes of Distant Thunder: Life in the United States, 1914–1918* (New York: Kodansha, 1996), 433–41 ("censorship, etc."); Ronald Schaffer, *America in the Great War: The Rise of the Welfare State* (New York: Oxford University Press, 1994), 13–30 ("dissent").

18 Gage, *The Day Wall Street Exploded*, 69–73 ("Haywood").

19 "The Centralia Massacre," Centralia Massacre Collection, University of Washington Libraries, https://content.lib.washington.edu/iwwweb/read.html, accessed August 6, 2018.

20 "The Centralia Massacre."

21 Asinof, *1919*, 197–203; Kennedy, *Over Here*, 291; *Washington Standard*, February 13, 1920, p. 12; "The Centralia Massacre: The Massacre"; "I. W. W. Band Routs Ex-service Men," *New York Times*, November 16, 1919.

22 "The Centralia Massacre"; Asinof, *1919*, 202–3 ("trial"); "Gen. Liggett to Send Troops to Scene of I. W. W. Trials," *New York Times*, February 25, 1920; "Self Defense to Be The Wobblies' Plea," *Washington Standard*, February 13, 1920, p. 12. It is not surprising that Liggett was called upon for help in maintaining order, since there was a long history of clashes between the US Army or state militias and unions, from Homestead, Pennsylvania (1892) to the Pullman Strike in Illinois (1894) and the Ludlow Massacre in Colorado (1914). Ellis, *Echoes of Distant Thunder*, 62–90 ("Ludlow Massacre").

23 *Arizona Republican*, November 19, 1919, section 2, p. 3.

24 Cullum, *Biographical Register*, vol. 7, *1920–1930*, 161; Statement of the Military Service of Hunter Liggett; *Reading Eagle*, December 30, 1935, p. 1; *New York Times*, March 23, 1921 ("Pershing").

25 "General Liggett Retires from Duty," *New York Times*, March 22, 1921; Cullum, *Biographical Register*, vol. 7, *1920–1930*, 161; *New York Times*, March 23, 1921 ("Birdsboro"); *Los Angeles Herald*, May 9, 1921 ("disabled veterans").

26 "Americans Arrive for Peru Centenary," *New York Times*, July 24, 1921; Statement of the Military Service of Hunter Liggett. As part of the delegation, Liggett was temporarily returned to active duty from July 3 through August 26, 1921.

27 *San Francisco News*, December 30, 1935.

28 "Forward," Liggett, *Ten Years Ago* ("Saturday Evening Post"); *San Francisco News*, December 30, 1935 ("too damn lazy"). Ironically, in 1931, Pershing published *My Experiences in the World War*, which would win the Pulitzer Prize for History the following year.

29 *Daily East Oregonian* (Pendleton), April 21, 1921, p. 4 ("American Legion"); *The Review* (High Point, NC), June 30, 1921.

30 *San Francisco Call-Bulletin*, December 30, 1935.

31 Hunter Liggett to George C. Marshall, April 22, 1924, GCML ("clubhouse"); *Assembly (West Point, N. Y.)* 1, no. 2:27 ("Association of Graduates").

32 Liggett to Albert N. Burkholder, June 1927, *Reading Eagle*, January 26, 1936.

33 Cullum, *Biographical Register*, vol. 7, *1920–1930*, 161; *New York Times*, March 23, 1921 ("Weeks"); "Would Make Liggett Lieutenant General," *New York Times*, February 18, 1928 ("Johnson"); "Would Raise Bullard and Liggett," *New York Times*, April 10, 1928 ("unanimous"); "An Omnibus Promotion Bill," *New York Times*, December 20, 1928; "Will Be Full Generals," *New York Times*, June 27, 1930 ("Hoover").

34 *Dictionary of American Biography, Supplement One*, 494–95; 1930 US Census, California, San Francisco County, City of San Francisco (Series T626, Roll 206, Page 20A).

35 Certificate of Death, January 2, 1936, Office of the County Clerk, City and County of San Francisco, CA; *Chicago Tribune*, December 31, 1935; *Reading Eagle*, December 30, 1935, p. 1; George W. Cullum, *Biographical Register of the Officers and Graduates of the U.S. Military Academy at West Point, New York, since Its Establishment in 1802, Supplement*, vol. 8, *1930–1940* (Chicago: Lakeside Press, 1940), 161.

36 Certificate of Death, January 2, 1936, Office of the County Clerk, City and County of San Francisco, CA. The cause of death was listed as "severe arteriosclerosis," along with "cardiac hypertrophy" and "auricular fibrillation." *San Francisco Call-Bulletin*, December 30, 1935; *Chicago Tribune*, December 31, 1935; *Reading Eagle*, December 30, 1935, p. 1; Cullum, *Biographical Register*, vol. 8, *1930–1940*, 161.

37 *San Francisco Call-Bulletin*, December 31, 1935 ("funeral arrangements"); *New York Times*, January 1 and 3, 1936.

38 *San Francisco Examiner*, January 3, 1936 ("driving rain"); "Gen. Liggett Buried after Coast Rites," *New York Times*, January 3, 1936; *San Francisco News*, January 3, 1936 ("Why did they let you go"); "Liggett Rites Tomorrow," *New York Times*, January 1, 1936; *New York Times*, January 3, 1936 ("Rock of Gibraltar").

39 *San Francisco Examiner*, December 31, 1935 ("deeply grieved"); *Hunter Liggett, Lieutenant General, US Army*, Nomination to Fort Leavenworth Hall of Fame (six-page typescript, n.p., n.d.), MHI ("in peace or war").

40 *San Francisco Call-Bulletin*, December 30, 1935 ("Rossi"); *San Francisco Examiner*, December 31, 1935 ("I want San Francisco").

41 *San Francisco Examiner*, December 31, 1935.

42 "To Aid Officers' Widows: Bills Ask Pensions for 11 Left by Army and Navy Leaders," *New York Times*, March 20, 1938; Yockelson, *Forty-Seven Days*, 326–27 ("veto");

Certificate of Death, April 29, 1939, Office of the County Clerk, City and County of San Francisco, CA ("generalized cerebral arteriosclerosis," "chronic myocarditis," and "auricular fibrillation"); Yockelson, *Forty-Seven Days*, 326–27.

EPILOGUE

1 *Reading Times*, May 18, 1937, p. 1. For an excellent recounting of the story, see a recent article by Ruth Shaffer titled "(Dis)Honoring a Hero: City Anti-war Socialists Reject Memorial for Reading-Born WWI Military Hero," *Historical Review of Berks County* 81, no. 4 (Fall 2016): 42–47.

2 *Reading Times*, May 18, 1937, p. 1.

3 Lynne Olson, *Those Angry Days: Roosevelt, Lindbergh, and America's Fight Over World War II, 1939–1941* (New York: Random House, 2013), 220–41.

4 *Reading Times*, May 19, 1937, p. 1; *Reading Times*, May 20, 1937, p. 1.

5 *Reading Times*, May 27, 1937.

6 *Reading Eagle*, September 13, 1937, p. 1; *Reading Eagle*, September 26, 1937, p. 1; "Accepts Liggett Plaque," *New York Times*, September 26, 1937.

7 "Dedication Service, Lt. General Hunter Liggett, Historical Marker, Sunday, December 30, 1984 at 3:00 p.m." (brochure), BHC. Sadly, upon a visit to the site in April 2016, I found that although the metal post remained, the historical marker itself was no longer in place. I have since been informed that the sign has now been replaced.

Other efforts were made to honor Liggett's memory. The US Army reconditioned and recommissioned the former Munson liner *Pan America* as the USS *Hunter Liggett*. Its maiden voyage took place on April 14, 1939. In 1941, the US Army established Fort Hunter Liggett at King City, California, and in August 1957, the US Army renamed "Building 100" at First Army Headquarters on Governors Island, New York, the Hunter Liggett Building. "Building Named for Liggett," *New York Times*, August 10, 1957. In March 1958, a delegation from the City of Reading, including Mayor Daniel F. McDevitt, traveled to Governors Island, New York, in order to present an enlarged photograph of Hunter Liggett to be hung in the library at First Army Headquarters. *New York Times*, April 15, 1939 ("UST *Hunter Liggett*"); *New York Times*, March 30, 1958 ("enlarged photograph").

8 Millett, *The General*, 314–15; Summerall, *The Way of Duty*, 117.

9 Harbord, "Personalities and Personal Relationships in the American Expeditionary Forces," 1 ("multiplier effect").

10 J. [Jefferson] R. Kean to Adjutant General of the Army, March 30, 1903, ACP.

11 McGovern, "The School of Experience," 423 ("interplay of talent, personal connections, and chance"); Kean to Adjutant General, March 30, 1903.

12 *Los Angeles Herald-Express*, December 30, 1935; Coffman, *War to End All Wars*, 325 ("comparatively green").

13 George Van Horn Moseley, quoted in Bland, *Papers of George Catlett Marshall*, 1:165.

14 Lengel, *To Conquer Hell*, 107.

15 George C. Marshall to Harriet Liggett, March 21, 1938, GCML.

SELECTED BIBLIOGRAPHY

ARCHIVAL SOURCES

Berks History Center, Reading, PA
  Hunter Liggett File
Florida National Guard and Department of Military Affairs, St. Augustine, FL
George C. Marshall Library, Lexington, VA
  The Papers of George Catlett Marshall
  Pierpont L. Stackpole Diary
Gettysburg National Military Park, Library & Research Center, Gettysburg, PA
Gray Research Center, US Marine Corps History Division, Quantico, VA
  James Guthrie Harbord Papers
Library of Congress, Washington, DC
  Prints and Photographs Division
Mansfield Library, Special Collections and Archives, University of Montana, Missoula, MT
  Montana Lou Grill Papers
Massachusetts Historical Society, Boston, MA
  Clarence Ransom Edwards Papers
Military History Institute, Carlisle, PA
  Hugh A. Drum Papers
  William August Kobbé Papers
  Hunter Liggett File
  Nelson A. Miles Papers
National Archives and Records Administration, Washington, DC
  Adjutant General of the Army, Record Group 94
Rutherford B. Hayes Presidential Center, Fremont, OH
  Webb C. Hayes Papers
University of Washington Libraries, Seattle, WA
  Digital Collections
US Military Academy, Special Collections and Archives, West Point, NY

PRIMARY SOURCES

Ahern, George P., ed. *A Chronicle of the Army War College*. Vol. 1. Carlisle, PA: US Army War College, 1919.

Annual Reports of the Secretary of War. Washington, DC: Government Printing Office, miscellaneous years, 1879–1921.

Ball, Harry P. *Of Responsible Command: A History of the U.S. Army War College, the School That Shaped the Military Leaders of the Free World*. Carlisle Barracks, PA: Alumni Association of the US Army War College, 1994.

Bland, Larry I., ed. *The Papers of George Catlett Marshall*. Vol. 1, *"The Soldierly Spirit," December 1880–December 1939*. Baltimore: Johns Hopkins University Press, 1981.

Bullard, Robert Lee. "Impressions of Service with the 2d Division in Texas." *Infantry Journal* no. 11 (November–December 1914): 353–59.

———. *Personalities and Reminiscences of the War*. Garden City, NY: Doubleday, 1925.

Carter, Robert G. *On the Border with Mackenzie, or Winning West Texas from the Comanches*. Austin: Texas State Historical Association, 2007.

Cullum, George W. *Biographical Register of the Officers and Graduates of the U.S. Military Academy at West Point, New York, from Its Establishment, in 1802, to 1890*. Vol. 3. 3rd ed. Boston: Houghton Mifflin, 1891.

———. *Biographical Register of the Officers and Graduates of the U.S. Military Academy at West Point, New York, since Its Establishment in 1802, Supplement*. Vol. 4, *1890–1900*. Cambridge, MA: Riverside Press, 1901.

———. *Biographical Register of the Officers and Graduates of the U.S. Military Academy at West Point, New York, since Its Establishment in 1802, Supplement*. Vol. 5, *1900–1910*. Saginaw, MI: Seemann & Peters, 1910.

———. *Biographical Register of the Officers and Graduates of the U.S. Military Academy at West Point, New York, since Its Establishment in 1802, Supplement*. Vol. 6A, *1910–1920*. Saginaw, MI: Seemann & Peters, 1920.

———. *Biographical Register of the Officers and Graduates of the U.S. Military Academy at West Point, New York, since Its Establishment in 1802, Supplement*. Vol. 7, *1920–1930*. Chicago, IL: Lakeside Press, 1930.

———. *Biographical Register of the Officers and Graduates of the U.S. Military Academy at West Point, New York, since Its Establishment in 1802, Supplement*. Vol. 8, *1930–1940*. Chicago, IL: Lakeside Press, 1940.

Funston, Frederick. *Memories of Two Wars: Cuban and Philippine Experiences*. Lincoln: University of Nebraska Press, 2009.

Harbord, James G. *Leaves from a War Diary*. New York: Dodd, Mead, 1925.

———. "Personalities and Personal Relationships in the American Expeditionary Forces," Lecture delivered at the Army War College, Washington, DC, April 29, 1933.

Heitman, Francis B. *Historical Register and Dictionary of the United States Army from Its Organization, September 29, 1789, to March 2, 1903*. Washington, DC: G. P. O., 1903.

Liggett, Hunter. *A.E.F.: Ten Years Ago in France*. Cranbury, NJ: Scholar's Bookshelf, 2005.

———. *Commanding an American Army: Recollections of the World War*. Boston, MA: Houghton Mifflin, 1925.

Marshall, George C. *Memoirs of My Services in the World War, 1917–1918*. Boston: Houghton Mifflin, 1976.

Official Register of the Officers and Cadets of the U. S Military Academy, West Point, N. Y., June 1876–1879.

Parker, James. *The Old Army: Memories, 1872–1918*. Mechanicsburg, PA: Stackpole, 2003.

Pershing, John J. *My Experiences in the First World War*. New York: Da Capo, 1995.

Stackpole, Pierpont Langley. *Diary of Lieutenant Colonel P. L. Stackpole, A.D.C. to General Liggett, January 25, 1918, to August 3, 1919* (unpublished typescript).

Summerall, Charles P., and Timothy K. Nenninger, ed. *The Way of Duty, Honor, Country: The Memoir of General Charles Pelot Summerall.* Lexington: University Press of Kentucky, 2010.

US Army Center of Military History. *Order of Battle of the United States Land Forces in the World War: American Expeditionary Forces, Divisions.* Washington, DC: G. P. O., 1988.

———. *United States Army in the World War, 1917–1919.* 17 vols. Washington, DC: G. P. O., 1968.

Wright, William M., and Robert H. Ferrell, ed. *Meuse-Argonne Diary: A Division Commander in World War I.* Columbia: University of Missouri Press, 2004.

OTHER WORKS

Ambrose, Stephen E. *Duty, Honor, Country: A History of West Point.* Baltimore: Johns Hopkins University Press, 1999.

Andrist, Ralph K. *The Long Death: The Last Days of the Plains Indian.* New York: Collier, 1993.

Asinof, Eliot. *1919: America's Loss of Innocence.* New York: Donald I. Fine, 1990.

Brands, H. W. *Bound to Empire: The United States and the Philippines.* New York: Oxford University Press, 1992.

Britten, Thomas A. *A Brief History of the Seminole-Negro Indian Scouts.* Lewiston, NY: Edwin Mellen Press, 1999.

Chase, Joseph Cummings. "High Commanders of the A.E.F.: James Guthrie Harbord." *Recruiting News* 24, no. 1 (January 1942): 2–3 and 18.

Coffman, Edward M. *The Old Army: A Portrait of the American Army in Peacetime, 1784–1898.* New York: Oxford University Press, 1988.

———. *The Regulars: The American Army, 1898–1941.* Cambridge, MA: Harvard University Press, 2007.

———. *The War to End All Wars: The American Military Experience in World War I.* Madison: University of Wisconsin Press, 1986.

Cooke, James J. *The All-Americans at War: The 82nd Division in the Great War, 1917–1918.* Westport, CT: Praeger, 1999.

———. *Pershing and His Generals: Command and Staff in the AEF.* Westport, CT: Praeger, 1997.

———. *The Rainbow Division in the Great War, 1917–1919.* Westport, CT: Praeger, 1994.

Davis, Richard Harding. *Cuba in War Time.* Lincoln: University of Nebraska Press, 2000.

Duane, James T. *Dear Old "K".* Boston: Thomas Todd, 1922.

Eisenhower, John S. D. *Intervention: The United States and the Mexican Revolution, 1913–1917.* New York: Norton, 1993.

Eisenhower, John S. D., and Joanne T. Eisenhower. *Yanks: The Epic Story of the American Army in World War I.* New York: Free Press, 2001.

Ellis, Edward Robb. *Echoes of Distant Thunder: Life in the United States, 1914–1919.* New York: Kodansha, 1996.

Ferrell, Robert H. *America's Deadliest Battle: Meuse-Argonne, 1918.* Lawrence: University Press of Kansas, 2007.

———. *Five Days in October: The Lost Battalion of World War I.* Columbia: University of Missouri Press, 2005.

———, ed. *In the Company of Generals: The World War I Diary of Pierpont L. Stackpole.* Columbia: University of Missouri Press, 2009.

Feuer, A. B. *America at War: The Philippines, 1898–1913.* Westport, Conn.: Praeger, 2002.

Finnegan, Terrance J. *A Delicate Affair on the Western Front: America Learns How to Fight a Modern War in the Woëvre Trenches.* Gloucestershire, UK: Spellmount, 2015.

Gage, Beverly. *The Day Wall Street Exploded: A Story of America in Its First Age of Terror.* New York: Oxford University Press, 2009.

Gates, John M. *Schoolbooks and Krags: The United States Army in the Philippines, 1898–1902.* Westport, CT: Greenwood, 1973.

Grotelueschen, Mark Ethan. *The AEF Way of War: The American Army and Combat in World War I.* New York: Cambridge University Press, 2007.

———. *Doctrine under Trial: American Artillery Employment in World War I.* Westport, CT: Greenwood, 2001.

Hagedorn, Ann. *Savage Peace: Hope and Fear in America, 1919.* New York: Simon & Schuster, 2008.

Harris, Stephen L. *Duffy's War: Fr. Francis Duffy, Wild Bill Donovan, and the Irish Fighting 69th in World War I.* Washington, DC: Potomac, 2006.

History of the One Hundred Second Field Artillery. Boston: n.p., 1927.

Karnow, Stanley. *In Our Image: America's Empire in the Philippines.* New York: Ballantine, 1989.

Kennedy, David M. *Over Here: The First World War and American Society.* New York: Oxford University Press, 1982.

King, Charles Francis. "General Hunter Liggett." Master's thesis, University of Oklahoma, 1964.

Lengel, Edward G. *To Conquer Hell: The Meuse-Argonne, 1918.* New York, Henry Holt, 2008.

Linn, Brian McAllister. *Guardians of Empire: The US Army and the Pacific, 1902–1940.* Chapel Hill: University of North Carolina Press, 1997.

———. *The Philippine War 1899–1902.* Lawrence: University Press of Kansas, 2000.

Macmillan, Margaret. *Paris 1919: Six Months That Changed the World.* New York: Random House, 2003.

Mattes, Merrill J. *The Great Platte River Road: The Covered Wagon Mainline via Fort Kearny to Fort Laramie.* Lincoln: University of Nebraska Press, 1987.

McCallum, Jack. *Leonard Wood: Rough Rider, Surgeon, Architect of American Imperialism.* New York: New York University Press, 2006.

McGovern, Rory M. "The School of Experience: George W. Goethals and the U.S. Army, 1876–1907." *Journal of Military History* 81, no. 2 (April 2017): 395–424.

Miller, Edward S. *War Plan Orange: The U.S. Strategy to Defeat Japan, 1897–1945.* Annapolis, MD: Naval Institute Press, 1991.

Millett, Allan R. *The General: Robert L. Bullard and Officership in the United States Army 1881–1925.* Westport, CT: Greenwood, 1975.

Morris, Edmund. *Colonel Roosevelt.* New York: Random House, 2011.

———. *Theodore Rex.* New York: Random House, 2001.

Olsen, Lynne. *Those Angry Days: Roosevelt, Lindbergh, and America's Fight over World War II, 1939–1941.* New York: Random House, 2013.

Palmer, Frederick. *Newton D. Baker: America at War.* Vols. 1–2. New York: Dodd, Mead, 1931.

Paschall, Rod. *The Defeat of Imperial Germany, 1917–1918.* Chapel Hill, NC: Algonquin, 1989.

Pogue, Forrest C. *George C. Marshall: Education of a General, 1880–1939.* New York: Viking, 1963.

Rickey, Don, Jr. *Forty Miles a Day on Beans and Hay: The Enlisted Soldier Fighting the Indian Wars.* Norman: University of Oklahoma Press, 1973.

Risch, Erna. *Quartermaster Support of the Army: A History of the Corps 1775–1939.* Washington, DC: Center of Military History, 1989.

Schaffer, Ronald. *America in the Great War: The Rise of the Welfare State.* New York: Oxford University Press, 1994.

Shaffer, Ruth. "(Dis)Honoring a Hero: City Anti-War Socialists Reject Memorial for Reading-Born WWI Military Hero." *Historical Review of Berks County* 81, no. 4 (Fall 2016): 42–47.

Shay, Michael E. *Revered Commander, Maligned General: The Life of Clarence Ransom Edwards, 1859–1931.* Columbia: University of Missouri Press, 2011.

———. *Sky Pilots: The Yankee Division Chaplains in World War I.* Columbia: University of Missouri Press, 2014.

———. *The Yankee Division in the First World War: In the Highest Tradition.* College Station: Texas A&M University Press, 2008.

Silbey, David J. *A War of Frontier and Empire: The Philippine-American War, 1899–1902,* New York: Hill and Wang, 2007.

Smith, Gene. *Until the Last Trumpet Sounds: The Life of General of the Armies John J. Pershing.* New York: Wiley, 1998.

Smith, Mark A. "The Politics of Military Professionalism: The Engineer Company and the Political Activities of the Antebellum U.S. Army Corps of Engineers." *Journal of Military History* 80, no. 2 (April 2016): 355–87.

Smythe, Donald. *Guerilla Warrior: The Early Life of John J. Pershing.* New York: Scribner, 1973.

———. *Pershing: General of the Armies.* Bloomington: University of Indiana Press, 2007.

Stallings, Laurence. *The Doughboys: The Story of the AEF, 1917–1918.* New York: Harper, 1963.

Taylor, Emerson Gifford. *New England in France 1917–1919: A History of the Twenty-Sixth Division USA.* Boston: Houghton Mifflin, 1920.

Thompson, Robert Smith. *Empires on the Pacific: World War II and the Struggle for the Mastery of Asia.* New York: Basic Books, 2001.

Trask, David F. *The AEF and Coalition Warfare, 1917–1918.* Lawrence: University Press of Kansas, 1993.

———. *The War with Spain in 1898.* Lincoln: University of Nebraska Press, 1996.

Utley, Robert M. *Frontier Regulars: The United States Army and the Indian, 1866–1891.* Lincoln: University of Nebraska Press, 1984.

Weintraub, Stanley. *A Stillness Heard Round the World: The End of the Great War, November 1918.* New York: Oxford University Press, 1987.

Welsome, Eileen. *The General and the Jaguar: Pershing's Hunt for Pancho Villa, a True Story of Revolution and Revenge.* New York: Little, Brown, 2006.

Wooster, Robert. *Frontier Crossroads: Fort Davis and the West.* College Station: Texas A&M University Press, 2006.

———. *Nelson Miles and the Twilight of the Frontier Army.* Lincoln: University of Nebraska Press, 1993.

Yockelson, Mitchell. *Forty-Seven Days: How Pershing's Warriors Came of Age to Defeat the German Army in World War I.* New York: New American Library, 2016.

Zimmermann, Warren. *First Great Triumph: How Five Americans Made Their Country a World Power.* New York: Farrar, Straus & Giroux, 2002.

NEWSPAPERS

Arizona Republican
Birdsboro (PA) Dispatch
Bismarck (DT [ND]) Weekly Tribune
Chattanooga (TN) News
Chicago Tribune
Daily East Oregonian (Pendleton)
Daily Enterprise (Livingston, MT)
Daily Yellowstone Journal (Miles City, MT)
Devils Lake (DT [ND]) Inter-Ocean
Evening Public Ledger (Philadelphia)
Evening Star (Washington, DC)
Forest Republican (Tionesta, PA)
Harrisburg (PA) Telegraph
Helena (MT) Herald
Jamestown (ND) Weekly Alert
Los Angeles Herald
Los Angeles Herald-Express
New York Sun
New York Times
Oakland (CA) Tribune
Omaha Daily Bee
Reading (PA) Eagle
Reading (PA) News-Times
Reading (PA) Times
The Review (High Point, NC)
River Press (Fort Benton, MT)
San Francisco Call
San Francisco Call-Bulletin
San Francisco Chronicle
San Francisco Examiner
San Francisco News
Sausalito (CA) News
Semi-Weekly Miner (Butte, MT)
St. Paul (MN) Daily Globe
Washington Standard (Olympia)
Worcester (MA) Evening Post

INDEX

Page numbers followed by *f* and *m* refer to figures and maps, respectively.